MOVIE MAKING
COURSE

2ND EDITION

MOVIE MAKING COURSE

2ND EDITION

EXPANDED AND UPDATED FOR THE DIGITAL GENERATION

Ted Jones

Chris Patmore

A QUARTO BOOK

This edition published in
North America in 2012 by
Barron's Educational Series, Inc.

Copyright © 2005 & 2012 Quarto Inc.

All inquiries should be addressed to:
Barron's Educational Series, Inc.
250 Wireless Boulevard
Hauppauge, NY 11788
www.barronseduc.com

ISBN: 978-1-4380-0112-8

Library of Congress Control Number:
2012938878

QUAR:NMMC

Conceived, designed, and produced by
Quarto Publishing plc
The Old Brewery
6 Blundell Street
London N7 9BH

Editor: Lily de Gatacre
Art director: Caroline Guest
Copy editor: Liz Jones
Designer: Tanya Goldsmith
Proofreader: Ruth Patrick
Indexer: Ann Barrett
Picture Researcher: Sarah Bell

Creative director: Moira Clinch
Publisher: Paul Carslake

Color separation in Hong Kong by
Modern Age Repro House Limited
Printed in China by 1010 Printing
International Limited

9 8 7 6 5 4 3 2 1

CONTENTS

INTRODUCTION

This book is a handbook, a daily working manual for anyone wanting grounded, practical information about making digital films with little or no money. Keep this book handy because it provides a basic but pragmatic approach to the processes and techniques utilized by professionals to realize a cinematic vision. Consider this book your encyclopedia of filmmaking. This book assumes you have already decided that you are a storyteller; your vision and passion are not driven by pursuits of fame and fortune. Your motivation is guided by telling a good story. In this business of making films, it is always about the story first. Fame and fortune may come—but much later. For now, it is about learning the craft.

Action!

Long before you can say "Lights, Camera, Action!" you have to put some very personal and hard work into identifying and understanding yourself as a filmmaker. What is a filmmaker? Simply, it is someone who wants to tell a story and does so via the motion picture medium. Specifically, a filmmaker is comprised of three essential personas: The writer, the producer, and the director. The hardest part is deciding which parts of the writer–producer–director you see yourself as. The idea that you can be all things to your film is a mistake. Gaining a clear understanding of your own strengths and weaknesses is the key to being a successful filmmaker.

How do you make this determination? You could attend film school classes, take workshops, study, and read everything you can about filmmaking. It is the best way to figure out where your natural creative instincts lie. For example, if you immerse yourself in some of the activities mentioned, you will discover all sorts of things about yourself as a filmmaker. The bottom line is finding what you like to do, what sparks your creative mind, and what you want others to do for you. This is a team sport, and being clear about your position on your team is of utmost importance to successful filmmaking.

This book aims to give you a solid base of understanding about the process of making a film. You will also gain the knowledge and confidence to make your films with very little money. Fear not! It can be done. The ideology that will emanate from this book is that you should strike the perfect balance between being a book-smart filmmaker and a street-smart filmmaker. What this means is that reading books on filmmaking is valuable, but actually hitting the street and making a film is crucial.

Be practical

Filmmaking is, for the most part, a collaborative effort. However, there are a couple of areas within the team environment that will see you working alone. Developing the story and writing the script is primarily a solo effort, as is cutting the footage together for the first rough cut. The rest of the filmmaking process asks, and will demand, that you be practical with your efforts. That means, be a collaborator and ask for help. If you don't, isolation can take hold and you will lose your creative vision.

You are making a film. It does not matter if you have a ton of money or not. It involves the same approach and the same mechanics, and the issues you will encounter along the way will be no different. Drive your film, be in control of all its elements, and know when to lean on like-minded collaborators that share your creative vision and understand the pragmatics of filmmaking.

There are three distinct stages of making a film: preproduction, production, and postproduction. This book will address these broad categories and the details contained within each stage, as well as the basics of storytelling and deploying your finished film. Sprinkled throughout each section are low-budget tips. They contain helpful hints about how to access, secure, beg, borrow, and grovel for the things you'll need to get the job done.

Ted Jones

ABOUT THIS BOOK

The book guides you through the entire process of making a film: From developing your story, through preproduction, production, postproduction, and development of your finished product. The final sections include a selection of projects to help you hone your moviemaking skills, a list of 50 great movies to see before you try it yourself, useful resources, and advice on starting your career in the entertainment arts industry.

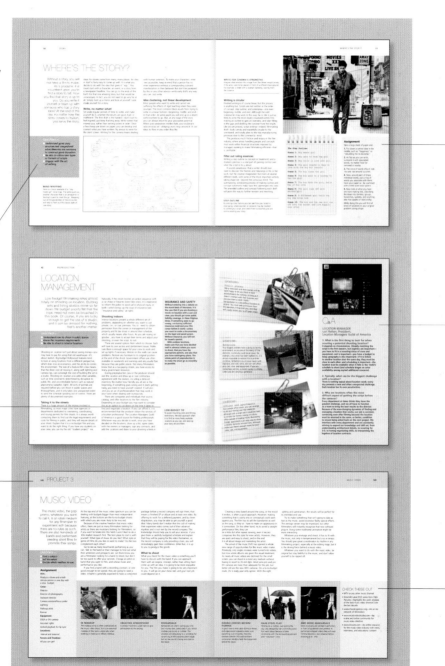

Objectives summarize the main teaching points and the skills you will acquire in each section.

Low-budget tips offer advice on how to create a professional-looking film without breaking the bank.

Six practical projects will give you experience in working in a variety of genres, and help you to develop your filmmaking skills.

Throughout the book, assignments allow you to develop the skills that you are learning, and help you to apply them in a practical way.

Get advice, and tips and tricks from industry professionals in a variety of fields within the moviemaking industry in the Q&A sections.

"Check these out" panels point you toward books, movies, or websites for guidance, resources, and examples of great moviemaking.

1

It is often said that a good film will have an incredibly solid base of preproduction attached to it. Writers will argue that a good film is all about good writing. Both are equally valid arguments. The writing and the organization of a film are simultaneous events that move toward the same goal. That goal is "going to camera" or "principal photography."

STORY

Finding the idea, developing it into a story, and writing the script is an integral part of the process. It can take weeks or even years to find a story to tell. This is a complex and arduous task, but it is the one thing that always comes first. Nothing else. The process of preproduction that flows around the script sets the tone and pace of your success in lifting your story off the written page and into the cinematic realm. To that end, this section starts off with the writing process and then moves into preproduction.

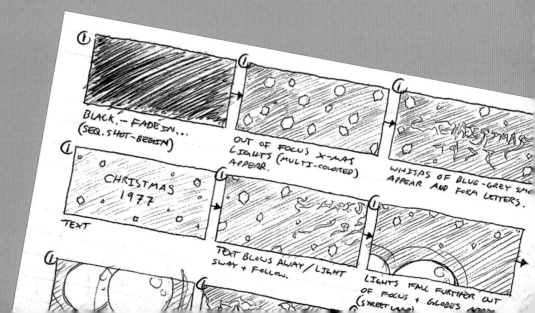

WHERE'S THE STORY?

Without a story, you will not have a film to make. As a producer, it is incumbent upon you to find a story to tell. How you find that story is up to you. Do you write it yourself or team up with someone who has a story idea? At the end of the day, no matter how the story comes to fruition, you serve the story.

Ideas for stories come from many, many places. An idea in itself is fairly easy to come up with. It is what you decide to do with the idea that gives it "legs." You could start with a character, an event, or a story from a newspaper headline. You can go to the ends of the Earth for that one amazing story, but that would be unnecessary. In fact, you do not need to go very far at all. Simply hold up a mirror and look at yourself. Look inside yourself for a story.

Write, no matter what!
Set aside regular periods of time to write, and make yourself do it, whether the results are good, bad, or indifferent. The first draft is the hardest—don't wait to feel inspired, just keep hacking away. Write scenes that interest you, rather than writing scenes in order. Once a few things are down on paper, you can develop and connect what you have written. Try always to write for the silent screen. Writing for the camera means dealing

with human exteriors. To make your characters' inner lives accessible, keep in mind that a person has no inner experience without a corresponding outward manifestation in their behavior. But don't be paralyzed by this or any other advice—write early drafts any way you can. Just write.

Idea clustering, not linear development
Most people who want to write and cannot are suffering the effects of rigid teaching when they were younger. The most common block results from trying to write in a linear fashion—beginning, middle, and end—in that order. At some point you will end up in a desert with nowhere to go. But, at any stage of the story you can always resort to your associative potential. When your pedestrian intellect fails, your exuberant subconscious will obligingly runs rings around it. Allow ideas to flow in any order they like.

MIND MAPPING
Here is a classic example of a "boy meets girl" mind map. The setting acts as another character that is an antagonist in the boy's quest to meet the girl. Mapping out all the possibilities of the encounter will help to flesh out this classic style of love story.

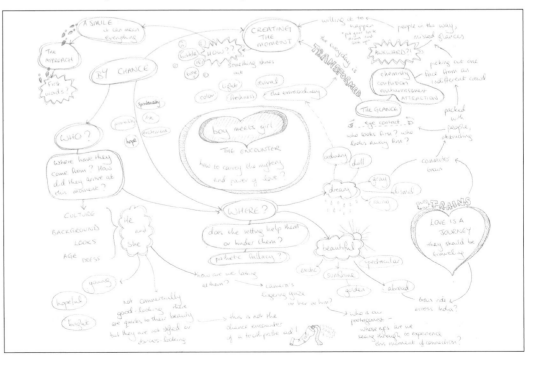

WRITE FOR CINEMA'S STRENGTHS

Imagine what emotion this image from *Taxi Driver* would convey if the actor were to be placed in front of a different background. For example, a street with a woman standing, waving from the distance.

Writing is circular

Finished writing is of course linear, but the process is anything but. Scripts are not written in the order of concept, step outline, and screenplay—nor even beginning, middle, and end. Although the odd screenwriter may work in this way, he or she is just as likely to write the most clearly visualized scenes first, making an outline to gain an overview, and later filling in the gaps and distilling the concept from the results. Like any art process, script writing—indeed, filmmaking itself—looks untidy and wastefully circular to the uninitiated, and totally alien to the tidy manufacturing processes dear to the commercial mind.

This produces much friction and misery in the film industry, where artists handling people and concepts must work within financial structures imposed by managers wanting to make filmmaking efficient—that is, profitable.

Filter out ruling essences

Writing a step outline (a concept or treatment) and a dramatic premise is a vital part of gaining control over what the script is truly about.

It sounds paradoxical that a writer should ever need to discover the themes and meanings in his or her work, but the creative imagination functions at several different levels, with some of the most important activity taking shape well beyond the conscious mind. The summarizing, windowing process of making outline and concept statements helps raise the submerged into view. The amended outline and concept following each draft will point the way to further revision and rewriting.

STEP OUTLINE

By writing a step outline you can see how your script is developing, where rewrites or revisions may be needed to control your script, and check how successfully you are communicating your story.

The Step Outline:

Scene 1: Boy meets girl

Scene 2: Boy gets to know the girl

Scene 3: Boy falls in love with girl

Scene 4: The girl starts to fall in love with the boy but resists

Scene 5: The boy loses the girl

Scene 6: The boy goes on a journey to find the girl

Scene 7: The boy finds the girl, tells her of his love

Scene 8: The girl runs off with another girl

Scene 9: A different girl tells the boy she loves him

Scene 10: The boy and the new girl run off into the sunset and live happily ever after

Assignment

Take a large sheet of paper and…

1. Put down a central idea in the middle, such as "happiness" or "rebuilding the relationship."

2. As fast as you can write, surround it with associated words, no matter how far-removed or wacky.

3. The circle of words should look like satellites around a planet.

4. Now, around each of these individual words, put a ring of words you associate with them. Soon your paper will be crammed with a little word solar system.

5. Now look at what you have and start making lists, classifying the ideas into families, groups, hierarchies, systems, and anything else that speaks of relationship.

While doing this you will find all kinds of solutions to your original problem taking shape.

FIRST DRAFT

INT. HOUSE - NIGHT

    A guy, DAVE, in his late teens wearing big frame glasses, a watch, dressed in typical nerdy clothes, is alone in the living room. He sits down on the chair and works on the computer on the table with table lamp.

    We hear a knock at the door.

Dave checks the time on his watch, gets up, walks to the door.

              DAVE
         Who's this?

              JASON (V.O)
      Hey dude, it's me. Jason. Open the
        damn door.

    Dave unlocks and opens the door.

    A tall, black silhouette of a male appears, takes a step inside a room, and we can see his face.

JASON, in his late teens, wearing dirty T-shirt and torn jeans, carrying a bag in one hand and an open 40 ounce Jack Daniels bottle in the other, stands at the door looking drunk and smiling.

              DAVE
    Hi Jason, I wasn't expecting you.

Jason forcefully lets himself in, places the bag on the table, and sits on the sofa.

             JASON
    Dude, I know your little secret, I
    was stalking your hot neighbor next
    door when I saw your parents leave.
    So let's have fun. I brought you some
        booze and stuff.

    Dave stands by the open door.

              DAVE
    No no no no no Jason, I don't want
    to drink. Remember last time
       what happened?

             JASON
    Don't be such a girl, man.
    Nothing will happen to you. You are
     always damn busy with your
       stupid computer.
         (MORE)

FROM FIRST DRAFT TO SHOOTING SCRIPT

The difference between a first draft and final draft of a script will vary depending on the complexity of the film. Scenes, locations, and characters can be dropped or added among myriad other changes. The biggest change occurs close to or at the final draft stage. That is the addition of scene numbers. When these numbers are added, the script officially becomes a "shooting script." Small changes to dialogue may occur after this, but nothing else. Hence we call this script a "locked final draft," and it is from this script that the scheduling can commence.

LOCKED FINAL DRAFT

1.   INT. HOUSE - NIGHT   1

    The place is clean and tidy with minimum furniture. There are books and puzzles in an open cupboard by the computer table.

JASON, a typical nerd in his early twenties, is in the living room reading an article about sleep apnea on his computer.

    We hear a knock at the door.

    Jason gets up, opens the door just a little bit.

              JASON
    Oh hey Dave, what brings you here
        my friend?

    A tall, black silhouette of a male appears, takes a step inside the room, and we can see his face.

DAVE. A jock guy, almost drunk, carrying a bag, stands at the door smiling.

             JASON (CONT'D)
        You stink!

    Jason moves away looking disgusted.

              DAVE
    Let me in, dude, I've gotta take a
    leak. Damn these cold beers, here take 'em.

Dave forcefully lets himself in, handing the bag to Jason, and runs to the back of the room.

Jason shuts the door and places the bag on the table. He then continues the reading on his computer.

    Dave comes in, stands behind Jason, reading over his shoulder.

             DAVE (CONT'D)
    What are you doing, man?

    He kneels and looks at his computer.

             DAVE (CONT'D)
    Sleep anemia. What is that?

    Jason turns back to Dave.

These outlines work as important way stations between drafts that make analysis unavoidable and development inevitable.

Work to create mood

Settings that are bland or unbelievable compel the audience to struggle against disbelief with every scene change, something the theater makes us do each time the curtain rises. Using locations and sound composition intelligently will provide a powerfully emotional setting and thrust the audience into the heart of a situation.

Write for the cinema's strengths

To avoid a theatrical film, turn conversations into behavioral exchanges comprehensible to a foreigner. Where you are forced to use dialogue there is probably a real need, and in any case a screenplay with sparse dialogue raises words to a higher significance. We are impressed most by a person's acts because the verbal is abstract and uncommitted until endorsed by acts. Decide for yourself what you like about the cinema and consciously compose to take advantage of these strengths.

Write with the audience in mind

If drama is to reach beyond the egocentricity of therapy, the writer must be aware of the broader implications of the material for an audience. To write for an audience is not about exploitation but about trying to conceive works that participate in modern thought and modern dilemmas, and that prompt questions and ideas that cut across conventional thinking.

Test your assumptions

A writer writes from experience, imagination, and intuition, as well as from assumptions stored in the unconscious. The writer knows that his character, Harry, would never perjure himself in court—but the audience knows nothing of the sort unless Harry's honesty is first established.

To do this, the writer might make Harry go back into a store to pay for a newspaper he unthinkingly carried out with the groceries. In this way his honesty is demonstrated.

It is important to stress that any form of writing creates significant spaces that the audience must constantly fill in based on their own values, imagination,

HELP YOUR AUDIENCE UNDERSTAND

Think about the main character traits that need to be portrayed for each of your central characters. You must then create moments in the script that allow these traits to be successfully communicated to the audience, allowing them to fully understand the characters.

Name:	Characteristic:	How to show:
Harry	Honesty	He speaks from his heart
Sally	Tough	She is loud and brash about everything
Ginger	Shy	She is afraid to say how she really feels
Jack	Dishonest	He will say anything to get what he wants

and life experience. A film audience does not have to visualize the physical world of the story, but it is constantly deciding on the character's motives and morals.

For the writer, anything that is to be implied must first be named, if there are not to be counterproductive ambiguities and contradictions. Then the writer must figure out how to make each intention reach the audience, and how to make each event or implication fit into the character's logic. A piece of fiction, though it is a self-contained work with its own set of rules governing the characters' lives, cannot capriciously violate what the audience knows from life.

It must be interesting, representative, and consistent if it is to suggest the depth of real life. This requires that the creators share a body of knowledge that is a great deal more complete than what appears in the film itself. It also means withholding just enough of that information to keep the audience guessing and involved, but not baffled or confused.

Assignment

Ask yourself the following questions about your story:

- What do I want to say?
- Why do I want to say it?
- Who do I want to say it to?
- How much does my prospective audience know about the subject?
- Is it liberal or conservative with regards to politics, art, or morals?
- What age group is it for?
- What are its notable prejudices?
- Can I describe in detail the personality of a typical member of the audience?

THE ART OF STORYTELLING

Whether your story is fiction or nonfiction, telling it within a designated time frame commits you to the principles of storytelling.

OBJECTIVES >>
- **Understand the importance of a clear story structure**
- **Know the needs and goals of your protagonist**
- **Develop a sympathetic character**

Through your story, you are trying to elicit emotion based on a sequence of events that you are authoring. Unless your intention is to place enough cameras to capture a 360-degree view of the full event in its entirety, you are, like it or not, editorializing. Therefore, for the sake of interest, brevity, and creative focus, a clear understanding of storytelling is paramount in making movies. Following are some guiding principles.

Clear structure

Structure in this case refers to the foundation of your story. The most proven type of structure is the three-act variety. Within the first act, the protagonist (your main character) must be introduced to the audience and an event must take place that changes the course of his or her life. This event changes all the subsequent decisions and actions of the characters, and raises the central question of the story that needs to be answered.

Some questions to consider:
- Does the story start at the beginning and end at the end, and does it follow logically?
- Does the audience have the necessary exposition early enough in the story to clearly understand what follows?
- Is there anything in the plot that is implausible?
- Does the conflict have great significance to the protagonist?
- Is the audience able to see the conflict? Is it internal or external?
- Does the conflict increase in intensity as the story progresses?
- Does every scene reveal new information about the characters or the main action of the story?
- Does the story reach an emotionally and visually satisfying climax and resolution?

Sympathetic protagonist

A sympathetic protagonist is someone with whom the audience can identify. If they do not care about the outcome of the protagonist's situation, they probably won't be involved in the film. This doesn't mean that the protagonist must be likable, but the audience must be intrigued and curious enough to want to know how the story ends.

Some questions to consider:
- What are the needs of the protagonist?
- What is the protagonist capable of doing?
- Have you generated empathy, or a sufficient level of interest in your protagonist?
- Do you know everything that there is to know about your protagonist—beyond what is necessary for the story that will appear on-screen?

The protagonist's goal

This goal is what the protagonist is trying to achieve by the end of the film; it is the reason for everything the protagonist does. The goal can be the choice of the protagonist or it may be thrust upon him or her. It might be simple to achieve or close to impossible. However, it must be important to the protagonist and, ultimately, to the audience.

A question to consider:
- Is the goal important to the protagonist?

Interesting obstacles

An audience's attention is sustained by a series of interesting obstacles that the protagonist must overcome. The obstacles can be minor or major impediments and may be self-imposed or external, but they must be interesting.

A question to consider:
- Are the protagonist's obstacles interesting?

KNOW YOUR PROTAGONIST
In order to have a story worth telling, the protagonist and his or her journey must be of interest to your audience. Here, we apply a few key questions to some iconic movie characters to show the importance of knowing the needs and goals of your character.

Q. What is the emotionally and visually satisfying climax and resolution?

A. Ripley's strong distrust of her fellow crewmate Ash after he disobeys her order not to let the infected Kane back on the ship is vindicated when it is revealed that the survival of the crew is not his priority. The movie shows that women can be strong action heroes that can measure up to the toughest of their male counterparts. Ripley (along with Jones the cat) is the only survivor of the crew's encounter with the Alien. In the ending climax of the story, Ripley finally prevails over the Alien creature.

Q. What are her needs?

A. Ripley has only one need, and that is to survive. As she realizes that her fellow crewmates are not capable of making good decisions, she responds to the growing disasters with characteristic resourcefulness and courage. Her subconscious desire or need is to become a caring person, and the audience sees that as she rescues the cat, Jones.

ELLEN RIPLEY
Alien quadrilogy.
Played by Sigourney Weaver.
Survivor, mother, host.

MICHAEL CORLEONE
The Godfather trilogy.
Played by Al Pacino.
Mobster, husband, father.

Q. What is the central conflict for the protagonist and what is the significance to him?

A. He is a tragic figure. His power and talent unravels due to his character flaws. His desire for vengeance quickly surrounds him so deeply that he cannot escape or change. Further, to his dilemma, is the fact that he sees himself as having the ability to hold his love interest by becoming legitimate, which, of course, he never does.

Q. How/why does the audience feel empathy for or interest in the character?

A. His character, although evil, maintains a visible genuine motivation to become a good husband and father. His resistance to the "family" in the early stages makes him likable enough. The audience wants to see him triumph over evil. In the end the audience moves from empathy to sympathetic pity because he is his own worst enemy.

Q. What is he capable of?

A. We know the character has certain given capabilities because he is a police officer. What the audience sees is he is capable of a lot with very little at his disposal. One of the joys in watching this film is seeing how John McClane continues to wage war with the terrorists. Of course, his capabilities are all driven by his need to rescue his estranged wife from the terrorists.

Q. What is the central conflict for the protagonist and what is the significance to him?

A. McClane is conflicted because he is arriving to patch things up with his estranged wife. His conflict is about how he does that as a husband and not a police officer. The two entities come together when Holly is taken hostage and McClane must rely on his policing instincts to save his wife. The central conflict is external to the McClane character and, by no mistake of his own, he has to literally fight the good fight to get his wife back.

JOHN McCLANE
Die Hard series.
Played by Bruce Willis.
New York cop, husband,
borderline alcoholic.

THE SCREENPLAY PARADIGM

Film is a visual medium that dramatizes a basic story line; it deals in pictures, images, bits and pieces: a clock ticking, a window opening, someone watching, two people laughing, a phone ringing.

LANGUAGE OF FILM

Dramatic premise
is what the screenplay is about. It poses a question or creates circumstances, which provide the dramatic thrust that drives the story to its conclusion.

Dramatic need
is defined as what your main character wants to win, gain, get, or achieve during the screenplay. What drives him or her forward through the action?

Resolution
does not mean ending; resolution means solution.

Dramatic structure

The dramatic structure of the screenplay may be defined as a linear arrangement of related incidents, episodes, or events leading to a dramatic resolution. How you use these structural components determines the form of your film. There is only form, not formula. The paradigm is simply a model, example, or conceptual scheme; it is what a well-structured screenplay looks like, an overview of the story line as it unfolds from beginning to end.

Beginning, middle, and end—this is the foundation of dramatic structure. A screenplay is a story told with pictures, in dialogue and description, and placed within the context of dramatic structure. This basic linear structure is the form of the screenplay; it holds all the elements of the story line in place. Think in terms of parts that make up the whole. A story is a whole, and the parts that make it—the action; characters; scenes; sequences; Acts I, II, and III; incidents; and so on—are what make up the story. It is a whole. This is the paradigm of dramatic structure. A paradigm is a model, example, or conceptual scheme.

The three-act structure described here applies more strongly to feature films than to shorts, which can be two, or even just one, act. But, you need to learn the rules before you can start to break them.

Plot points

We've established that beginning, middle, end; Act I, Act II, Act III; and setup, confrontation, resolution are the parts that make up the whole. If these are some of the parts that make up the screenplay, then how do you get from Act I to Act II? The answer is simple: create a plot point at the end of each act.

A plot point is any incident, episode, or event that "hooks" into the action and spins it around into another direction. A plot point usually occurs at the end of Act I, at about pages 20 to 25 of the screenplay, and another at the end of Act II—usually at about page 85 to 90 of the screenplay.

The average feature film is roughly 120 minutes in length. A page of screenplay equals approximately one minute of screen time. It doesn't matter whether the script is all action, all dialogue, or any combination of the two.

BEGINNING | ACT I

THE SETUP, PAGES 1–30

Act I, the beginning, is a unit of dramatic action that is approximately 30 pages long and is held together by the dramatic context known as the setup. Context holds the content of the story in place.

• These first 30 pages are used to set up the story, the characters, the dramatic premise, and the situation, and to establish the relationships between the main character and the other people who inhabit the landscape of his or her world.
• The first ten-page unit of dramatic action is the most important part of the screenplay because you have to show the reader who your main character is, what the dramatic premise of the story is (what it's about), and what the dramatic situation is (the circumstances surrounding the action).

THE PARADIGM APPLIED TO
THE SHAWSHANK REDEMPTION

THE SETUP
In 1947, banker Andy Dufresne (Tim Robbins) is convicted of murdering his wife and her lover, and is sentenced to life imprisonment at Shawshank State Penitentiary. Andy befriends "Red" (Morgan Freeman), an inmate known for obtaining contraband. He asks Red for a rock hammer, and later on, a large poster of Rita Hayworth. Andy befriends the guards by offering them financial advice. He builds a prison library in exchange for helping Warden Norton (Bob Gunton) to illegally launder money under a false identity.

PLOT POINT 1
pages 20–25
A plot point usually occurs at the end of Act I, at about pages 20 to 25. It is a function of the main character—something happens to further his or her struggle.

PLOT POINT 2
pages 85–90
A plot point occurs at the end of Act II, at about pages 85 to 90. Again, this creates a further struggle or conflict for the main character.

MIDDLE | ACT II

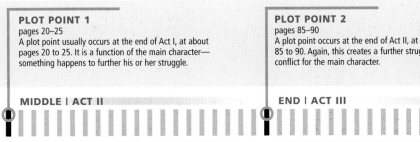

THE CONFRONTATION, PAGES 30–90

Act II, the middle, is a unit of dramatic action that is roughly 60 pages long and is held together by the dramatic context known as confrontation. All drama is conflict. Without conflict you have no character; without character, you have no action; without action, you have no story; and without story, you have no screenplay.

• The main character encounters obstacle after obstacle that keeps him or her from achieving his dramatic need.
• If you know the character's dramatic need, you can create obstacles to that need, and the story becomes the main character overcoming obstacles to achieve (or not achieve) his or her dramatic need.

END | ACT III

THE RESOLUTION, PAGES 90–120

Act III, the resolution, is a unit of dramatic action, of about 30 pages that is held together by the dramatic context known as resolution. Resolution does not mean ending; resolution means solution.

• What is the solution of the screenplay? Does your main character live or die? Succeed or fail?
• Act III resolves the story; it is not the ending. The ending is that specific scene, shot, or sequence that ends the script; it is not the solution of the story.

THE CONFRONTATION
Twenty years later, newcomer Tommy Williams tells Andy that in prison he talked to an inmate, Ernie, who said he killed a banker's wife and her boyfriend but that it was framed on Andy. Andy tells Norton, who fears that Andy might tell of his corruption if he is released, and refuses to cooperate. Norton then has Tommy shot, claiming an attempted escape.

THE RESOLUTION
One morning, Andy is gone from his cell. The guards reveal a tunnel, hidden behind the poster, that Andy had dug over the last twenty years using his rock hammer. The night before, Andy had escaped through the tunnel and a sewage drain during a thunderstorm. He takes the money accumulated from the scam and sends evidence of Norton's corruption to a local newspaper. The police attempt to arrest the warden, who commits suicide. Red passes his parole board and reunites with Andy in a Pacific Mexican town.

Assignments

1. Write a one-page story that contains a beginning, middle, and end. Use the "boy meets girl, boy gets girl, boy loses girl" scenario. Or, try to write a script for a commercial—this is a good example of extreme short storytelling.

2. If you are interested in writing, read screenplays to expand your awareness of the form and structure.

3. Watch movies and see if you can determine the breakdown of each act. Find the plot points at the end of each act and see how they lead to the resolution.

Ten films that illustrate great classic story structure
• *The Godfather*
• *Forrest Gump*
• *Titanic*
• *The Lord of the Rings: The Return of the King*
• *Gladiator*
• *The Shawshank Redemption*
• *Star Wars: The Empire Strikes Back*
• *The Matrix*
• *Fight Club*
• *Braveheart*

See pages 162–167 for 50 movies that demonstrate excellence in some of the main areas of filmmaking, and are must-sees for all budding moviemakers.

GOOD SCREENPLAY ESSENTIALS

Because a screenplay is a blueprint, not a literary narrative, it should not be overwritten. Very detailed descriptions condition your readers (money sources, actors, crew) to anticipate particular, hard-edged results. The director of such a script is locked into trying to fulfill a vision that disallows all variables, even those that would contribute positively.

OBJECTIVES >>
- ■ **Learn to keep your screenplay writing pared down**
- ■ **Learn how to "road test" your script**

It is important to exclude embellishment. A good screenplay:
- Doesn't include any direct thoughts, instructions, or comments from the writer.
- Avoids qualifying comments and adjectives that will too precisely condition what the reader imagines.
- Leaves most behavior to the reader's imagination and instead describes its effect (for example, "he looks nervous" instead of "he nervously runs a forefinger around the inside of his collar and then flicks dust off his dark serge pants").
- Never gives instructions to actors unless a line or an action would be unintelligible without them.
- Contains little or no camera or editing instructions.

The experienced screenwriter is like an architect supplying the shell for a building, knowing that the occupant will build his own walls and interiors, and select his own colors and furnishings. The inexperienced screenwriter feels compelled to specify everything down to the doorknobs and the pictures on the wall. This makes the building uninhabitable to everyone but himself or herself. The writer–director might seem a different case. Being in a position to know exactly what

---

Prose-style scene setting is better suited to literary fiction than to film.

THE WRONG WAY
A badly written script is very difficult to follow. The actors' dialogue disappears into the page. For the director, there are too many instructions, and scene changes are too hard to find.

Start with black and the sound of deep breathing. Then the sound of a child shouting.

LAURA: Daaad!

Rambling, long-winded camera directions lack clarity.

Inside a bedroom in the early morning.

Shoot over the shoulder of the girl with a close-up of a man's unshaven face. The girl, Laura, is lifting up one of the man's eyelids.

The camera changes to what the man sees—a girl with the morning sun shining through the window highlighting her beautiful long, curly hair.

LAURA: Dad. I want my breakfast.

To avoid confusion, character names should be kept completely separate from your dialogue.

Wide-angle shot of the bed from a higher angle.

Camera direction is far too detailed. The writer is trying to do the director's job.

The man, Matt, rolls over, trying not to lose his eye in the process, and pulls the bedcover over his head.

MATT (in a tired, slightly jaded voice, but as a voice-over): Why is it on school days children never want to get out of bed, but come the weekend they're up before the birds?

A different wide-angle, overhead shot of the bedcover sliding down the bed and the mischievous laughter of two children. Matt sits up and looks at his peacefully sleeping wife, Ami. Would look good as a moving crane shot.

MATT (thinks in voice-over): Faker. This is my payback for all those nights of sleeping through the feeding and changing.

Matt gets out of bed, pulls the cover back over his wife, and gives her a kiss on the cheek. He turns to follow the children out of the room. Shoot it handheld and following him.

AMI (in a quiet, sleepy voice): Have a shave this morning, dear.

MATT (mumbling to himself): It's the weekend. Why do I have to shave?

New scene in the kitchen. Close-up of Matt drinking a large glass of water, which pulls back to show him absentmindedly pouring cereal from a box into two bowls.

New scene of dining room. Matt places the two bowls of over-sugared cereal in front of the already overexcited children and walks toward the bathroom. Tripod shot that pans to follow the action. Wide angle.

New scene in bathroom. Over the shoulder, close-up shots of Matt staring in the mirror.

Inadequate margins.

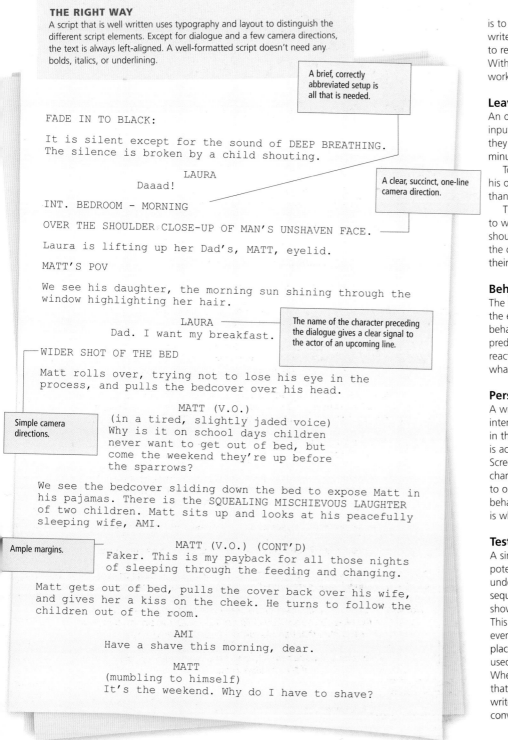

THE RIGHT WAY
A script that is well written uses typography and layout to distinguish the different script elements. Except for dialogue and a few camera directions, the text is always left-aligned. A well-formatted script doesn't need any bolds, italics, or underlining.

A brief, correctly abbreviated setup is all that is needed.

```
FADE IN TO BLACK:

It is silent except for the sound of DEEP BREATHING.
The silence is broken by a child shouting.
                    LAURA
            Daaad!

INT. BEDROOM - MORNING

OVER THE SHOULDER CLOSE-UP OF MAN'S UNSHAVEN FACE.

Laura is lifting up her Dad's, MATT, eyelid.

MATT'S POV

We see his daughter, the morning sun shining through the
window highlighting her hair.
                    LAURA
            Dad. I want my breakfast.

WIDER SHOT OF THE BED

Matt rolls over, trying not to lose his eye in the
process, and pulls the bedcover over his head.
                    MATT (V.O.)
            (in a tired, slightly jaded voice)
            Why is it on school days children
            never want to get out of bed, but
            come the weekend they're up before
            the sparrows?

We see the bedcover sliding down the bed to expose Matt in
his pajamas. There is the SQUEALING MISCHIEVOUS LAUGHTER
of two children. Matt sits up and looks at his peacefully
sleeping wife, AMI.
                    MATT (V.O.) (CONT'D)
            Faker. This is my payback for all those nights
            of sleeping through the feeding and changing.

Matt gets out of bed, pulls the cover back over his wife,
and gives her a kiss on the cheek. He turns to follow the
children out of the room.
                    AMI
            Have a shave this morning, dear.

                    MATT
            (mumbling to himself)
            It's the weekend. Why do I have to shave?
```

A clear, succinct, one-line camera direction.

The name of the character preceding the dialogue gives a clear signal to the actor of an upcoming line.

Simple camera directions.

Ample margins.

is to be shot, even where and how, it seems logical to write very specifically. But this overlooks the concessions to reality that everyone must make during filming. Without unlimited time and money, nothing ever really works out much as you envision.

Leave things open

An open script challenges the cast to create their own input. The closed framework signals to the actors that they must somehow mimic the actions and mannerisms minutely specified in the text, however alien.

To challenge actors means getting each to work from his own, different, and distinct personal identity rather than taking it from the script's common pool.

The good screenplay leaves the director and players to work out how things will be said and done. These should be greatly influenced by the personal qualities of the cast members and the chemistry between them and their director.

Behavior instead of dialogue

The first cowboy films made their impact because the early American cinema recognized the power of behavioral melodrama. The good screenplay is still predominantly concerned with behavior, action, and reaction. It avoids static scenes where people talk about what they feel.

Personal experience must be recast

A writer needs to draw a conscious line between the intensity of life as lived and what is moving or exciting in the cinema. In a moving personal experience, one is actively involved and feels the stresses subjectively. Screen drama must, however, be structured so that characters' inner thoughts and emotions communicate to outsiders through the characters' outwardly visible behavior. Drama is doing. What matters on the screen is what people do.

Testing for cinematic qualities

A simple (sometimes deadly) test of a script's screen potential is to ask how much of it the audience would understand with the sound turned off. Examining each sequence in this way produces a kind of "relief map," showing how much is really radio drama with pictures. This is not to deny that people talk to each other or even that many transactions of lifelong importance take place through conversation. But, dialogue should be used when it is necessary, not as a substitute for action. When you are writing dialogue you must be mindful that the way people speak is different than how they write. It's important to take the time to listen to real conversations so that your dialogue will be convincing.

SCRIPT FORMATS

A script, as a written description of a proposed production, has two purposes: One is to provide sufficient information for the production to be adequately planned and scheduled. The second is to serve as a guide or plan for the director to follow as the production is shot.

OBJECTIVES >>

■ **Learn to apply the different formats to suit your production**

Script elements

A script is a description, in words, of what will ultimately be shot. There are many types of scripts. If you are writing a script for yourself, you may use almost any method that is understandable to you. For everyone else involved in filmmaking the script must be formatted in an unambiguous and readable fashion.

People need to understand clearly what the script refers to; as a result, certain conventions have developed for conveying the following necessary information:

• The location where the scene takes place.
• The time of day when the action takes place.
• Scene number.
• The angle or point of view—how we see the scene.
• Who is in the scene.
• Description of the action and camera movement—what is happening.
• Words spoken by actors and narrators.
• Special effects directly related to the action.
• Transitions from one scene or shot to the next.

Almost any comprehensible arrangement of the above information results in a usable script. Two of the most common arrangements are the A/V, or split column, format and the full-page, or master scene, formats.

A/V SCRIPT EXAMPLE

This format allows for a quick reference to the shots required. It is used solely for commercial production and sometimes documentaries. In the case of this example, a storyboard would go hand-in-hand with the A/V script.

Formatting programs

Just about every serious screenwriter uses one of two software packages: Final Draft or Movie Magic Screenwriter. These programs format your screenplay using industry-standard layouts and terminology, keeping lists of all your characters, scenes, locations, and so on, easily accessible. They can also track your changes (and believe me, there will be plenty) in different colors. Demo versions are downloadable from the Internet. Try out both of them to decide which suits you.

The split-column format

The A/V format is used for very specific purposes: commercial or documentary production. The A/V format is not used for feature or episodic production. In some cases this format is good for quickly jotting down a series of shots for a scene.

When reading a split-page script, it is always a challenge to maintain continuity. Your eyes must continually jump backward and forward between the two columns. To understand the writer's intended relationship between image and sound, the reader must be capable of visualizing and willing to make the effort to "see" as he or she reads. Many producers and potential sponsors don't have the ability to hold mental images clearly as they read, and consequently end up reading only the right-hand (audio) column to "get the story." The inevitable feeling is that something is missing from the script—because of the fact that they have not "seen" the visuals as they read. As a general rule the A/V format works best for narrated productions.

LOW-BUDGET TIP

If you cannot afford to purchase the Final Draft software bundle, then any text editor package will do. Follow the "Master Scene" example to set up the tabulations and indents needed for a professionally formatted script.

The date of the script

The name of the client

Shot number

Each shot listed in order

Description of shot—"WS," "CU," "MS" (see pages 88–89)

Content of shot—such as "man walking in park"

Transition between shots—such as "cut to," "dissolve to"

Any camera moves.

"Super" indicates graphics and text

Date: 11/21
Client: Miles, Inc
Product: One-a-Day
Job No: MI43257

Title: "Portraits—Umbrella"
Director: John Smith
Length: .30
Status: OC

VIDEO	AUDIO
	(MUSIC UP AND UNDER)
1. OPEN ON OVERCRANKED CU, MOM GIVING YOUNG DAUGHTER PIGGYBACK RIDE.	AVO: EVER WONDER HOW ONE-A-DAY
2. CUT TO MCU ELDERLY MAN ON PORCH, SMILES.	GOT THE IDEA TO MAKE DIFFERENT
3. CUT TO MS OWNER IN FRONT OF RESTAURANT.	VITAMINS FOR DIFFERENT PEOPLE?
4. CUT TO MCU WOMAN, SMILES TO CAMERA MISCHIEVOUSLY	ISN'T IT OBVIOUS?
5. CUT TO MCU BLACK MAN AND YOUNG DAUGHTER.	PEOPLE HAVE DIFFERENT NEEDS.
6. CUT TO MCU ASIAN WOMAN ON COUCH.	BECAUSE WOMEN NEED MORE CALCIUM,
7. CUT TO MCU WOMAN WALKING DOWN STREET, DX WOMEN'S FORMULA OVER SCENE.	ONE-A-DAY GIVES THEM MORE THAN ANY OTHER VITAMIN.
8. CUT TO MS MAN PICKING UP HUNTING DOG, DX MEN'S FORMULA OVER SCENE.	FOR MEN, WE INCREASED ANTIOXIDANT LEVELS.
9. CUT TO MS GROUP OF OLDER WOMEN AT MAKEUP TABLE.	AND OUR 55-PLUS FORMULA.
10. CUT TO PAN MS GROUP OF OLDER WOMEN, DX 55-PLUS FORMULA OVER SCENE.	HAS MORE OF EIGHT ESSENTIAL VITAMINS THAN CENTRUM SILVER
11. CUT TO DAD PLAYING WITH SON IN BOOTH.	PEOPLE ARE DIFFERENT.
12. CUT TO BLACK WOMAN WITH YOUNG DAUGHTER ON PORCH. SUPER: "WE'VE GOT THE ONE FOR YOU," DX FULL LINE OF PRODUCTS OVER THE SCENE.	SO IS ONE-A-DAY. WE'VE GOT THE ONE FOR YOU.

Callout labels (right margin):
- The name of the program
- Name of the producer or director
- Duration of the program
- Music and/or sound FX—uppercase, underlined.
- Who is speaking—uppercase, underlined
- Narration or dialogue—uppercase

The master-scene format

Most dialogue scripts work best in the full-page, or master-scene, format as shown on the right. Sometimes it is useful to put a narrated script into full-page format to force the reader into reading scene descriptions as well as the narration. When narration and scene description follow one directly below another, it's difficult not to read everything. The reader may still not be able to visualize well, but there is less inclination to feel that there is something missing, and at least to see the relationship between narration and description. Normally, it is more convenient to format a narration-type production as a split-page script. It is much easier to shoot and time with the picture directly across from the narration.

Certain conventions in the layout of a master-scene script have developed over the years. Conventional drama was originally built according to the rules of continuity that prevailed on the stage for over 2,000 years. Dialogue dominates action, and the feature script concentrates on developing the story through what the characters say rather than what the camera sees and how it moves. Feature film differs from stage presentation in the way that a story can be

CHECK THESE OUT

- www.finaldraft.com—Web site for Final Draft software
- www.screenplay.com—Web site for Movie Magic Screenwriter software
- www.simplyscripts.com—Links to free, downloadable movie scripts
- www.writersstore.com—Books and software for screenwriters and filmmakers

portrayed to an audience. Onstage, an entity such as a flashback or dream sequence must be portrayed through dialogue, but film can express this visually. Also, film has fades, wipes, dissolves, and other special effects available to further enhance the visual element. Camera scale and movement is largely left to the discretion of the director and the director of photography in a feature film.

Assignment

Study a scene from a film, or even a still from a film, such as this one from *Run Lola Run*, and write a page of script based on this. Write a sample typescript using the master-scene format, imagining what the script would be.

Take a large sheet of paper and draw a line down the middle of the page. Make two column headings: "Picture" on the left and "Sound" on the right. With your story in mind, brainstorm your ideas onto the A/V script.

Scenes—these are numbered and included on the top line of each scene; the numbers should appear on both sides of the page. This can be done by the production manager at the initial budget stage, and it indicates that the script is "locked" and is a final shooting script.

Slug line—this is the first line of each new scene and includes the location where the scene takes place. INT (interior) and EXT (exterior) indicate the desired setting. The slug line is capitalized.

Any character names that appear in descriptions are capitalized on first mention.

Dialogue—this usually follows description. The speaker's name is printed in capitals in the center of the page. The person's name should be repeated each time their dialogue is interrupted by description or action.

To the right of the speaker's name there might be screen directions, specifically if the dialogue is delivered offscreen (O.S). Longer and more detailed descriptions belong in the descriptive paragraph separated from the lines of speech. Lines of dialogue follow the parentheses (if any), offset slightly further to the left.

MASTER-SCENE EXAMPLE

Notice how easy it is to see the various sections, making for an easy read.

34

3.

3.   CONTINUED:

                    GRANT
          Two thousand?!

                    NICHOL
          Damn right -- y'get two for the
          price of one Irishman, and they pay
          for their own food and camp.

Grant gives Nichol a look - the man's talking his language.

As the businessmen continue up the slope, the Chinese foreman
steps into frame watching them, eyes cold with distaste; his
face disfigured by a brutal scar. This is BOOK MAN.

                                                    4.

4.   EXT.   MOUNTAIN RANGE - DAY

Nichol and Grant crest the ridge. In the loose shale, Grant
jockeys for a footing, sending a cascade of stones bouncing
and rolling into the canyon a hundred feet below

Nichol grabs Grant's arm to steady him.

                    NICHOL
          You wanted to see it? Look -
          there it is.

Grant looks out, awestruck at the vista before him.

                    GRANT
                  (annoyed)
          Dammit all, man. How do you think
          y'can cross that in a year?

                    NICHOL
          I'll do it. Tell your directors
          not to worry.

                    GRANT
          They don't need to worry, Alfred.
          You do -

REVEAL: A sweep of plunging cloudy canyon that dwarfs them,
then rises into a seemingly impenetrable wall of mountains.

                    GRANT (O.S) (CONT'D)
          - if you don't make it, the bank
          will take every penny of your
          assets and receivables.

                    NICHOL (O.S)
          I swear I'm gonna drive a railroad
          through there...if it kills me and
          every man under me.

                                          CUT TO:

STORYBOARDS

The script is the written blueprint for your movie, and the storyboard is the visual guide. Screenplays are best presented in the correct standardized format, but storyboards aren't necessarily placed under such rigid constraints.

OBJECTIVES >>
- **Be able to explain concepts**
- **Make sure the film works**
- **Understand storyboard formats**

Why storyboards?

One of the primary reasons for using storyboards is to convey your ideas to other members of the production team, especially the director of photography (or cinematographer or cameraman). It may also be useful for explaining concepts to the visually illiterate, such as some producers and money people. When the Wachowski brothers were trying to get *The Matrix* made, they had to get elaborate storyboards drawn because the people who could green-light the project didn't understand the script.

Although it is not necessary to storyboard every shot, having a detailed storyboard can make the shoot run a lot more smoothly. It does not mean that you have to adhere rigidly to what you've drawn, because unexpected things will happen during the shoot—or someone, including you, may come up with a better idea. In these situations, if you aren't flexible you will probably end up either going crazy or missing a special, magical shot.

Each director has his or her own approach to storyboards, from making highly detailed drawings of every shot to simple napkin scribbles of the most complex scenes. How you use storyboards will depend on your experience and particular working methods.

Setting the pace

A storyboard is useful in preproduction for checking the flow and pacing of the story. This can be done with an animatic, which involves making a video of the

TRACKING PROGRESS
As the director shoots, he or she checks his or her storyboards and will eliminate or check off shots as needed.

LOW-BUDGET TIP
If you cannot afford to purchase (or don't have access to) Microsoft Excel or Adobe Illustrator, then simply use a pen or pencil, a ruler, and paper to create your paperwork. Or, you can download Open Office Suite. It is free and has the same word processing power as Excel. www.openoffice.org.

STORYBOARDS
This storyboard shows three very long shots and what happens as each shot progresses toward and into the house for the opening sequence. Shot 1: Exterior shows 12 distinct visual points in its development (and movement). Shot 2: Exterior on house, although shorter, shows six distinct visual points. Shot 3: This shot is shorter than the previous two but establishes the main character asleep on the couch. This is an effects-heavy sequence and required a highly detailed storyboard in order to get the visual elements across to the director of photography.

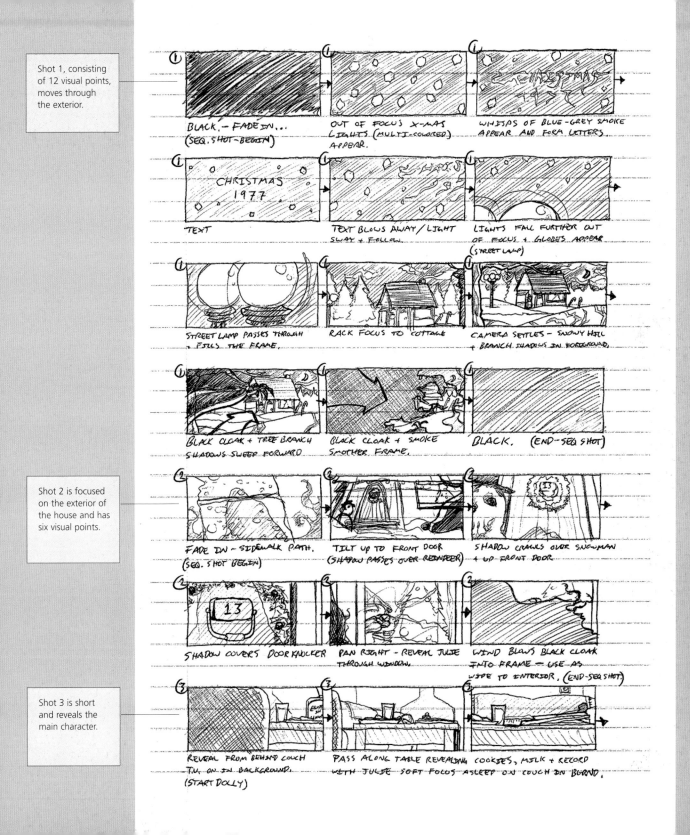

Shot 1, consisting of 12 visual points, moves through the exterior.

Shot 2 is focused on the exterior of the house and has six visual points.

Shot 3 is short and reveals the main character.

1 BLACK. – FADE IN...
(SEQ. SHOT – BEGIN)

1 OUT OF FOCUS X-MAS LIGHTS (MULTI-COLORED) APPEAR.

1 WHISPS OF BLUE-GREY SMOKE APPEAR AND FORM LETTERS.

1 TEXT

1 TEXT BLOWS AWAY / LIGHT SWAY + FOLLOW.

1 LIGHTS FALL FURTHER OUT OF FOCUS + GLOBES APPEAR (STREET LAMP)

1 STREET LAMP PASSES THROUGH + FILLS THE FRAME.

1 RACK FOCUS TO COTTAGE

1 CAMERA SETTLES – SNOWY HILL + BRANCH SHADOWS IN FOREGROUND.

1 BLACK CLOAK + TREE BRANCH SHADOWS SWEEP FORWARD

1 BLACK CLOAK + SMOKE SMOTHER FRAME.

1 BLACK. (END – SEQ SHOT)

2 FADE IN – SIDEWALK PATH. (SEQ. SHOT BEGIN)

2 TILT UP TO FRONT DOOR (SHADOW PASSES OVER REINDEER)

2 SHADOW CRAWLS OVER SNOWMAN + UP FRONT DOOR.

2 SHADOW COVERS DOOR KNOCKER

2 PAN RIGHT – REVEAL JULIE THROUGH WINDOW.

2 WIND BLOWS BLACK CLOAK INTO FRAME – USE AS WIPE TO INTERIOR. (END – SEQ SHOT)

3 REVEAL FROM BEHIND COUCH T.V. ON IN BACKGROUND. (START DOLLY)

3 PASS ALONG TABLE REVEALING WITH JULIE SOFT FOCUS

3 COOKIES, MILK + RECORD ASLEEP ON COUCH IN BGRND.

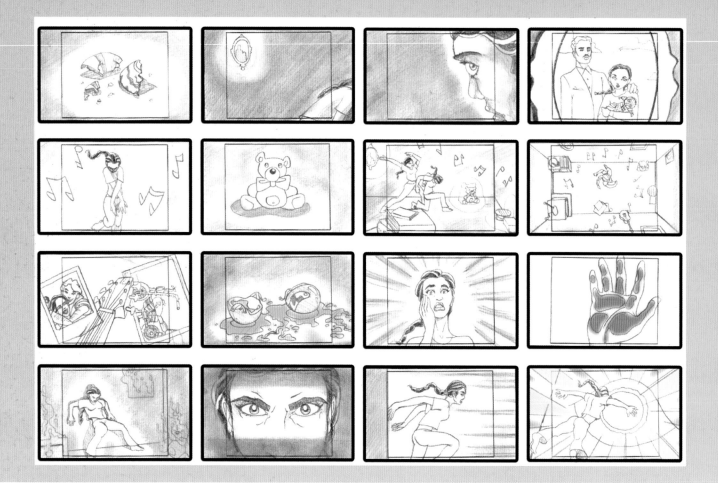

WORDLESS BOARD

This storyboard shows a series of shots showing a progressive approach to the entire story. Some storyboards will not contain sound or dialogue, just enough visual information (such as angle, frame, and action) to get the idea across. Coverage of each frame could be an option. Note the 4:3 aspect ratio box within the 16:9 frame (see pages 82–83). This is done to maintain correct wide-screen ratios in case the project is deployed accordingly. This is an experimental art film and is silent.

storyboards and adding the dialogue from the script. You can either shoot each storyboard frame to the requisite length with your video camera, or use a scanner and edit the images together on your computer, dubbing the sound on later. The animatic will give you a good idea of the film's running time, and any superfluous scenes or shots will become immediately evident.

For short films, where time is at a premium, storyboards and animatics will help to ensure that the film works. Editing a feature film to a manageable length is a matter of cutting minutes at a time from it, but when you are only working with minutes, you have to make the most of every second.

In traditional animated films, storyboarding is a vital stage because you don't have the luxury of retakes or reshoots. Experimenting with different angles is not a viable option when there are thousands of drawings involved. 3-D CGI (computer-generated image)

animation does offer more flexibility to experiment before the final render, but it is still a time- and labor-intensive activity. Shooting live action, on the other hand, especially on video, does afford you the luxury of multiple takes, which can ultimately be resolved in the editing suite—usually.

Details

As storyboards are visual reminders, how detailed you make them is entirely up to you. Plain white record cards are an ideal medium; they are also useful when developing your script. You can make your sketches on one side and write notes on the other. Cards can be pinned to a wall or notice board (which is where the name "storyboard" comes from), and are easily shuffled around. Alternatively, you can draw some boxes to your screen ratio and print them from your computer, or photocopy them. These sheets can be bound into a folder, to avoid losing them. Don't worry if you can't

Board built using Poser Pro (Smithmicro), Vue (Eon Software), and Photoshop.

The camera cranes down from wide on the boy and his grandfather to a tighter shot.

draw, because the quality of the pictures is not that important: even stick figures will do, as long as the idea is conveyed.

Going digital

Naturally, in this digital age, there are software solutions too. Two companies are competing for the market share (much as in scriptwriting): Power Productions' Storyboard programs, which come in three versions—Storyboard Quick, Storyboard Artist, and Storyboard Artist Pro—each with an increasingly complex range of features, and FrameForge 3D.

All these programs let you create storyboards from libraries of scenes, props, and characters, or you can add your own digital photos of locations. Some can integrate with scriptwriting software and also produce an animatic, so you can have a clear idea during preproduction of how your movie should work. These programs produce rather generic results that lack the

charm of hand-drawn boards, but they are reasonably economical, quick, and easily edited, which makes them worth considering as an option.

Whichever method you choose, storyboards are a vital part of the production process. They will make your work, and that of others, much easier, no matter which role(s) in the production you choose.

Assignment

Create a series of screen boxes on your computer and print them. Then, sketch in the shots with any notes you might want. The drawings don't need to be elaborate—they're simply to remind you what you want to shoot.

DIGITAL BOARDS

Joint film directors Ian and Dominic Higgins favor digital boards because they "get to play around with lighting schemes and camera angles in a virtual world." Most 3D software allows you to change the camera focal length of your "virtual cameras" to help mimic different lenses and you can add as many or as few lights as you want and reposition them, change their angle, and alter their intensity. It's helpful to be able to experiment with shots this way without a cast and crew breathing down your neck.

Q&A

STORYBOARD ARTIST
Rachel Garlick

1. How important are storyboards to the low-budget filmmaker?
One of the most important uses of storyboards to the low-budget filmmaker is exactly the same as that of the high-budget filmmaker in that the process allows the director to hone and focus his or her vision of the script, saving a huge amount of time (which as we know equals money) on set. It means all of the deliberating gets done before the camera rolls and provides a document for all other crew in the preproduction/production process that allows them to work more efficiently with the director. Lots of questions are answered by storyboards up front, and that means the project runs in a more streamlined and labor-saving way.

2. What is the simplest approach to creating storyboards for the first-time filmmaker.
The simplest approach to storyboarding for a first-time filmmaker is to draw basic thumbnails (stickmen could suffice) for your boards and annotate them to convey technical needs, such as shot size, camera movement, etc. Arrows are also useful to add camera movement or movement within the frame.

82.1   INT. Bramwell Hosp. Noah's Room - Morning
M/S Noah lies in bed in the fetal position. He looks pale and sweaty. He has a journal in his hands.

82.2
C/U journal page.
There is a small photo of his mother and next to the photo is a pencil rendition of it.

SCENE 82 FILMED
SCENE 82.1 48 MINS 39 SECS

SCENE 82.2 48 MINS 55 SECS

3. What is the minimum amount of information that should appear on a storyboard?

The minimum amount of information that should appear on a storyboard would be a sketch of what's being shot within the frame and then annotations underneath the frame to describe shot size, camera movement, and the basic action in that frame. Do not forget to label every frame according to the scene number within the script so that everyone viewing the storyboards knows exactly what it relates to.

4. What is the most important part of a storyboard artist's job?

The most important part of a storyboard artist's job is to be able to interpret what's in the director's head and put it onto paper. It doesn't matter how great a draftsperson you are if the image you end up with does not represent what the director has asked for, because its importance as a document is that every member of the crew who views it should have a clear idea of the director's vision.

FROM STORYBOARD TO SCREEN

In the sequence below we see four shots from a storyboard and their corresponding frame grabs in the final film. Note how some shots match exactly, while some were altered from the intended vision slightly as the practicalities of production dictated.

82.3
C/U   Noah looks at the drawing

82.4B Cont. Camera Jib Up
...his mother sitting at the end of his bed in the exact same pencil form that she is in his journal (rotoscope animation).
MUM "Mind if I smoke?"

SCENE 82.3 49 MINS 07 SECS

SCENE 82.4 49 MINS 23 SECS

2

Arguably, preproduction (perhaps the critical phase of filmmaking) starts at the point of having a locked final draft of a script in hand. Once you have a scripted story, the "war" of preproduction can begin in earnest. Realistically, preproduction is defined as containment. You need to be prepared to push, pull, and drag your script before the camera no matter what happens. And yes, the script will fight you every step of the way. All of the events that happen prior to shooting your film will need to be carefully and assertively maneuvered into their proper place within a schedule.

PREPRODUCTION

Preproduction is the preserve of highly organized individuals who dissect, break down, budget, and make the script a viable prospect. It is composed of numerous activities and skill sets: planning, organization, and management (as well as things like intuition, leaps of faith, prayers, and good old-fashioned communication skills). The size of your show (meaning your budget or number of pages you intend to shoot) does not matter—the script does not discern between large or small. Eventually, battle by battle, although it will sometimes feel impossible, you will win the war on containment and be ready to shoot.

THE BUDGET

BUDGET TIPS

- Using a spreadsheet such as Microsoft Excel is the easiest way to produce a budget. You can add an extra column for actual expenses, taken from your receipts, if you want to compare them with your projected costs. An Excel spreadsheet template for a large-budget film shoot, listing all the items you could ever need to purchase, is available to download from http://makingthemovie.info.

- The categories listed below are a great guide to what you need to take into account in your budget. However, this is just a starting point, and there are many items inside each category and a great deal of miscellaneous expenses.
  - Story and script
  - Producer and director
  - Performers
  - Production staff
  - Production equipment
  - Location and studio
  - Sound and music
  - Editing and finishing
  - Marketing and PR

Money makes the world go 'round, as the saying goes, and when it comes to making movies it seems to be a major criterion. In Hollywood, a movie's merits are judged by its finances: "This film cost $100 million to make"; "That film grossed $100 million at the box office" (of course, if it was the same film, it actually lost money).

OBJECTIVES >>
- ☐ Know how to research
- ☐ Understand how to factor in all expenses

There is the other extreme, which usually applies to first-time Indie films, where there seems to be competition based on how little it cost to shoot (such as the $7,000 it cost to make *El Mariachi*). These are the positive spins. The negative production comments usually tend to revolve around how much over budget a movie went. So how do you avoid this?

One way is simply not to discuss the budget with anyone. This could be tricky if someone else is funding your film. Naturally, they will want to know where their money is going, or went. Chances are, for your first films you will have no funding, personal or otherwise, and, although it is possible to make a movie for almost no money, drawing up a hypothetical budget is an excellent exercise.

One reason to start with short films is to learn as much as possible about all aspects of the filmmaking process, and drawing up a budget is something that will help prevent you from being ripped off in the future. If you know how much everything costs, you are not going to be tricked into paying more than you should.

Be accountable

It is best to set up your budget using a computer spreadsheet. It doesn't have to be very complex: one column for the names of items, one for their list prices, a column for what you expect to pay, and, most importantly, one for what you actually paid.

Your first unavoidable expenses are going to be equipment and consumables. The question of rental or purchase is covered on pages 68–69, but you should factor in a cost even if you purchased your camera. The other inescapable cost is your talent (the actors) and the crew. Even if they are working for nothing, you have to pay their travel expenses and feed them. Find out what the minimum union rates are for the people you are using, and include it in your budget. The normal cost of time or services when donated is usually known as "payment in kind." This can be very useful if you ever

MONEY MATTERS These two movies had vastly different budgets. Look at each picture and you can see the money in the shots. *El Mariachi* (1993, budget of $7000, below left) is sparse, whereas *Pirates of the Caribbean: At World's End* (2007, budget of $300,000,000, below right) looks full of life, including a big-name cast and an elaborate set. Filmmakers always throw the money in front of the camera to make it look good.

want to apply for a grant or other non-commercial funding, as it counts as part of your financial contribution to a project.

The list in the panel to the left suggests some broad categories that could be a starting point for your budget, although there are expenses in each of these categories and many miscellaneous costs too. You will need to factor in not just your performers but also catering, costumes, and makeup. Within editing you would need to consider things such as titles, optical effects, and digital color-correction. Construction, art supplies, transportation, lighting, props, location and studio fees, and publicity would all need to be accounted for. The list can go on and on, so just be sure that you consider everything that you will need throughout the whole process. For your first films, you will probably be getting a lot of your resources for nothing, but as you become more professional, every aspect of the production has to be accounted for. It is worth getting into the habit of accounting for everything while it is easy. When you start on properly financed films, all these items become deductible expenses, so always keep receipts. And if you find the thought of doing all this number crunching a bit daunting, find someone else to do it for you. Remember that they, too, become a deductible expense.

LOW-BUDGET TIP
The main philosophy is to always barter, deal-make, borrow, and beg for your show. With the right positive approach you will be surprised how many individuals and companies will support your film.

BUDGET SUMMARY SHEET

Even no-budget filmmaking incurs expenses, and while it may be possible to eliminate most of these by getting the cast and crew to pay their own way, it is not the best idea if you want to work with them again. This budget is for a ten-minute film with four actors and four crew over three days, and came to just over $500.

Finding cast and crew was done using a filmmakers' Internet bulletin.

Auditions had to be recorded to help with selections.

Some cash for emergencies.

Apart from feeding the cast and crew, paying their travel expenses is the least you can do. Allow the same for everyone even if they choose to walk or cycle, but make sure they live locally to keep the cost down. Actor 1 "donated" his car as a prop so he received a little extra for fuel.

Supplying a copy of the finished film to all participants is vital so they can use it for their audition tapes.

A local amateur theater hired out one of their spare rooms for auditions.

Camera and sound equipment was borrowed. No extra artificial light was needed.

Feeding the cast and crew is important and need not be expensive.

Even using your own printer will need ink and paper

Item	Quantity	Unit cost	Total	Notes
PREPRODUCTION				
Advertising for cast and crew	1	0.00	0.00	
Audition space per day	2	20.00	60.00	
Tapes for audition	3	5.00	15.00	
PRODUCTION				
Camera rental	1	0.00	0.00	
Microphone rental	1	0.00	0.00	
Light rental	0	0.00	0.00	
DV tape stock	3	5.00	15.00	
Script Photocopies	10	0.50	5.00	
Props	3	7.00	21.00	Toy guns
Wardrobe	0	0.00	0.00	
Makeup	1	5.00	5.00	Fake blood
Catering for 8 per day	3	40.00	120.00	
Petty cash			30.00	
TRAVEL EXPENSES PER DAY				
Actor 1	3	10.00	30.00	Includes gas for car used in movie
Actor 2	3	7.50	22.50	
Actor 3	3	7.50	22.50	
Actor 4	3	7.50	22.50	
Cameraman	3	7.50	22.50	
Sound recordist	3	7.50	22.50	
Makeup	3	7.50	22.50	
Director	3	7.50	22.50	
POST-PRODUCTION				
Editor	1	0.00	0.00	
DVD-R	20	1.50	30.00	For cast, crew, and marketing
Marketing/PR	10	2.00	20.00	Printing press pack
Total			**508.50**	

COMING UP WITH A STRATEGY FOR CONTAINMENT

Whether you are shooting a short or a feature film, you will have to organize a huge number of elements and overcome multiple obstacles before you can start production. Here, we look at the strategy you will need to employ and the key personalities in the war of containment. Over the following six pages, we will look in more depth at some tools you can utilize to get your script in front of the camera.

OBJECTIVES >>

- To understand and be able to execute preproduction and contain your script
- Know who your key crew members are in the preproduction process.

Contain the Beast

Imagine for a moment that the script can be viewed as a gnarly, nasty beast. It has two arms and two legs and is ready to tear you apart and stop your film at any time. Those legs and arms represent the four basic elements requiring containment, a paranoid watchful eye, and precision-honed organizational skills. These elements, in order of importance, are:

- locations
- actors
- crew
- equipment

Inclusive to these four elements are all the other hundreds of things requiring containment. The diagram at right gives you an idea of how many considerations there are when dealing with the Beast. The Beast will do anything necessary to prevent you from putting it in front of the camera. Your job is to contain the Beast.

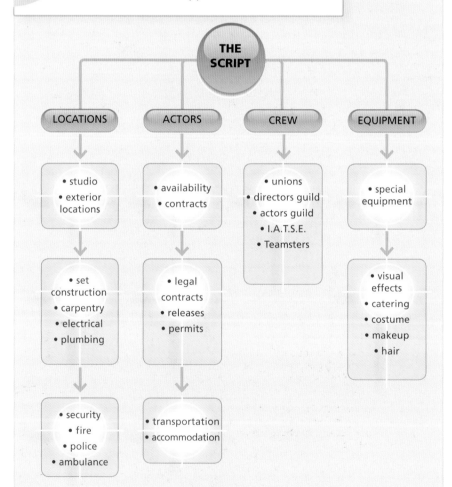

THE BEAST CONTAINED— AT LEAST ON PAPER
It may not be possible to slot every script consideration into a linear framework as here but your job is to contain the Beast whichever way you can.

THE SCRIPT

LOCATIONS	ACTORS	CREW	EQUIPMENT
• studio • exterior locations	• availability • contracts	• unions • directors guild • actors guild • I.A.T.S.E. • Teamsters	• special equipment
• set construction • carpentry • electrical • plumbing	• legal contracts • releases • permits		• visual effects • catering • costume • makeup • hair
• security • fire • police • ambulance	• transportation • accommodation		

THE SCRIPT

The chain of command

When approaching preproduction it is important to understand the chain of command, or who the four principal creative personalities are. These are the department heads. It is their creative vision that will drive the process of preparing and shooting the film. Figuratively speaking, on a small short film you will have to play the role of department head for all areas. Wherever possible, enable people to assist you in filling a role as the lead department person.

Preproduction is about relationships and how well everyone communicates. Each department has a responsibility to hold up their end of readying their department for the rigors of making a film. The panel at right gives a view of a typical chain of command or the heads of departments.

The one person that keeps all of this contained and moving toward the same end is the production manager. This is a critical hub or center of the creative team. He or she is responsible for making the rubber hit the road in a timely and efficient manner. This person is invaluable because he is often the first person hired by the producer to examine the script and determine a budget.

Assignments

1. Take a few moments to write down who you think are your creative principles. Decide your role in and among your principal creative crew.

2. Write down on a sheet of paper your perception of the biggest risks or your biggest containment issues. As you write them down, think about whether you have missed anything.

The four principal creative personalities "above the line" set the vision for the film. Everyone else "below the line" either manages or assists creating the vision.

PRINCIPAL CREATIVES

Producer
Story and budget

Director
Actor casting and performance and production manangement

Director of photography
Lighting and cameras

Production designer
Aesthetics and palette

PRODUCTION CREW

Production manager/ 1st Assistant Director
Responsible for overseeing production

All other crew
Reports to the 1stAD

FIVE STEPS TOWARD CONTAINMENT

Once the script is written, approved, and locked, there are five steps to filmmaking preproduction—the blueprint of containment of the script. These steps are designed to do one thing, and one thing only: get the script in front of the camera. It is basic in its intent but incredibly detailed in its execution. One mistake can result in delays and turmoil that can ultimately derail the filmmaking process altogether.

OBJECTIVES >>

☐ **Understand the five steps of preproduction**

CHECK THESE OUT

- www.junglesoftware.com Gorilla scheduling and production software. Demo available.
- www.entertainmentpartners.com MovieMagic Scheduling. Demo available.
- www.filmmakersoftware.com A comprehensive scheduling and budgeting software for great value (requires Microsoft Excel).

Even though all departments and sub-departments follow the steps of the battle plan, the production manager (PM) and first assistant director (1stAD) are responsible for the process of containment, or production management, every step of the way. The PM is the first to arrive and will help to determine the budget. The 1stAD is next on the scene to work toward scheduling the script. These two individuals represent the production office (PM) and the set (1stAD), and you need to make sure they're rock-solid individuals.

1. Script reading

Script reading is not done from a creative or inspirational point of view at this stage, but rather in order to see the management issues inherent to getting the film made. The master scene script is read twice—once for a general sense of the requirements and a second time for detail. Practical questions will begin to arise and notes will be made to determine the possible answers.

2. Script markup

This is the first step in formulating a scheduling game-plan after thoroughly reading the script a couple of times. A script markup has potentially three distinct purposes: for budget, creative elements, and generating a schedule.

Production managers are frequently hired to mark up a script in order to determine the budget. Producers rarely do this because they are in the business of getting money, not figuring out what it costs. A smart producer will hire the PM to mark up the script and have him or her continue through preproduction and going to camera.

The PM and the 1stAD will do a markup for scheduling. This is done to coincide with the prep time of the principal creative leads. If the production designer says sets will take a certain number of days or weeks to construct, then the schedule is driven to include those parameters. In fact, the four basic categories mentioned earlier (locations, actors, crew, and equipment—see page 34) drive the overall planning arc of the schedule.

2. THE SCRIPT MARKUP
Color-coding is used to "lift" the elements off the page.

Each department is color-coded so responsibility for each implicit script element can easily be assigned.

Set deck means set decoration—anything that contributes to the look of the set but is not handled by the actors: furniture, books on a shelf, photographs, etc.

Any small item that will need to be picked up, handled, or used by the actors is categorized as a prop.

Each element is coded only the first time it is mentioned in the script.

Although it is used by the actors, furniture is set decoration, not a prop.

SCRIPT

░	Location
■	Character
■	Props
▒	Set deck
■	Vehicles/Transport

```
1        INT. HOUSE - NIGHT                                      1

         The place is clean and tidy with minimum furniture. There are
         books and puzzles in an open cupboard by the computer table.

         Jason, a typical nerd in his early twenties is in the living
         room reading an article about sleep apnea on his computer.

         We hear knock at the door.

         Jason gets up, opens the door just a little bit.

                              JASON
                   Oh hey Dave, what brings you here
                   my friend?

         A tall, black silhouette of a male appears, takes a step
         inside the room and we can see his face.

         DAVE a jock guy, almost drunk carrying a bag, stands at the
         door smiling.

                              JASON (CONT'D)
                   My god, you stink!

         Jason moves away looking disgusted.

                              DAVE
                   Let me in dude, I've gotta take a
                   leak. Damn these cold beers, here
                   take'em.

         Dave forcefully lets himself in, handing the bag to Jason and
         runs to the back of the room.

         Jason shuts the door and places the bag on the table. He then
         continues the reading on his computer.

         Dave comes in, stands behind Jason, reading over his
         shoulder.

                              DAVE (CONT'D)
                   What are you doing man?

         He kneels and looks at his computer.

                              DAVE (CONT'D)
                   Sleep anemia, what is that?

         Jason turns back to Dave.
```

FRIDAY NIGHT

Every creative department involved in a film will also complete a script markup. It raises questions and issues all focused around the creative look and feel of the movie and has nothing to do directly with the production schedule. The technique of underlining in color is used to identify all the different elements of the script. A legend or key is configured to clearly show what elements are as these might be numerous. For example, there could be many different colors used to identify the many different elements just within the hair and makeup department.

Within this script markup, there are two main categories to identify—the "implicit" and the "explicit" elements. It is the implicit ones that will catch you off-guard. These are the elements the "beast" deploys to throw your plans into turmoil. For example, the script may describe a man walking down the street at night. The explicit elements are the walking man, the street, and nighttime. Those implied are the details about the man (tall, short, bald, skinny, heavy-set?), what the street looks like, and what is in the street. The implicit elements can be identified and clarified when the entire creative group and key personnel have a production meeting. The 1stAD leads the meeting by reading each line of the script, resulting in all departments clearing away the implicit elements in their script markups.

3. Script breakdown

You will need to break the script down into its basic constituent parts—scenes, locations, and actors—but also keep a note of shot length (this is done by dividing the script page into eighths and marking how many eighths a scene requires), props, effects, and camera equipment. Take all of the markup items and place them on a breakdown sheet. Each scene (not each page) gets a breakdown sheet. The entries you make are encoded as basic information. For example, your actors will now be assigned a number, starting with the principal actors at 1, 2, and so on. This effective means of categorization breaks the script down into manageable

3. THE BREAKDOWN SHEET

Each scene has its own breakdown sheet full of important information.

pieces. The pages themselves are color-coded:

Yellow Exterior Day
White Interior Day
Green Exterior Night
Blue Interior Night

Typically, a production budget cannot be prepared until a script breakdown is created. However, what happens first in budget preparation and script breakdown will depend on the most pressing needs of the preproduction. A breakdown for budget only is completed first. A breakdown for schedule will come later, after the production is funded.

Several formats of script breakdown sheets are used in the industry, but the differences are mainly in the manner in which the information is arranged on the page. The function of the breakdown sheet, as the name implies, is to break down the information contained on the script page into its component physical requirements. Each department completes this process of breakdown as it relates to their specific needs. The example shown to the right is a breakdown sheet used by the production manager for the purposes of budget and creating an initial schedule.

4. Production board

The production board is a graphic representation of the entire script. Although not yet day- or time-specific, it moves the script into the realm of the shooting schedule. It is a look at a living, breathing script ready to go before the camera. This representation comes in the form of cardboard strips encoded with information for each master scene from the breakdown sheets, and laid out in a flat frame. The strips are vertically aligned to show the number of scenes to be shot in a given day or week. You can also buy software for this purpose, if you don't want to make a physical board, called MovieMagic Scheduling, the result of which can be seen opposite.

Once the PM has reduced the script information onto breakdown sheets, it is possible to arrange the script's basic units into a shooting sequence. The 1stAD is

---

BREAKDOWNS

BREAKDOWN SHEET

BREAKDOWN PAGE # 1 _____

SHOW Friday Night _____   PRODUCTION # Preeti _____
EPISODE _____   DATE _____
LOCATION House _____

SCENE #"S		DESCRIPTION		NO. OF PAGES
	(INT)(EXT)		(DAY)(NIGHT)	
1	INT	Dave comes to Jason's house and compels him to	DAY	1, 2
		drink beers with him.		
			TOTAL	2

NO.	CAST	BITS/DOUBLES	ATMOSPHERE
1 2	Dave Jason	-	quiet at first, fun, party

WARDROBE	PROPS/SET DRESSING
Full sleeves, flannel shirt & regular jeans	Computer, beer bottles, four glasses. two energy drinks, bag / table, books, puzzles, open cupboard, computer table
T- shirt & torn jeans	
SPEC. EFFECTS	TRANS/PIC VEHICLES
-	-

STUNTS	MUSIC/SOUND/CAMERA	WRANGLERS/LIVESTOCK
-	Sound- Camera-	-

HAIR/MAKE-UP	SPECIAL REQUIREMENTS
Hair Makeup	Minimum furniture in the living room. Place is clean and tidy. Sleep Apnea article on computer.

FRIDAY NIGHT

Production data appears at the top of the sheet.

Cast members listed and assigned numbers.

Scenes and page count are listed.

Categories _____

Production data always appears at the top of the sheet.

Different colors are used to denote lighting and location.

4. DIGITAL PRODUCTION BOARD

Here, we see a production board that has been created using MovieMagic Scheduling software. On the next page you can see a traditional production board created with cardboard strips.

Assignment

Create your own breakdown sheet using Excel or a simple piece of lined paper. Apply your markup from the previous activity to the breakdown sheet.

generally responsible for the preparation of the production board, and sometimes the PM.

By transferring the most pertinent details of the breakdown sheets onto thin strips and arranging these within a frame, it is possible to view the film as a whole. The strips laid side-by-side present a continuum of the entire production and also constitute a flexible tool, for the strips can be rearranged at will to accommodate the changing needs of preproduction and production.

Each vertical strip is used to represent the continuous action of a master scene. This master may consist of one or several actual scene numbers from the script. The strips are lined to form boxes for encoding information. A header on the left side of the board acts as a key or legend to the entries in the boxes. With the information filled in and laid out, the board resembles a mosaic, as each unit contributes to forming the whole picture.

Each strip, like the breakdown sheet from which it is derived, begins with a discrete unit. These may be master scenes that run for several pages or an establishing shot that barely qualifies as an eighth of a page. The most fundamental concept remains that of continuous action from the same camera angle. The board preparer may be well aware that the director plans to shoot many shots to cover a given master scene. The purpose of the production board, however, is to continue the process of the breakdown sheet in extracting and encapsulating the action of the script scenes.

There are two sizes of board strips in use: 15 inches (380 mm) and 18 ¼ inches (460 mm) high. The widths vary from ³/₁₆ inches (45 mm) to ⁵/₁₆ inches (79 mm). Many board preparers use colored strips for quick identification of lighting and location. There is no

Master scene strips are grouped into shooting days

		No.	EXT STREET	EXT CITY MALL	EXT STREET	EXT STREET	INT DAY	INT TALK SHOW	INT CORRIDOR (ESTABLISH)	INT CORRIDOR 12	INT CORRIDOR 12	INT CORRIDORS	INT CORRIDOR	INT BOARD ROOM	2ND DAY / INT COCKPIT	INT ANNIE'S OFFICE	INT ANNIE'S OFFICE	INT ANNIE'S OFFICE	INT ANNIE'S OFFICE	INT MAIN CONTROL ROOM
Date Breakdown page			49	47	45	48	43	2	85	66	100	10	47A	81	8	73	50A	19	80
Day or Nite			D	D	D	D							D						
Period Pages			7/	4/	4/	✓	7/	✓	✓	✓	✓	2/	6/	✓	3⅜	1⅜	2⅞	✓	✓
Sequence																			
Scene #			53	50A	50	52	45	2	101	76ft	23A	10	51	96	8	99	57	20	75

Title: "The Creature Wasn't Nice"
Director: Bruce Kimmel
Producer: Mark Haggard
Asst. Dir.
Script Dated 2/24/81

Character	Artist	No.																		
Annie		1														1	1	1	1
John		2								2	2						2		
Jameson		3																	
Rodzinski		4														4			
Dr. Stark		5															5		
Creature		6								6	6								
Max (V.O.)		7																	
Old Man		8	8	8	8	8							8						
Linda		9						9											
Grace		10						10											
Margie		11						11											
Board Member		12											12						
Punk		13		13															
Hood #1		14	14																
#2		15	15																
#3		16	16																
#4		17	17																
Person		18																	
Narrator (V.O.)		19	19	19	19	19													
News Announcer (V.O.)		20																	
Body Trans.		21						21											
Atmosphere - Bits		22					1						4						
- General		23	12	12	12		X												
Driver		24				X													
Add'l Camera		25																	
Video Playback		26																	
Cart/Cars		27	X		X	X													
Crane		28		X	X														
Playback		29																	
FX: Vertigo		30																	
Shuttle (Miniature)		31																	
Computer		32																	
Cockpit Lights		33												33					
A) Slender		34																	
B) 2001		35																	
C) Flying		36																	
D) Planet		37																	
E) Terrain		38																	
F) Three Shuttle		39																	
		40																	

Production data is listed at the top of the board.

People and objects are listed and assigned numbers.

4. PRODUCTION BOARD

A traditional working schedule of the shoot comprised of cardboard strips that can be moved around to keep the board up to date.

standard code, but, as with the script breakdown sheets, the four most common are: yellow for exterior day, white for interior day, green for exterior night, and blue for interior night. Various kinds of black strips may serve as dividers and may have white areas for marking the shooting day.

The operative method in the preparation and updating of the production board should be one of expedient and positive annotation. This means the board preparer, whether the PM or the 1stAD, must reanalyze the raw data of the script and the refined data of the breakdown sheet to reduce them further in both logical and economical fashion. Although this process is essentially subjective, the underlying assumptions are commonly held by most industry professionals.

Each strip of the production board should contain only a clearly encoded representation of the content and basic physical requirements of the scene to be filmed.

5. The call sheet

The call sheet is the official shooting schedule—the call to work. This final document describes each day's planned shooting schedule in detail and informs everyone on the production of where, when, and how the day's work is planned to be completed. The word "planned" merits emphasis, because the call sheet, like all the production paperwork, is always subject to change. Unlike other forms, the call sheet is the culmination of all the preproduction scheduling and deal making—the implement by which production itself is initiated. The call sheet is the direct line of communication from the set to the departments. It is the document that officially releases work calls and requisitions equipment; placing a request for anything, from a camera crane to coffee and donuts, by writing it on the call sheet, means that they will arrive at the appointed time and place without any further action. Because the call sheet has such impact, it must allow for all the significant needs of a given day's work to be clearly inscribed. If a call sheet is unclear, turmoil and confusion will ensue.

5. THE CALL SHEET

This official document is signed off by the PM and the 1stAD. It serves to inform everyone working on the production of the planned schedule for each day.

The main reason for having a shooting schedule is economic. Even if there is no money involved, there is time. Without a properly coordinated schedule, you are going to waste a lot of time, which can lead to frayed tempers and even missed shots. For example, if you have a location that is only available for one day but appears at different times in the script, you will have to shoot everything required on that one day with all the right costumes, props, and actors (with the all-important continuity person noting every detail).

A common operating procedure is for call sheets to be signed or initialed by the production manager before being copied and distributed. The second assistant director is generally responsible for preparing the call sheet. This is accomplished by consulting the production board and shooting schedule. This implies a final check with the 1st assistant director to make sure that everything is up to date. Since the call sheet for a given day must be distributed to the cast and crew affected on the day before, the call sheet must be prepared 24 hours ahead of the work that it details. The most important information on the call sheet is as follows:

1. The sets or location
2. Scene numbers
3. Cast numbers
4. Page count.

Since everyone relies on the accuracy of the call sheet to prepare the day's work, double or even triple checking it may be essential. The originator's last step should be a thorough review of the scenes by rereading the script and verifying that all production elements are listed on the call sheet.

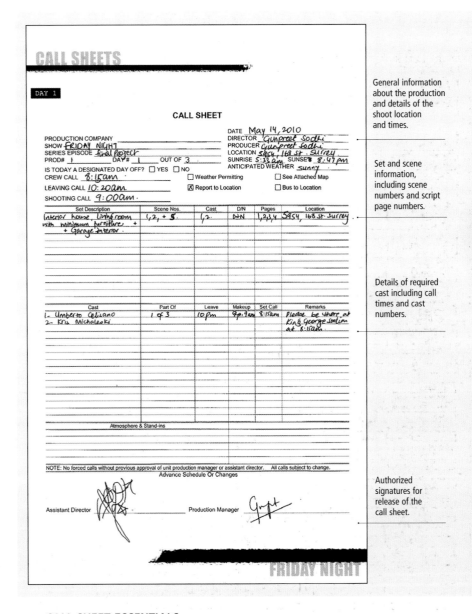

General information about the production and details of the shoot location and times.

Set and scene information, including scene numbers and script page numbers.

Details of required cast including call times and cast numbers.

Authorized signatures for release of the call sheet.

CALL SHEET ESSENTIALS

There are many different formats of call sheets, but each should allow for the following data to be entered:

1. Basic heading information
2. Script information
3. Cast information
4. Crew information
5. Special information or remarks
6. Transportation information
7. Advance schedule information
8. Production staff information.

LOCATION MANAGEMENT

Low-budget filmmaking relies almost totally on shooting on location. Building sets and hiring studios come so far down the budget priority list that the topic need not even be broached in this book. Of course, if you are lucky enough to get the use of a studio, and it can be dressed for nothing, that's another matter.

OBJECTIVES >>
- **Understand how to shoot in public spaces**
- **Know the insurance requirements**
- **Be able to shoot in interior locations**

Shooting on location isn't just about saving money—you may have to pay for using that old warehouse—it's about realism. Big-budget Hollywood features tend to look at using locations from a different perspective, which does involve economics, and the ability to control the environment. The size of a feature-film crew means that the sheer cost of moving it, along with lighting and camera rigs, can outweigh the cost of building the set in a studio. Shooting on location also adds other variables, such as time constraints determined by disruption to public life, and uncontrollable factors such as natural phenomena (weather, light). All sorts of permits are required before you can shoot in public spaces and thoroughfares, and it only takes one unexpected event to send the schedule spiraling out of control. There are plenty of documented examples.

Taking it to the streets

There is a huge amount of the money involved in filmmaking, so most major cities have agencies or departments dedicated to overseeing, coordinating, and issuing permits for film shoots. It is always worth contacting them to find out the legal requirements and costs for filming in public, and they will require details of your shoot. Explain that it is a no-budget film and you want to do the right thing. If you have any students on your crew, you can try the old "student project" line.

Naturally, if the shoot involves an action sequence with a car chase or firearms (even fake ones), it is imperative to inform the police to avoid jail or physical injury, or both—which brings up the issue of insurance (see "Insurance and safety" at right).

Shooting indoors

Interior locations present a whole different set of problems, depending on whether you want to use private, civil, or civic premises. You still need to obtain permission from the owner or management of the property and fit the shoot in around their schedule, which usually means after hours. As you are relying on goodwill, you have to accept their terms and adjust your shooting, or even the script, to suit.

There are several options from which to choose. Each will have its own access and containment issues. Make sure there is enough space for your crew to work and set up lights if necessary. Mirrors on the walls can cause problems. Restore any furniture to its original position at the end of the shoot. Government offices are often available on weekends and evenings and are usually free because they are public places. Not many filmmakers know that as a tax-paying citizen, you have access to many government resources.

During preproduction, you or the producer should visit the location and draw up a clear contractual agreement with the owners, including a detailed inventory. No matter how friendly you all are in the beginning, if something goes wrong and it starts getting nasty, you need to have yourself covered. It will also lend you an air of professionalism that may work in your favor when dealing with bureaucrats.

There are companies and individuals that source, catalog, and offer locations to the film industry. Depending on your budget you may want to consider this as an option to cut down on the time it takes to find and negotiate a location. If you can afford it, it is recommended that the producer obtain the services of a location professional. The Location Managers Guild of America is a good source for finding professionals. Whichever way you decide to work, once you have decided on the locations, draw up a list, agree dates with the owners or managers, sign any contracts, and add the locations and dates to your shooting schedule.

INSURANCE AND SAFETY

Without entering into a debate on the moral basis of insurance, it is the case that if you are shooting a movie on location with a cast and crew, you should get some public liability coverage. In these litigious times, if something were to go wrong, not having sufficient insurance could end your film career before it starts—unless you want to make a documentary on the legal and penal system. Without insurance, you will not be issued a permit.

With outdoor locations, make sure that you have decided well in advance where you want to shoot, that you have the appropriate permits, and also that you have contingency plans. The whole point of preproduction is to make the shoot go as smoothly as possible.

LOW-BUDGET TIP

To avoid mounting costs and filming restrictions, the best approach often is to find as many freely available locations as you can, and develop your story around them.

LOCATIONS:
Public places

Many restaurant and store owners will be quite happy to let you shoot in their establishments for nothing, as long as it doesn't interfere with their business and you give them a credit. Public transportation is a very difficult location to acquire. You must seek permission from the operators, it may cost you, and they will usually restrict you to off-peak times.

LOCATIONS:
Exteriors

Your biggest problem here is going to be the environment, as you are at the mercy of the elements. Continuity could be an issue; for example, once snow has been walked on, it is almost impossible to restore it to a pristine condition. Reflections could cause havoc with exposure, and cold, wind, and rain will affect your cast, crew, and equipment. If you are somewhere remote, a power supply is unlikely, unless you are carrying a generator.

LOCATIONS:
Offices and apartments

For a simple office shoot, you can arrange to do your filming over the weekend, although with a small cast it could be hard to imitate the frenetic energy of a busy office outside of trading hours. Borrowing friends' apartments is an easy way to show a realistic domestic environment, although make sure there's enough room for your crew, cast, and equipment.

Q&A

LOCATION MANAGER
Lori Balton, President, Location Managers Guild of America

1. What is the first thing to look for when scouting a potential shooting location?
It depends on circumstances. Visually matching the script is the first concern, but logistics are important—you have to fit in a traveling circus of crew and equipment; cost is important—you have a budget to keep; geography is also important—if it is linked to another location shot the same day, they must be close to each other; and scheduling is important—the location must be available when it falls in the 1stAD's schedule to shoot (and schedule hinges on actor availability among myriad additional concerns).

2. Typically, what can be the biggest challenge with a location?
There is nothing typical about location work; every day presents a new and often unexpected challenge. Each location has its own peculiarities.

3. Why are locations often the most difficult aspect of getting the script before the cameras?
Every department at times thinks they have the greatest challenge, and we all have to function as a team to bring the best results to the director. Because of the ever-changing dynamics of finding and managing a location that works, our job is constant, continuing even after filming because the location must be returned in the same, or better, condition to ensure being asked back on the next project. We interface with every department and are constantly striving to expand our knowledge and skill set, from understanding architectural details, to scouting for 3-D, to honing negotiating skills, to interpreting the legalese of location contracts.

CASTING AND REHEARSALS

Assuming that your foray into films is neither a documentary nor animation, you are going to need some actors (or "talent"). Finding a competent, experienced crew (whom you don't know), willing to work for nothing, is difficult—mainly because if they are any good, they are already earning a living.

OBJECTIVES >>
- **Be able to source talent**
- **Know about audition protocol**
- **Understand the importance of rehearsal**

Competition among actors for the few paying roles out there is fierce. When actors say "break a leg" to each other, they mean it. Most actors between jobs will be happy for the chance to appear in low-budget films, even without payment, because it will give them material for their résumés. Of course, it is up to you to make it something they would want to include.

So, how do you go about finding actors who are between jobs?

Casting on the net

There are websites, such as shootingpeople.org, that run daily bulletins for actors and filmmakers. Subscribers to the site can display a "card" outlining their skills, experience, and other personal data. This makes it an excellent starting point, especially as subscribers are already in the lo-no budget mind-set.

Another excellent resource is a local theater group or theater workshop. Signing up to take part in actors' workshops is a good way to meet actors, and learning

ACTOR'S RÉSUMÉ
This document, usually one page in length and presented along with a headshot, briefly shows the actor's experience, training, and skills.

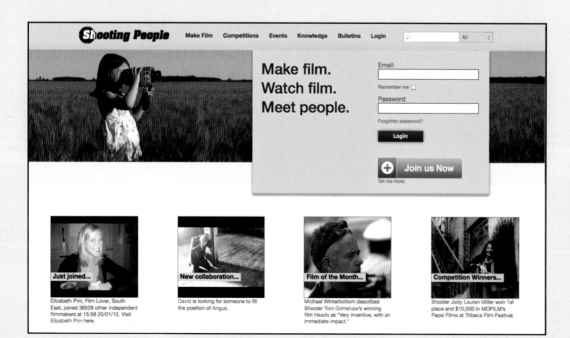

TALENT ON THE INTERNET
With a little research and creative discovery, you can use online sources to find your actors. Many websites, such as shootingpeople.org have links to talented actors looking for work. Some may even consider acting in low- or no-budget productions on which they can cut their teeth. Other online avenues you could explore include Craigslist, acting school alumni or graduate websites, or professional websites such as LinkedIn and Plaxo.

Kyle Elmsworth

SAG-AFTRA
Height: 5' 11" **Weight:** 150 lb
Hair: Brown **Eyes:** Green

Phone: 555 764 9471
E-mail: KyleElmsworth@gmail.com
Agent: Bruce Smith Associates, Los Angeles 555 764 9101

Training

- Vancouver Academy of Dramatic Arts. Dramatic Arts Program. Simon Longmore/Tony Alcantat
- Camera Acting Technique at the Studio on the Drive & UBCP, Vancouver, BC
- Physical Theatre skills with Rough Cut Theatre Co.
- St Thomas of Villanova High School. Dramatic Arts. Various.

Skills

- **Accents:** Standard American, American South, British, Russian
- **Sports:** Soccer, basketball, hockey
- **Other:** Strong improv background, Certified PADI Open Water Scuba Diver, Drivers license
- Will do nude scenes.
- Can play ages from late teens upward.

Experience

Film & Television:

Last Chance Casting	Principle	Whitlock World Entertainment Inc.
Fated	Lead	Vancouver Film School
Tequila and Double Doubles	Lead	Vancouver Film School
Out of Port	Lead	Vancouver Film School
Fred and Ginger	Principle	The Art Institute of Vancouver

Theater and Stage:

Joseph and the Amazing Technicolor Dreamcoat	Simian/Guard	St Thomas of Villanova
***You Don't Know Jack**	Lead/Jack	St Thomas of Villanova
Bedtime Stories	Jack Balintyne	University of Western Ontario
Office Hours	Racetrack Owner	University of Western Ontario
Departures and Arrivals	Frenchman/Janitor	University of Western Ontario

Awards

***You Don't Know Jack**	Best Actor	Sears Regional Drama Festival

---

Being a member of an actors' union shows that they have at least done some professional work.

These personal details are not enough unless accompanied by a full-length photo.

If an actor has additional or unusual skills, he or she will list them. Be wary of actors who say they can do something that isn't on their résumé. They may be capable of learning, but you won't have the time or the budget for that. If you want nude scenes, it is best to state this in the casting call, and the actor should also state his or her willingness (or unwillingness) to do it on the résumé.

Theater experience does mean they are capable of remembering lines, but theater and film acting have different methods. The venue should be a good indication of whether it was an amateur or professional production.

Make sure they include a cell phone number and email address in their personal contact details.

It is much easier to deal with an agent, although they may not want to handle no-budget jobs. Most actors doing unpaid work will not tell their agents about it.

Training does not equal experience or ability. When working with children, using untrained actors will give more natural performances, and they will often take direction better.

Film and TV experience should be supported by an audition tape. There is a good chance an actor's role was a non-speaking, "background artist" (extra) part if there is no accompanying audition tape. Either way, it shows they have experience of being on a film shoot.

some basic acting skills and techniques will help you as a director. If you understand, first-hand, the acting process, you will be able not only to relate to the talent but also to coax better performances from them. Acting for theater and film are two slightly different disciplines. Film requires short bursts of acting, often understated, that may have to be repeated several times in a short space of time, whereas the stage demands sustained and "large," almost exaggerated, performances. Film acting is more intimate, as you are performing to a very small audience that scrutinizes your every word and movement. Some stage actors have problems adapting to film because they are too theatrical, an approach that appears unnatural on camera. It is therefore very important to hold auditions.

CLINT EASTWOOD

6 ft 2 in (188 cm)

Selected films: *Unforgiven*, *A Fistful of Dollars*, *Gran Torino*, *Dirty Harry*

TILDA SWINTON

5 ft 10½ in (179 cm)

Selected films: *Constantine*, *The Chronicles of Narnia*, *The Curious Case of Benjamin Button*

ANDY SERKIS

5 ft 8 in (173 cm)

Selected films: *Ink Heart*, *The Rise of the Planet of the Apes*, *Death of a Superhero*

MEYRL STREEP

5 ft 5 in (165 cm)

Selected films: *The Iron Lady*, *Sophie's Choice*, *Silkwood*, *The Devil Wears Prada*

DANNY DEVITO

4 ft 9 in (145 cm)

Selected films: *L.A. Confidential*, *Batman Returns*, *Get Shorty*

Auditioning

Your initial selection will be based on age, gender, and physical attributes, and is usually made from the glossy pictures that actors send out. As they show only one pose, and are designed to represent the actor at his or her most glamorous, these are not always helpful. Always look at the actor's height. Unless you want big differences in height, trying to frame very tall and very short people in the same shot can be difficult.

Once you have chosen the actors you want to audition, make very clear to them any special demands you will be making—nudity, equestrian skills, working at heights—anything that is out of the ordinary. For paying jobs, actors will often lie to get the part, but with freebies, impress on them the importance of being honest, as you don't want to jeopardize them or the shoot. You will also need to know their availability.

For the auditions, find neutral territory and avoid private homes. A local theater may have a space you can use, which will also be useful for rehearsals.

During auditions it is a good idea to have someone of the opposite sex in the room to remove any possibility, or accusations, of impropriety. Having an actor with you to read any other roles is useful, as is someone to operate a video camera. Always get the actors to give their name at the beginning of the audition so you know who they are when you play the tape back.

There are many different approaches to auditioning. Some directors like to give the actors a script so they can prepare, while others like them to sight-read. You have to decide which method will give you the results you need to make the right decision.

After the initial audition, draw up a shortlist of the people you want to see again. Get them to perform with other actors you have chosen. The intangible and mysterious "chemistry" between performers does exist, and you need to do your best to find it, or at least something close.

CASTING DECISIONS
Actors come in all shapes and sizes. In the end you are looking for ability to act. You may have to compromise on the "look" in order to get a solid, experienced performance.

Audition etiquette

Apart from ensuring that there is at least one person of each sex present, there are levels of courtesy toward the actors that you should observe. Always thank them for coming, and be enthusiastic but professional about their performance, no matter how good or bad—this isn't *American Idol*. If they have come from an agent, tell them you will let their agent know, otherwise you have the thankless task of letting them know that they have not been successful. Don't do this until you have your cast firmly agreed; it is not very good to tell someone they haven't got the part, only to have to call them later to say that they have.

If your first choice can't do it, offer the part to your next choice, and so on until you have someone. Never reveal that an actor wasn't your first choice. Give all the actors a deadline for letting them know, and tell them either way.

Letting them down gently

Always do the actor the courtesy of letting them know if they did not get the part. A simple and well-written rejection letter will speak volumes about your professionalism. When composing a rejection letter or email, remember to keep it tactful and encouraging. You never know—the actor you disliked today might be perfect for a future production. Don't create enemies.

Rehearsals

Whether it's a feature film or a five-minute short, you are going to need some rehearsals. The actors will need to get a handle on their characters and establish a rapport with the rest of the cast. You may need only a couple of days, but even that will help when it comes to the shoot. It will also give you an idea of how you might want to alter the shoot to suit the talent.

As director, you must know what you are looking for in the performances. Because short films are often just snapshots from an ongoing story, you need to have a clear idea of the background and work through this with the actors. The genre and the script will dictate the nature of the rehearsals. An action piece will require one sort of rehearsal while a dialogue-heavy drama will need another. Let the actors feed you ideas; just remember who is in charge.

Cast well, rehearse well, and your shoot should go smoothly—or at least more smoothly than if you had cut corners. Rehearsals ultimately save time and money.

CONDUCTING AUDITIONS

To make the most of an audition, you should test the actor's skills and ability to get into character. Using these four methods should give you a good idea of what the actor is capable of.

- Send the actor a script and ask him or her to learn a designated passage for the audition. Alternatively, just send him or her one scene to learn, to see how he or she interprets the character from that scene. The piece should be from the script you intend to shoot. This will test his or her understanding of the character and ability to memorize lines.

- At the audition, give him or her an unseen piece, either of the same character or another character he or she might be suitable to play. Get him or her to read it through without preparation. When he or she has finished, get him or her to read it but with direction. This will test how quickly he or she can get into character and take direction.

- Discuss a possible backstory of the character with the actor and get him or her to improvise a scene, with another actor, that leads up to the one just performed or read. After the improvisation, get him or her to redo the scripted piece. This will test his or her ability to get into character and assess how he or she can contribute to the role.

- If there are any scenes that require special skills or handling of specific props, they should be performed for the camera.

CHOOSING CREW

Although its size depends on the complexity of your screenplay, you are going to need a crew with the specialized skills to help you realize your project.

At the lo-no-budget end of moviemaking, the fewer people you have working for you the better. This is primarily an economic consideration because, even if you aren't paying them, you have to at least feed them and cover their travel expenses.

If you can convince friends to help out willingly, without so much as a sandwich in recompense, that is another matter—and if they volunteer to work under those terms, better still. Of course, you don't want to surround yourself with dead wood either. You will need a small, tight-knit, multitasking crew that can work fast, anticipate situations, and solve problems.

As the size of the budget increases, so does the crew—and vice versa. You only have to watch the credits on a feature film to see the huge number of assistants, and assistants to the assistants, and so on *ad infinitum*. On small films it is best to get people each to do a variety of tasks—it is good experience for them

Producer

The producer runs practically everything, particularly the money side, and is the business face of the film. He or she usually comes from one of two angles. Either he or she has an idea for a film, or likes the idea of making a film, and hires all the necessary talent to bring it to fruition; or a writer/director wants to make a film and needs someone to take care of the business end, leaving him or her free to be creative. If you have good business sense and like dealing with all sorts of people, you should be able to take on the producer's role. The person who works with the production manager on the day-to-day running of the picture is called the line producer.

Director

Directing is perceived to be the glamour job. The director is ultimately responsible for the look and feel of the movie. The ideal is to be a writer–director, because this way the creative vision is taken from conception to completion. A lot of the director's work is organizational, ensuring that everything is ready for the shoot and is in the right place when "Action!" is called. Depending on his or her strengths, the director may take on many roles, but in Indie films (at least) the director is the boss, as long as he or she stays on budget. A good director needs to be a visionary… and something of a control freak.

Director of photography (DP)

The director of photography, or cinematographer, has the job of capturing the picture. More than just a camera operator, he or she has to work with the director on deciding the best angles, lighting, lenses, camera movements, and so on. If, as the director, you don't feel technically confident, an experienced DP will make a huge difference to the final look of your film. Nevertheless, learn to operate your own camera.

and it makes for a tighter, more manageable team. Too much specialization results in an incredible amount of standing around on film sets, and if people are not busy they want to eat—or talk. The busier everyone is, the more they will enjoy it and the greater their sense of achievement.

When you pick your crew, start with friends, or friends of friends. Acquaintances help break the ice and have the added advantage of recommendation, though this isn't always a guarantee of ability. An alternative is to join a local theater group, which will give you access to all sorts of resources and skills that can easily be translated to movies. Only get people to do the jobs you can't actually do yourself, physically or technically. This is your show, so try to do as much as possible; but once you do take someone on, let them get on with their job—providing they are not messing up. The important things to get across are first, that you are in charge, and

second, that you appreciate their help. Praise and thanks go a long way when there's no money.

In the coming pages, the various jobs will be covered in more detail, giving you a better idea of what is needed so that you can decide on the ideal size of crew for your project.

Local unions such as a Directors Guild or technical union are good sources for experienced crew. If your script is good, you might just get a few good union people on board for a negotiable fee. Knowing when local shows are on hiatus can be helpful. A lot of union people look for short, fun projects to work on between gigs. Also, film schools can be a good source for crew. Although film students may be inexperienced, they can more than make up for that with sheer enthusiasm.

Assistant director (AD)
ADs are the eyes, ears, and especially the mouth of the director. They run the set because they do all the necessary coordinating and managing work, while the director is occupied with the "vision." They are superfluous on a small shoot.

Camera operator
This is an important job because the shot must be executed according to the DP's instructions. He or she also reports any problems during the rolling of a take or shot.

Location sound
Unless you are making a silent or dialogue-free film, you will need a location sound person. This person is responsible for ensuring all sound and dialogue is recorded. He or she also functions as your boom operator. The boom operator is a person of great stamina and strength who has to hold a long pole with attached microphone over his or her head during a take, keeping it out of the frame but as close as possible to the actors. It's not as easy as it sounds.

Continuity/script supervisor

After the director, the continuity person has perhaps the most important role on the set; his or her effectiveness prevents your film from turning up on one of those movie-mistakes TV shows. His or her job is to make sure that everything matches up from shot to shot and take to take. A meticulous eye for detail, verging on the obsessive, is imperative. A digital still camera makes the job easier, but it is no substitute for observation.

Production assistants (PAs)

Perhaps the busiest members of the crew, the production assistants have to organize everything and make it happen. The AD is involved in the actual shoot, but the PAs have to oversee all the practical aspects of the film, making sure everyone and everything are where they should be, and as cheaply as possible.

Production designer/art director

The production designer is responsible for creating the look of the sets and getting them made, found, or bought. Get them to work with the PAs on sorting out props, etc.

GETTING TO GRIPS ON SET
Grips do a variety of things on set, including holding bounce boards or flex fills as shown in this photograph.

Extra crew

Gaffer: Chief electrician, responsible for lights. AKA "sparks."

Best boy: Gaffer's assistant.

Focus puller: Adjusts focus during filming.

Clapper loader: Writes details on clapperboard/slate.

Grip: Person who transports and sets up equipment and props. Operates equipment such as the dolly.

Key grip: In charge of grips.

Swing gang: People who set up and dismantle the sets.

Location manager: Books and oversees location shoots. Gets permits.

Runner: Runs, or drives, around delivering messages, cast, crew, or collecting props. Does anything no one else wants to. Paid slave wages.

Steadicam operator: Operates Steadicam—usually a specially trained camera person.

Costume

The wardrobe department not only needs to make the actor look the part; it has to be authentic. Detailed attention to time period, location, etc. are critical to giving a period film the credibility it needs to carry the audience into the story. For low-budget movies the best place to look are either movie costume shops or second-hand clothing or thrift stores.

Grip

Grips move and handle the camera and lighting equipment. They are often referred to as "intelligent muscle" because they can put lights and cameras in amazing places in order to get the right shot.

Editor

Although the editing comes after the shoot, it is advisable to get the editor involved as early as possible. A good editor can make your picture… and a bad one can ruin it. An experienced editor can give you invaluable advice about what to shoot (coverage) so that they have plenty of material to work with.

Makeup

Never underestimate the importance of makeup. Even something as simple as removing a shiny nose or forehead can be a nightmare under an inexperienced hand. Be sure your makeup artist has mainly television and film experience versus theatrical experience. The approach and design of film is different than the stage. A good place to look for an inexpensive makeup artist is film schools that instruct in makeup design and technique.

HOW MANY MAKE A CREW?

It is possible to make a film on your own (depending on how you intend to capture the sound), but that degree of autonomy is not always a good idea. The best plan is to go through the jobs listed and decide which ones you can do yourself, which you can delegate, and which will need someone with experience to advise and assist. A good starter, "bare bones" crew is listed below. Note that some positions can, and must, be combined.

- Writer/producer/director—you
- Production manager/assistant director
- Location manager/production assistant
- Script supervisor
- Director of photography/camera operator
- Key grip/key electrics
- Loction sound/post-sound designer
- Production designer/props/set decorator
- Wardrobe/hair/makeup

PRODUCTION DESIGN

When you write a script or read someone else's that you want to direct, you must have a very clear idea of what the movie is going to look like and where it will be shot. If you are the writer, you may already have specific locations in mind, or they may just be concepts based on places you've seen. If you haven't chosen anywhere, you may want to enlist the help of a production designer.

What does the production designer do?

The role of the production designer is to create the overall look of everything that appears in front of the cameras, from sets and props to costumes and even hairstyles. If you have the luxury of a studio shoot, the production designer, in consultation with the director, will devise the sets and oversee their construction and the buying or renting of props. For the lo-no budget movie, you are more likely to be shooting in borrowed locations, and on borrowed time if they are public property, so that sort of attention to detail is not always possible.

Scene stealing

If you are lucky enough to have flexible use of a location, you may need to "dress" it. This usually involves emptying the room and decorating it in a fashion that suits a character or the film. The production designer, along with a location manager, takes care of this. Sometimes this "dressing" goes beyond just changing the furniture to repainting the walls. This has to be negotiated and agreed on with the property owner, and usually entails restoring the location to its original color after the shoot—unless you can convince them how wonderful your taste in interior decorating is!

On lo-no budget movies, these sorts of cosmetic changes will add up to wasted time and money. Making the most of what you have is a very practical approach. A bit of uncluttering can help to remove unwanted distractions from the background, but anything else would be superfluous. Ideally, you don't want the setting to dominate the scene, or steal it from the actors, so it should be kept as natural as possible.

The type of film you are making will dictate your approach to production design. If the movie has lots of fast-moving action or fight scenes, the sets will have to be designed to accommodate the fight choreography, or vice versa. For exteriors, the production designer will make suggestions for locations, but with no budget you will not always be able to shoot in the place you want.

If the movie has lots of dialogue, with the focus on the actors, backgrounds may not be very important and shouldn't impose. On the other hand, because you have only a very limited time to develop a character's personality, a lot can be conveyed through the production design. Simple things like the pictures on the wall, the style of furniture, and general cleanliness (or lack of it) are all devices for conveying personality traits to the audience. One of the edicts of good writing and storytelling is to show, not tell (see page 19), and this is even more important, and easier, in visual media. Take advantage of it.

Q&A

PRODUCTION DESIGNER
Kevin Pierce

1. What is the art director/production designer's biggest challenge when dealing with a small budget?

When dealing with smaller budgets one of the biggest challenges is finding creative solutions to solve financial shortfalls without compromising the integrity of the scene or the look of the project. Typically this can mean sourcing inexpensive and/or free materials and reshaping or recycling them in as many different ways as possible. Creating a realistic budget based on a clear vision of the set design while having a healthy roster of resourceful people to work with are a few of the greatest assets a production designer can bring to any project.

2. What aspect of production design should you not stint on when working with a small budget?

A production designer should never stint on his or her design vision. Room should always be left, however, for compromise. Cost-effective solutions to creative problems can be solved many ways. For example, scaling down the size of a set, recycling construction and paint materials, building only what the camera will see, or shooting in locations that are well suited for the scene can allow for a significant reduction in labor and material costs. Oftentimes the solutions to budget issues are worked

out during conversations with the director of photography, the director, and the supporting art crew, who understand that filmmaking is a collaborative effort and production design goals are more readily attained when all the key players share input and ideas.

3. What are some good general sources for set decorating, set dressing, and general art direction?

The best general sources are the ones you most likely already know. Asking friends and family to help by donating items and materials can yield a great deal of low- or no-cost set dressing and props. Social networking websites like freecycle and craigslist as well as the yellow pages of your local telephone book can often bring some wonderful surprises when searching for materials and set dressing.

Film-friendly companies that advertise in sourcebooks such as the LA 411, NY 411, and Debbie's Book, which are all available online, are a fast (but not always cheap) way of sourcing materials. Most of the companies advertising in these sourcebooks have websites where you can view their products, and many will email you photos or video if you have specific items in mind. They'll also ship whatever you need to any location in the world. Other sourcebooks may be obtained through various State Film Commission offices.

4. What does the production designer focus on the most?

Visual communication and storytelling through texture, color, pattern, and scale (or dimension) as it pertains to floors, walls, windows, ceilings, and doors. In addition to managing the budget, set dressing details, and daily activities of the art crew, consideration should always be given to other department heads to ensure that the overall look of the film is in line with the director's vision. The basic job of the production designer is to set the palette and landscape for all of the other departments to come and work their magic.

5. Is there a production designer whose work you particularly admire?

Since 1969 Dante Ferretti has brought unforgettable beauty to the silver screen. His early works with Federico Fellini showcased the simplistic beauty of high contrast three dimensional art, which helped set the standard of form and function in production and costume design. His most recent works (*The Aviator*, *Sweeny Todd*, *Shutter Island*, and *Hugo*) continue to shine as a fine example of his mastery of color, dimension, texture, and storytelling via the ever-changing world of computer-assisted design.

Good production design should be invisible, just as the cinematography and sound should be, which means as the viewer you won't notice it. If you hear people talking about how great the picture looked, and nothing else, then you know your film didn't work. Everything has to be balanced so that they say, "What a great movie." It should look fantastic, for sure, but not at the expense of the story.

LOW-BUDGET TIP

Local studios can be very supportive of low-budget productions and will often lend out their space in return for credit in your film. Film schools can similarly be a good source of space.

CONCEPT SET FOR AMERICAN MOVIE CLASSICS (AMC) CHANNEL
The images above show the transformation of the concept from pencil sketch to colored pencil sketch to Adobe Illustrator and Photoshop drawings to the final 3D rendering in Maya.

COSTUME AND MAKEUP

OBJECTIVES >>

- Be able to source low-budget costumes and makeup
- Understand costuming logistics
- Know about production design

GETTING INTO CHARACTER
Once you have the cast dressed, it is up to the actor to make that character shine and really sparkle in order to be convincing.

LOW-BUDGET TIPS
- Thrift and cheap fashion stores are a great source of clothes for costumes, especially if you are after the "trashy" look.
- Local amateur theater groups may have elaborate costumes they will lend you, or rent at favorable rates, especially if you can offer your talents in exchange.

Once you've dressed the set, you have to dress the actors. The more ambitious your project, the more complex it becomes for the wardrobe department.

Gritty urban drama won't require much more than the clothes the actors themselves own, or a quick visit to the local thrift store. Once you start moving into genre movies, you will need to enlist the assistance of someone who is handy with a sewing machine, or the telephone number of your local costume rental store or amateur dramatic group.

For your first film, it's unlikely you are going to attempt a period costume drama. If you are, good luck. Contemporary drama is the most popular genre, followed by horror and sci-fi. The beauty of the last two is that they can be produced without elaborate costumes and makeup. It is often overlooked that science fiction is a story with a scientific base, and it does not have to involve futuristic space travel. Horror is about scaring people, and it does not need monsters; in fact, what you can't see is usually more frightening than any latex mask.

Makeup

Even without going into special effects (see page 94), you are going to need someone on your team to apply basic makeup. This is usually no more than face powder, to take the shine off skin under lights. They must also ensure that hairstyles remain consistent throughout scenes. Most women have experience applying their own makeup and should have no problem adapting their skill to making up others. If you want someone more skilled or professional but don't have the budget, try using your charms, and the mystique of movies, to approach the people who work as demonstrators at the cosmetic counters in department stores. If you are male, send your girlfriend or sister for a free makeover and ask them to drop the subject into the conversation.

Another potential source of labor is college students. Working with students has its advantages and disadvantages. They may be happy to get credits for their audition tapes, but they are also an obvious target for every low-budget and student filmmaker, so they can be in demand. Alternatively, approach an amateur dramatics association. These are great resources for budding filmmakers. Although stage makeup is more exaggerated than that for film, the principle is the same. These associations can also be a good place to find elaborate costumes.

All dressed up

Although every production is different, the basic rules and requirements remain the same. If your shoot is going to last more than one day, you will need a person to run your wardrobe. Even if your actors are supplying their own costumes, you need someone to coordinate the logistics. When a shoot lasts longer than a day, it is especially important that actors do not wear their costumes to the shoot—they must be left with the wardrobe person. Allowing actors to leave the shoot in their costumes is courting disaster, as the clothes risk being dirtied or, worse, being left at home. Polaroids were a standard tool of costume departments, used to keep a record of who wore what and how, but digital still cameras are a lot more convenient, economical, and efficient, especially if used with a laptop computer.

Apart from the organizational aspect, the wardrobe person/department has to work in conjunction with the production designer. Not only do the costumes have to fit the characters, but the choice of colors and patterns can influence the look and meaning of the finished movie. For example, in Warren Beatty's *Dick Tracy,* the costumes used bold, flat colors to enhance the overall "comic book" look of the film. These are subtle details that may go unnoticed but do make a difference, just as giving a character a particular color to wear can add symbolic meaning.

Getting the wardrobe and makeup organized before the shoot will make everything run that much more smoothly on the day of filming.

MAKEUP DETAILING
Full-face makeup such as the makeup shown here can take large amounts of time to complete, so factor that into your planning.

PLANNING MAKEUP
There are three main types or styles of makeup: fashion, fantasy, and creature. Each one of these styles has its own creative demands. Most makeup artists now create makeup designs in Adobe Photoshop from a head shot of the actor receiving the application.

3

After all the preproduction, the next phase—production—is almost anticlimactic. It is certainly the most intense part of the filmmaking process, and sometimes the shortest. When the preproduction is performed correctly, that is how it should be. Roughly speaking, preproduction and production make up only 25 percent of the entire process. Postproduction and distribution make up all of the rest.

PRODUCTION

As an independent filmmaker you are reliant on those you bring on board to help you. You must be cognizant of their time and the time you spend preparing. The less prepared you are, the less time those around you will be willing to give to you. Whether or not you have money for your production, you must be organized and clear about your plan. The best way to do this is to assemble experienced people and carefully lean on their expertise.

Never think that you can make your film alone. This is a huge mistake— filmmaking is inherently a collaborative process. This section of the book covers the theory and pragmatics of filmmaking, and provides insights on making the most of what you have to produce the best results.

DIRECTING: AN INTRODUCTION

The role of director is seen as one of the more glamorous and prestigious in the film industry. However, in reality it is all guts and no glory. Charged with driving the production forward, the director must be able to instill his or her vision, collaborate with the other visionaries, and bring the show to the screen—all within a specific time frame. No matter how glamorous directing appears to be, this is not an easy task.

OBJECTIVES >>
- [ ] **Understand the director's role**
- [ ] **Communicate your vision**
- [ ] **Work with talent**
- [ ] **Call the shots**

It's not part of the romanticized image, but a lot of the director's time is actually taken up by mundane administrative matters, and the larger the production, the more decisions a director must make. Never forget, the main job of a director is to get great performances out of his or her actors. In military terms, a director is like a general—responsible for strategy, giving orders, and overseeing the troops. What follows is a brief introduction to directing, followed, on pages 62–67, by a lengthier discourse of the approach a director must take to all the elements of filmmaking.

Auteurs

There are two specific types of director, independent of personality traits. Writer–directors are the elite, the auteurs of the film world, who take a film from conception to completion. They have a story to tell and a vision of how it should be told on screen. The other type will take a screenplay written by someone else and use their vision to interpret how it should be played out. Not all directors are capable of writing an original script, and even fewer writers have the personality needed to command a film crew.

Most first-time filmmakers tend to jump in as writer–directors. They want to make a film and usually have an idea for the story they want to tell, and this is as it should be. That story might be an adaptation, or one inspired by another story, but whatever the source, novice directors will have ideas they want to manifest.

No matter how multitalented or capable of multitasking he or she is, to bring the concept to reality, the director will need to enlist the help of others in the form of actors. It is the director's job to coax the best performances possible out of that talent.

The director's work with the actors begins with casting and auditions, and continues through into rehearsals. These are vital for establishing relationships between the actors—and with the director. It is the relationship between the director and the actors that will determine how good a performance the latter will give.

Two of a kind

There are two extreme kinds of directors—the total control freak and the go-with-the-flow type. You should aim to be somewhere in between. The control-freak director will want the actors to move and speak exactly as they are instructed, treating them as no more than puppets. The go-with-the-flow director will let the actors improvise as much as they want, often to the detriment of the original script. What is needed is for the director to allow the actors to explore their characters and make suggestions, tempering this with clarity of vision. Directors must find ways of communicating their perception of the character to the actors so they will be able to understand how the character would behave in the given situations.

Not making it big

Many actors come with stage training and experience (if they have any at all), where actions and voices have

PLAN THE PROCESS
The flow chart at right shows the director's role in making a low-budget movie, from the concept through to promotion. A visual tool like this can make the whole organization of your shoot easier. On a big-budget production, the director would not take on some of these tasks, such as creating the production or the shooting schedule.

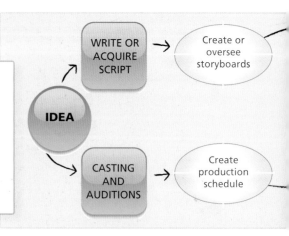

GETTING YOUR POINT ACROSS
The director has to be the great communicator on set. In the midst of shooting, the director must be most concerned with the actors' performances and realizing the vision with the director of photography (DP).

1. Director (Quentin Tarantino): Explains his vision for the shot in *Kill Bill* to the cast and crew.

2. DP: The director of photography has to visually interpret the director's ideas and capture them on film or video. His relationship with the director must be symbiotic.

3. Fight/stunt coordinator: Has to choreograph the action scenes in action films, hire stunt people, and train the actors. Safety is one of his primary concerns, even beyond getting the shot.

4. Actor: The director has to coax the best possible performances from the cast, whether physical or emotional. It is important to allow time for the actors to warm up, but without delaying the schedule.

---

to be "big." This does not work on film, where the proximity of the camera demands understatement, and exchanges between actors have to be more intimate and often more intense than on stage. But these are not the only differences. In movies, actors do not have to learn and recite huge chunks of dialogue. With scenes shot out of sequence, and multiple takes for coverage, it can demand a lot of energy for an actor to maintain focus on the character, which is why directors have to be empathetic with their talent, praising their efforts while finding diplomatic ways of getting exactly what they want.

One of the best ways is to talk to the character—that is, to address the actor as the character. Ask characters questions about their actions in order to elicit the appropriate emotion or response. The other method to

use is, "That was great but can we just try… ?" In the end a lot of it is about developing interpersonal skills and understanding each actor individually. What will work with one actor won't work with another. Unfortunately, it is something that can only be learned through trial and error, and experience. A lot of actors and directors continually work together because they understand and respect each other.

If you can establish that sort of relationship, your movies will develop in ways that you could not have imagined.

Directing isn't just about drawing the right emotions out of the actors; you have to do it in relation to the camera. This means orchestrating the movement of the actors in front of the camera while maintaining control over framing and the movement of the camera itself.

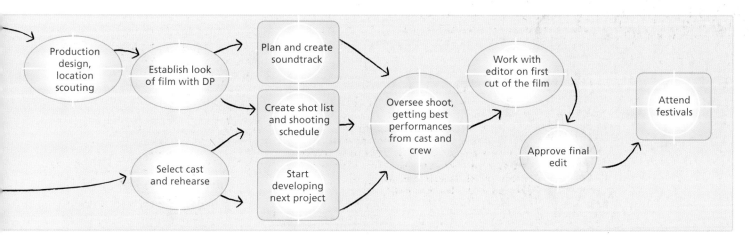

SHOT LIST

Scene 1: INT.HOUSE - NIGHT

Set Up	Shot No"s	Shot Size	Description
#1	1, 9	Wide Shot / Master	Jason & Dave (Est. Shot to End of Scene)
	2, 4, 13, 14, 16, 19, 21, 22, 24	Medium Shot	Jason looking at the monitor to End of scene
	12	Dolly Left	Dave kneels and looks at the computer
2	5, 8	Medium Shot	Jason walks and opens the door to Dave "Lemme in dude, I've gotta take a leak, damn these cold beers here, take 'em."
	6,	MCU / Long Angle	Jason "Oh hey Dave, what brings you here my friend?"
	10	Dolly Left / Pan / Medium Shot	Jason shuts the door, places the bag on the table & continues to work on his computer.
3	7	Medium Shot/ OS of Dave	Jason "My God, you stink!"
	11	Medium Shot	Dave comes in and stands behind Jason and walks to the other side.
4	17, 18	Close Ups	Jason "No, Dave I'd rather finish my puzzles to fall asleep." Dave spills the beer on himself. Dave "Dude, trust this ain't life."
Inserts	3, 15, 20, 23	Inserts/ CUs	Sleep Apnea info on monitor, beer bottles, pouring drink into glass, holding glass.

FRIDAY NIGHT

SHOT LIST

This is a list of planned coverage, the shots that the director wants. It is his or her vision of what the scene needs to remain true to the story. The shot sheet (see page 79) is a record of what was ultimately shot. This can vary wildly or remain fairly similar to the shot list.

Cinematography

When it comes to cinematography, some directors are very hands-on, often operating the camera at the same time as directing the actors. This allows the director to make snap decisions about composition, which works well on lo-no budget shoots where video-assist isn't available. It also speeds up the process, as the need to explain everything to the DP or camera operator is eliminated, as is the need for extra retakes.

One of the perceived problems of filming and directing at the same time is the difficulty of giving enough attention to what the actors are doing. Much of this depends on how comfortable you are behind the lens. It also depends on how much faith you have in your actors. If you have rehearsed with the actors and are pleased with their performance, then just shoot it. One advantage of video is that you can shoot and shoot, but it is also a disadvantage, because in the days of shooting on film there was more of an incentive to make sure that the take is right the first time.

As the director, you have to decide what needs to be shot in terms of coverage—establishing shots, medium shots, close-ups, and cutaways. You can get plenty of coverage, as much as your cast and crew will tolerate (see page 78).

Call to action

All the preproduction meetings, the rehearsals with actors, and the hours of overseeing setups culminate in the moment when the director gets to call "Action!" There is actually a protocol that has to be followed before those words are shouted, depending on the equipment. First the 1stAD calls (yells) "Stand by/Lock it up," followed by, "Quiet on set!" and "Roll camera."

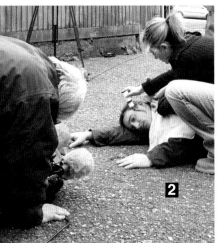

1. TALKING IT THROUGH
The director will discuss the shot with the DP/camera operator, explaining precisely what he or she wants.

2. GETTING THE SHOT
Once explained by the director, the DP will position the camera ready to shoot, while the director checks the shot on a field monitor (if available). The makeup artist applies the special effect just before the shot.

The camera operator will call "Speed" or "Locked," and then the director calls "Action!"

From this point on, the director is in charge, and everything carries on until he or she calls "Cut!" The DP is the only other person permitted to call "Cut!" and only if there is a technical fault with the camera or lights. Even if an actor misses his or her lines, it is the director's decision whether to continue with the take or start again. Once he or she has called "Cut!" the director decides if he or she is happy with the take, and will check with the DP that the shot was technically sound. A good director will usually praise the actors if it was a good take, and may ask them if they were pleased with it, as a courtesy. Generally, a director should not ask the cast or crew for their opinion of the take, as this can undermine his or her authority. If there is any doubt, the director may decide to reshoot, making any suggestions to the actors on ways to improve the scene. If the actors, who are notoriously self-critical, are happy, the director will often let it go and shoot the scene from a different angle or with a different lens. And so it goes on, setup after setup, until there is enough footage in the can to call it a wrap.

Now that we've established the basic role of the director, over the next six pages we will delve more deeply into the intricacies of this vital role.

INT. KITCHEN -- MOMENTS LATER

Matt is drinking a large glass of water and absentmindedly pouring cereal from a box into two bowls.

Insert close up of cereal pouring into bowl.
Insert Pour of guru pic with vitamans etc
INT. DINING ROOM -- MOMENTS LATER

Matt places the two bowls of over-sugared cereal in front of the already over-excited children and heads toward the bathroom. *get kids to improv chat*

CUT TO:

INT. BATHROOM -- MOMENTS LATER

4 OVER THE SHOULDER CLOSE UP OF MATT STARING IN THE MIRROR

maybe too long *keep it tight in edit.*

SERIES OF QUICK CUT SHOTS *Shot as if camera is mirror* **3**

Matt is inspecting his eyes, tongue, nose, receding hairline and three-day stubble then lathering up and shaving. *may have to cheat shot*

Once Matt has finished shaving he opens the bathroom cabinet and deliberates over which after shave to use.

                    MATT
               (Talking to
               himself)
5   This'll be the only decision I'll get to a say in make today. *Try both versions*

He wipes the fog off the mirror, applies the after shave, combs his hair and gives himself a feigned look of approval.

                              DISSOLVE TO:

INT: DINING ROOM -- LATER

Matt is sitting at the table which is covered with empty *cutaway* bowls and plates. He is still drinking a cup of tea and reading the morning paper. The two children are harassing him to let them watch television. He is trying *cu* **2** to ignore their pleas.

1   LAURA
                    Can we watch TV?

make sure they are whispery. Try some improv
                    ANDY
                    Come on dad, just a bit.

                    LAURA
                    Yeah dad. I really need to watch
                    Scooby Doo.

SCRIPT CAPTIONS AND NOTES
No matter how many amends a script has before the shoot, on the actual day the director can still make changes, especially if he or she wrote it. Although amends will appear on the shot sheet, making notes on the script will help during the editing process. Write plenty of notes because, with so much happening, you may forget what you did or why.

1. Directing note for actors

2. More shooting notes to be added to shooting list

3. Something to be discussed with DP

4. Note for editor

5. Dialogue change

THE INTRICACIES OF DIRECTING

AT A GLANCE

1 THE SCRIPT

2 FIRST IMPRESSIONS

3 DETERMINE THE GIVENS

4 BREAK THE SCRIPT INTO MANAGEABLE UNITS

5 PLAN TO TELL THE STORY THROUGH ACTION

6 DEFINING SUBTEXTS

7 THE DISPLACEMENT PRINCIPLE

8 AMBIVALENCE, OR BEHAVIORAL CONTRADICTIONS

9 DEFINING A THEMATIC PURPOSE

10 REHEARSAL

11 FIRST READ-THROUGH

12 KEEP NOTES

13 DIRECT BY ASKING QUESTIONS

14 FIRST DISCUSSIONS—FOCUSING THE THEMATIC PURPOSE

15 GIVEN CIRCUMSTANCES

16 BACKSTORY

17 NATURE OF CHARACTERS—WHAT EACH CHARACTER WANTS

18 NATURE OF ACTS

19 NATURE OF EACH CONFLICT

20 FINDING THE BEATS

21 CHANGES IN A CHARACTER'S RHYTHM

22 OBLIGATORY MOMENT

23 FUNCTION OF EACH SCENE

Now that the overall arch of directing has been covered, it is time to get down to the finer details. Directing is never about showing the actors how to do it; it is about explaining the story and characters to your actors. It sounds simple enough, but this river we call directing runs very deep; you cannot simply dip your big toe in and feel the surface—you have to jump in all the way. Your immersion in the script will help you to easily communicate your ideas to the actors.

It is your passion and ability to communicate that indicates your commitment to the actors, and your commitment will signal to the actors that you are a true collaborator, a visionary, and trustworthy. Let your actor run with the role, inject their take on the character, and blend in your commentary. The results will be astounding if you give the actor freedom to act. That is why a good director will never show an actor how it is done. It gets in the way of a good performance and signals to the actor that you do not trust his or her process. All you have to do is watch some of your favorite movies, or those that have won awards for directing, to fully understand the stamp of the director on a film. What follows over the next six pages are the main topics or areas a successful director must have a solid grasp of.

1 THE SCRIPT
As the director you must be absolutely conversant with the script's inner workings and practical implications. Since the screenplay is skeletal and open to a wide spectrum of interpretation, you will need to further assess your script's potential and to build upon it methodically and thoroughly.

2 FIRST IMPRESSIONS
If the screenplay is new to you, read it quickly and without interruption, noting any random first impressions. These can be a vital resource later when essentials become blurred through over-familiarity with detail. First impressions are intuitive and, like those you might form about a new acquaintance, become increasingly significant with greater familiarity. Make a step outline showing each sequence's function and how it defines the film's concept.

3 DETERMINE THE GIVENS
Reread the script slowly and carefully and determine what is given—that is, what is directly specified in the screenplay. This is your

hard information, which includes locations, time of day, character details, and words used by the characters. All these are fixed and serve as the foundations determining everything else.

Much is deliberately and wisely left unspecified, such as the movements and physical nature of the characters and the treatment to be applied to the story in terms of camerawork, sound, and editing. The givens must be interpreted by the director, cast, and crew, and the inferences each draws must eventually harmonize to be consistent.

To each actor, for instance, the script provides everything known about his or her character's past and future. A character, after all, is like the proverbial iceberg—four-fifths being out of sight.

What is visible (that is, in the script) allows the actor to infer and develop what is "below the water line" (the character's biography, motives, volition, fears, ambitions, vulnerabilities, and so on).

4 BREAK THE SCRIPT INTO MANAGEABLE UNITS
Next, divide the script or treatment into workable units by location and scene. This helps you to plan how each unit of the story must function and initiates the process of assembling a shooting script. If, for example, you have three scenes in the same day-care center, you will shoot them consecutively to conserve time and energy, even though they are widely spaced in the film.

When production begins, everyone must be well aware of the discontinuity between the three scenes, or actors may inadvertently adopt the same tone, or the camera crew will shoot and light in the same way. In storytelling, one is always looking for ways to create a sense of contrast, change, and development.

5 PLAN TO TELL THE STORY THROUGH ACTION
Cinematic film remains largely comprehensible and dynamic even with the sound turned off, so you should devise your screen presentation as if for a silent film. This way you will tell your story cinematically rather than theatrically—through action, setting, and behavior rather than through dialogue exchanges. This may necessitate rewriting.

6 DEFINING SUBTEXTS
The notion that every good text is a lifelike surface hiding deeper layers of meaning or "subtext" is invaluable. It reminds us that as dramatists we must always search out the submerged stream of heightened significance flowing beneath life's surface.

7 THE DISPLACEMENT PRINCIPLE
In life, people very rarely deal directly with the true source of their tensions. Instead, what takes place is a displacement. Two elderly men may be talking gloomily about the weather, but from what has gone on before, or from telltale hints, we learn that one is adjusting to the death of a family member and the other is trying to bring up the subject of some money owed to him.

Although what they say is that the heat and humidity might lead to a storm, what we infer as the subtext is that Ted is consumed by feelings of guilt and loss, while Harry is realizing that once again he cannot ask for the money he badly needs.

The scene's subtext can be defined as "Harry realizes he cannot bring himself to intrude his needs upon Ted at this moment, and that his situation is now desperate." We cannot interpret the subtext here without knowledge gained from earlier scenes, and this demonstrates how drama that is well conceived builds and interconnects.

REHEARSAL SPACE
Some directors like to rehearse in a more formal setting, for example, a theatrical stage.

READING THE SCRIPT
The first read-through generally takes place around a table in a very informal setting.

8 AMBIVALENCE, OR BEHAVIORAL CONTRADICTIONS

Intelligent drama exploits the way each character consciously or otherwise tries to control the situation, either to hide his or her underlying intentions and concerns or, should the occasion demand it, draw attention to them. Once we know the subtext, we can contrive behaviors for each character to indicate the contradictions between his or her inner world and outward self-presentation.

Ambivalence is the cinema audience's main evidence of a character's hidden and underlying tensions. When actors begin to act upon (not merely think about) their character's conflicts and locked energies, scenes move beyond the linear, superficial notion of human interaction and we begin to truly feel the character's emotions. The dramatic work now begins to imply the pressurized water table of human emotion below the aridly logical top surface.

9 DEFINING A THEMATIC PURPOSE

Another concept vitally important to the director is that of the thematic purpose, or "super objective," to coin a phrase. This describes the authorial objectives powering the work as a whole. One might say the super objective to Orson Welles' *Citizen Kane* is "to show that the child is father to the man, that the power-obsessed man's course through life is the consequence of childhood deprivation that no one around him ever understands." It is mandatory that you define a thematic purpose for a work in script form if you are to truly capitalize on the script's potential. Usually one has a strong intuition about what it is, but it should emerge when you link up each scene's subtext. A script's thematic purpose is to some degree a subjective entity derived from the author's outlook and vision.

In a work of some depth, neither the subtexts nor the thematic purpose are so fixed and limited. Indeed, these choices are built into the way the reader reads and the audience reacts to a finished film, because everyone interprets selectively what they see from a background of

particular experiences. These are individual but they are also cultural and specific to the mood of the times.

Kafka's disturbing story *Metamorphosis*—about a sick man who discovers he is turning into a huge beetle—might be read as a parable about the changes people go through when dealing with the incurably sick, or it might read more from a science-fiction perspective as a grisly "what if" experiment in locking the human sensibility into the body of an insect.

In the first example, the thematic purpose might be to show how utter dependency robs the subject of love and respect, while the second shows how compassion goes out to a suffering heart only when it beats inside a palatable body.

Whatever you choose as your thematic purpose, it must be articulated, be consistent with the text, and eventually be acceptable to your creative collaborators.

Divergent, unexamined readings produce contradictory interpretations, so finding a shared understanding of the story's purpose is a prerequisite for integrated storytelling.

10 REHEARSAL

"Rehearsal" is a misunderstood activity. The difficulties begin with the word itself, and its unfortunate associations with repetition and drilling. A much better word would be "development." To forgo rehearsal prior to shooting actors' performances is to forgo development and therefore depth. Because films are shot piecemeal, it is often assumed that film performances, unlike theater, need little or no rehearsal; indeed, that rehearsal damages spontaneity. This belief may be a rationalization for minimizing costs or perhaps people think that theater plays rehearse to overcome the problems of a continuous performance, such as mastering lines and movements. Preparation is the key to success. If top-notch professional film actors find it necessary to prepare, novices must be ready to work even harder. Few beginning

1. What do you think your character's main motivation is?
2. Why do you think he or she is motivated in this way?
3. What is the emotional range of your character?
4. Do you see yourself in this character in any way?
5. What part of the character calls out to you?
6. Where do you want to go with this character?
7. What does your character look like physically?
8. Why do you think your character behaves in a certain way?
9. Do you have enough of the backstory on this character to develop it?
10. Do you like or dislike your character in this story?
11. What are his/her redeeming qualities?
12. What do you dislike?

ASK QUESTIONS
Directing by asking questions is the best way to guide your actors to discover their character's intricacies.

filmmakers seem aware of this, and the acting in student films is usually appalling. Too often student directors believe editing is the alchemy that will magically produce gold from lead. Before something good can emerge from the rehearsal process, the director must understand the importance of tapping into the actors' creativity, and not to think of them, however privately, as puppets. They must have the time to become comfortable and interested in each other.

You as the director need to make your actors into an ensemble, with its own dynamic of relationships and its own history that makes up in intensity what it might lack in duration. The actors can begin to absorb dramatic situations into authentic reality. Fiction and actors' relationships become indistinguishably real. That is our aim in this developmental work.

11 FIRST READ-THROUGH

After everybody has had time to study the script, the first read-through will show how each actor interprets the piece and how well the characters are fitting together. You should also expect to get first glimpses of where your biggest problems lie, in particular scenes, particular actors, or both.

Encourage actors to use as much natural movement as they can, both during the read-through and subsequently, even though the primary focus is on the meaning of the words. Holding a script will inhibit movement, but the emphasis on doing reminds the cast that it is vital to act with the whole body, not just the voice or the face. Depending on the length and complexity of the screenplay, read it through in sections, or all in one go if possible. Have a list of fundamental questions ready for the actors. Give little or no direction; you want to see what ideas and individuality each spontaneously brings to his or her role and to the piece. Show that you expect actors to be partners in seeking answers to problems, for problem solving is at the heart of creativity. This also discourages actors from passively depending on minute instructions, not

usually a problem if your casting is good. Although you may have strong ideas of your own, be receptive to your actors' input and individuality. It shows you expect them to dig into the piece and thoroughly explore what kind of people the characters are.

They will have to judge what motivates each to do what he or she does, and to define what purposes lie behind the script as a whole. Any serious actor will find this approach attractive and challenging because it acknowledges his or her intelligence.

12 KEEP NOTES

A tough part of directing is holding on to important impressions during a rehearsal. Because you must monitor so many things simultaneously, early impressions can be erased by later ones, and you can easily turn to the actors with a mind drained of everything except the last set of impressions.

Avoid this humiliation by carrying a large scratch pad and, without taking your eyes off the performance, scribble a key word or two. Then glance down and place your pen at a starting point ready for the next note. Afterward you will have several pages of large, wobbly prompts. These should trigger the necessary recall.

TEST YOUR VISION
Although rare, readings of the script can also take place in front of an audience, for example at film festivals, where feedback, audience reactions, and discussions can help you to focus your vision.

GUIDING YOUR ACTORS
As a director, you will need to guide your actors to the places in the script that require good listening and timing.

13 DIRECT BY ASKING QUESTIONS

Through probing questions you can guide the cast to discover what you may already know (it also gives you time to think). Because of the energy and diversity a group brings to any enterprise, this flushes out aspects that may never have occurred to you. Learning becomes a two-way street. Throughout production, even when everyone feels there can be nothing left to discover, the piece will continue to deepen, growing stronger as you and your cast stumble upon even more meanings and interconnections. Here lies much of the exhilarating sense of shared discovery and closeness that can develop between cast and crew.

Asking challenging questions is always a more effective way of briefing and coordinating a group than simply reeling off instructions. Orders, not least because of their authoritarian nature, are easily resisted or misunderstood, especially when they prove inadequate and must be modified or superseded.

But people seldom forget what they discover for themselves.

14 FIRST DISCUSSIONS—FOCUSING THE THEMATIC PURPOSE

A theme represents an authorial system of values and beliefs that lies within the director's interpretation of the screenplay.

To communicate yours on the screen, you will have to effectively argue it. Stating the thematic purpose of one's piece really means defining the steps and focus of this argument.

A story represents a limited but intense vision. Such a vision is made coherent and integrated, however subtly, by an underlying philosophy of cause and effect. Many, and perhaps most, stories are experimental in the sense that telling a story is really a way of constructing a working model of one's beliefs.

If others are moved to conviction, the principles behind the model have been shared, acclaimed, and may have merit. That is the best anyone can hope to do.

A thematic purpose for your work need not try to encompass universal truth or be morally uplifting. Audiences will feel they are being preached at, especially when the scope of the film falls short of the global nature of its message.

Modest, solid, specific, and deeply felt aims are the most practical. Your thematic statement may focus the motivation for telling the tale onto a simple principle with profound consequences ("though his ideologue is honest and sincere, he is dangerous to those that love him").

By taking a small truth and deeply investigating it, you can invest it with life and indicate larger truths of wider resonance. Put another way, a thoroughly absorbing and convincing microcosm will effectively create the macrocosm.

Your notion of the piece's thematic purpose will come from your study of the text, but that does not guarantee that it will be shared by those who matter most: your cast.

A wise approach is to form your own ideas and then either parlay your cast into accepting them, or form alternatives that are as acceptable or (do not tell anyone) even superior.

Now that the cast has had time to study the script:

- Ask the players to discuss the purpose of the whole story, or the scene in relation to the whole story. This reveals what spectrum of opinion exists. Encourage all points of view and impose none of your own at this time. You want the cast to reason things out for themselves. Not only will this bring them closer, but you will acquire additional insights, since each is an advocate for single character.
- Ask the cast to formulate the "backstory" (what may ostensibly have happened before the film begins).
- Ask each actor to describe his or her character and to prepare a brief biography for that character.
- Turn the cast's attention to successive key scenes or the scene being worked on, and ask the players to develop the subtext.
- Ask the cast to review the main themes of the piece or scene; say

what you think their hierarchy is. During this process you should try to unify the body of opinion into a coherent thematic purpose for the piece.

15 GIVEN CIRCUMSTANCES

Know the script so you're quite certain what location, time frame, character details, acts, and so on are exactly specified, and what other detail is only implied or must be supplied by director and cast.

16 BACKSTORY

Using your intimate knowledge of the script, infer what took place prior to the script's action. This is the backstory.

17 NATURE OF CHARACTERS—WHAT EACH CHARACTER WANTS

It is vital to go beyond what a character "is" and to know what he or she wants. This conception gives the character not just a fixed, static identity worn like a glove, but an active, evolving quest that mobilizes willpower to gain each new end, moment to moment. A succession of small, precise goals utterly transforms a person's acting by releasing his or her character's inner life into visibility.

18 NATURE OF ACTS

Since behavior is so important in the cinema, it helps to create a unique identity for each act under discussion, even the tiny ones. These labels or similes function as a potent directive when briefing or redirecting actors. To say that a man leaves the table during a family feud is not enough, for it provides an instruction lacking special identity. Give the nature of the act a precise and imaginative coloration.

19 NATURE OF EACH CONFLICT

Because drama is powered by conflict, the director must know where and how each situation of conflict develops. It can appear as: tension within each character of interest, conflict between characters, or conflict between characters and their situations.

For any conflict to exist, a pattern of oppositions must emerge: tension builds in stages (rising action), reaches a climax, and then is resolved (falling action). When a scene's resolution leads to harmony, this is usually only a temporary lull before a fresh set of tensions develops, starting a new cycle.

20 FINDING THE BEATS

A scene of tension between individuals is like a fencing match—much strategic footwork and mutual adaptation punctuated by strikes. Each moment of impact alters the balance of power and puts the match's outcome in a new light.

In drama, likewise, a scene's nature and apparent premise change at each impact moment or beat. It is a moment of high significance for at least one character, and is shared by the audience. This is the beat, the heightened moment or "crisis adaptation" toward which the scene has been working. There may be several cycles in a scene. Mark the beat points in your script, and see how the scene's forward movement becomes a waveform charting a series of dramatic onslaughts upon the audience's emotions.

21 CHANGES IN A CHARACTER'S RHYTHM

Every character has his or her own rhythms for speech and action. These vary according to mood. It is an actor's responsibility to keep the character's rhythms distinctive and vary them according to the character's inner state, which is likely to change at a beat point. Monotony is an invariable indicator of performing by rote.

22 OBLIGATORY MOMENT

This is the fulcrum on which the whole scene turns; the moment of change for which the whole scene exists. Subtract it and the scene is disabled or redundant.

23 FUNCTION OF EACH SCENE

Like a single cog in the gear train of a clock, each scene in a well-constructed drama has its correct place and function. Defining this early on enables you to interpret the scene confidently and to make it feed impetus into the larger pattern.

Giving a name to the scene helps transfer this information rapidly and forcefully to someone else. Dickens' chapter titles from *Bleak House* make good examples: "Covering a Multitude of Sins," "Signs and Tokens," "A Turn of the Screw," "Closing In," "Dutiful Friendship," and "Beginning the World."

CAMERAS

Today's cameras give you an infinite choice, from really decent consumer cameras all the way up to semi-professional (or prosumer) and professional cameras, and now DSLR (digital single-lens reflex) cameras. It all comes down to how much you know about cameras and how you want yours to perform. Purchasing a camera can often be out of the question for a beginning filmmaker, but renting can make many superb cameras available to you without the high cost of ownership.

OBJECTIVES >>
■ **Understand the camera components**

There are many different DV formats available, from the consumer miniDV up to the professional High-Definition Video (HDV) that has been used for films such as the *Star Wars* series.

Which format?

For our purposes, miniDV is most likely to be the first choice, although DVCAM, Digital Betacam, and the new range of HDV cameras are viable, if more costly, alternatives. It may be best to go for a mid-range digital video camera rather than some of the cheaper consumer cameras available because, apart from the low resolution of the consumer formats, there is the additional expense and inconvenience of transferring or digitizing footage to take advantage of computer desktop non-linear editing. The digital format has the ability to maintain the quality of the original no matter how many times it is copied.

Although miniDV has been used for major theatrical releases, including *The Blair Witch Project* (Eduardo Sánchez and Daniel Myrick), *Time Code* (Mike Figgis), *Full Frontal* (Steven Soderbergh), and *28 Days Later* (Danny Boyle), it has in these cases been chosen in order to exploit the fact that the movie was obviously not shot on film.

Camera manufacturers have moved away from analog miniDV tape recording. Memory cards capable of recording and playing back large amounts of data are now the norm. They are able to stream data and high rates with no degradation to the quality of the image, no matter how many times it is copied.

If your intention is merely to learn the craft of moviemaking and possibly to enter competitions or festivals, make DVDs, show on your local cable station, or broadcast over the Internet, then the DV format is perfect for you.

Buying or renting—advice

If you are buying your first DV camera, try to avoid the cheaper models. Their lack of important features—a quality lens, decent resolution, external microphone jack, and Fire Wire or DV in/DV out—may hinder your work. As technology and manufacturing improve, the quality-to-price ratio moves in favor of the buyer. Use the many consumer magazines available to ascertain which models offer the best value for the money. A price range of $1,000 and up is a good starting point for the kind of quality you will need.

Judicious use of money is one of the secrets of low-budget filmmaking, in contrast to Hollywood's approach to solving problems by throwing dollars at them. When buying a camera, don't spend more than you need to, but don't try to save money at the expense of useful features. On the other hand, don't use the lack of camera features as an excuse for not shooting a movie. Even the lowest-spec DV camera will have more features than some of the older pro models.

In fact, there is quite a lot to be said for using a simple camera, as it will make you concentrate on telling your story rather than being hung up on the technology. On the other hand, poor-quality pictures and sound are not going to impress an audience.

Don't rely on your tools

Whatever camera you choose to shoot your story, remember that garbage in = garbage out. Nothing can help you if your focus is bad or your color balance is off. Having a solid base of camera proficiency is incredibly important no matter what camera you use. Equipment is only a tool to help bring the story to life. It is not what makes a good story.

DIGITAL SINGLE-LENS REFLEX (DSLR) CAMERAS
DSLR cameras are growing in popularity due to their low cost, high definition image capture capabilities, and portability. Their limitations are single chip capture and poor audio input. As the demand grows, newer models are coming out with better sound-recording abilities.

CAMERA COMPONENTS

All video cameras are made of the same basic components, but each model has its own individual style and features. There are three main parts: the body, the lens, and the viewfinder. Less expensive cameras feature less functionality, whereas more expensive professional cameras will give you more control. The semi-professional camera sits in the middle and generally can give you the features of manual control you will need. You will want to look for manual control of the following components: iris or aperture, zoom, gain, and color temperature.

Microphone: Look for sockets for external microphones—these will give you a more controllable sound recording. XLR or balanced inputs are best but are found only on semi-professional cameras.

Zoom lens: Most cameras have uni-body lenses, except for more expensive professional models. Look at the optical zoom range (usually around 10x) and avoid using the digital zoom capability of the camera you choose. It will cause pixelation and distortion.

Lens hoods: Stop extraneous light from entering the lens and causing "flaring" bright beams of light that mar the image.

Focus ring: An easy-to-access manual focus will give your videos a more professional look.

Manual override buttons: These give more control of the camera's functions.

Viewing monitor: Adjustable screen that allows easy viewing from any angle or camera position. Generally not accurate enough for reliable color balance or exposure.

Viewfinder: Contains a tiny digital screen.

LOW-BUDGET TIP

Rent, don't buy. Unless you are an established freelance camera operator, there is no need to go out on a limb and buy a camera you will use just a few times. Many rental houses offer a standard five-day rental package and will charge you for only four days. This way you can keep your cost of overheads down and you'll also avoid locking into technology that changes every six months. If you are shooting a feature-length piece, it might make sense to buy a camera, or at least have access to one for the long haul. This is when becoming a member of a local film collective can be beneficial.

SEMI-PROFESSIONAL CAMERAS

These types of cameras are comprised of 3 CCD (charged-coupled devices); some have an interchangeable lens and balanced (XLR) audio inputs. They also have full manual functionality.

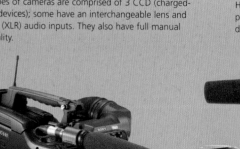

HIGH-DEFINITION (HD) CAMERAS

HD cameras are essentially the same as a semi-professional camera but are capable of high-definition acquisition.

TECH TIP

Be careful with high-definition production, because it means larger amounts of streaming data to produce an HD image. Computer editing for this format means you must have a machine with enough memory to be capable of handling the large amounts of data needed to reproduce the HD picture.

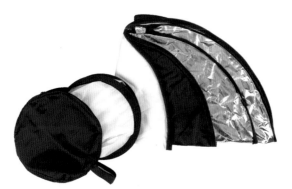

LIGHTING

The director of photography (DP), or cinematographer, has two very specific functions to fulfill on a shoot. The first and most obvious is operating, or at least directing, the camera. The second is lighting the shots, because without light, you would not be able to film.

A badly lit scene is going to ruin your movie as much as bad acting or poor sound. The way a scene is lit will change its mood and your audience's perception of what you are trying to express. For the low-budget filmmaker, having a truckload of lights is out of the question, so how do you get the best possible lighting without spending a fortune?

Natural light

The simplest way is to use existing light, the light that is around you. Natural daylight is best, although shooting in the noon sun is going to give very contrasting images. This can be overcome either by diffusing the sunlight through thin cloth shades or by using filler lights to remove hard shadows.

Alternatively, you can use reflectors, which are simply large reflective surfaces that bounce a source light onto your actors to soften shadows. Foldable reflectors can be bought from professional photography suppliers, or you can make your own reflector with a thin sheet of polystyrene foam or foam core board and some kitchen foil. Simply glue the foil onto one side of the sheet and leave the other side white. As they are a little more cumbersome to transport than the reflectors you can buy, if you plan to do lots of outdoor shooting involving traveling, you should definitely invest in the manufactured, foldable ones.

Natural light is also wonderful for daytime interiors. Unfortunately, it does change as the day progresses, and

REFLECTOR RANGE
Portable reflectors are indispensable, both in the studio and on location. They come in a variety of sizes and colors, and fold down into small cases.

you will need to plan your shoot carefully to take full advantage of it. Make use of reflectors here as well.

Artificial light

Using artificial light involves spending money. How much depends on the look you want or the amount of improvisation you are prepared to do. The majority of affordable lighting is tungsten, which has a lower color temperature than daylight (see chart below). You can simply change your camera's white balance to the tungsten preset. Avoid using auto white balance or trying to do it manually. If you mix light sources, unless you are really comfortable with what you are doing, it will create unnatural colors, as the daylight will get a blue cast using a tungsten-balanced medium.

If your largest source of light is daylight, convert your tungsten lights to daylight using Color Temperature Blue (CTB) gel.

OBJECTIVES >>
- **Use natural light**
- **Create affordable artificial light**
- **Understand lighting design**

COLOR TEMPERATURE

Video is affected by color temperature. The chart to the right is divided into Kelvins (sometimes called degrees Kelvin), and shows an approximation of how they look. You can obtain accurate color by adjusting the white balance on your camera. The chart clarifies why photos shot indoors on daylight film (5,500 K) appear orange, and sunsets always look so much more vibrant.

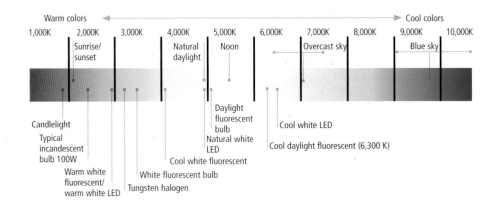

Warm colors ← → Cool colors

1,000K 2,000K 3,000K 4,000K 5,000K 6,000K 7,000K 8,000K 9,000K 10,000K

Sunrise/sunset

Natural daylight

Noon

Overcast sky

Blue sky

Candlelight

Typical incandescent bulb 100W

Daylight fluorescent bulb

Natural white LED

Cool white LED

Warm white fluorescent/warm white LED

White fluorescent bulb

Cool white fluorescent

Cool daylight fluorescent (6,300 K)

Tungsten halogen

ARTIFICIAL SUNLIGHT
This setup is a fantastic example of using artificial lighting that is balanced to match outdoor sunlight. These are large HMIs (Halogen Metal Iodides) without barn doors but are being controlled by flags seen at the left of the shot.

The cheapest form of artificial light is the high-wattage practical light bulb or photoflood available from photographic equipment suppliers. These will fit into most domestic light sockets and remain hidden. Other solutions are the tungsten or halogen floodlights used on construction sites. These give off a lot of light and heat that is difficult to control and work with, but they are inexpensive.

For low-budget filmmakers needing a decent artificial light source, redheads or Lowell Omnis are the most popular choices. These are available in a package with stands and barn doors and will cost you around $1,000 for three lights. They also give off a lot of heat.

Photographic fluorescent tubes provide an alternative. These are balanced for either tungsten or daylight. (Standard domestic tubes give off a green light, so they are not suitable.) Professional lighting rigs are available, but if you are handy or know an electrician, you can make your own. Fluorescents are much cooler than standard tungsten and use a lot less electricity but can take up more space, which may not be available in a small location. The two types of artificial lighting instruments, fresnel and open-face lights, are discussed below.

ARTIFICIAL LIGHTING INSTRUMENTS

FRESNEL
On a fresnel, the front of the housing contains a thick piece of glass. The glass focuses the light emanating from the bulb in a more defined manner than open-face lights, and the beam is more controllable and tighter in its throw. These lights can be found as a daylight- or tungsten-balanced instrument. Daylight-balanced lights are referred to as HMIs (Halogen Metal Iodides). Much like common fluorescent lights, they require a ballast to convert and control the AC current. The electrical current interacts with gas located inside the glass bulb, which then emits a "daylight" balanced light.

OPEN FACE
The housing of open-face lighting instruments does not contain any glass at the front. The throw of the light tends to be wider and more displaced than that of a fresnel light. These lights are tungsten-based and are commonly used as a portable system. Redheads made by Ianera or Lowell are good examples of portable tungsten lighting.

Remember, when designing your lighting it is important to make it look realistic and natural, unless you are deliberately trying to create an atmospheric mood or special effect. In addition to proper camera aperture setting, you must ensure you don't over-light, which causes the whites to burn out, or under-light, which results in grainy images with lots of artifacts. Get your lighting right and your movie will definitely look a lot more professional.

How many lights?

The basic lighting principle behind every photographic situation is a solid understanding of three-point lighting (illustrated below). The three lights you will need are: key (highest wattage), fill (half the wattage of the key), and backlight (the same wattage as the fill). The lighting ratio for three-point lighting is 2:1. So, if the key light is 1000 watts (1K) then the fill light and backlight are half the wattage, at 500 watts. A fourth light can be added in as a "background light." It creates further separation of the subject from the background and creates depth to the 2D photographic plane.

DIFFUSING LIGHT
Lighting is always about diffusion or bouncing the source. Here you can see a single source being readied for a softer look by loading it with some diffusion.

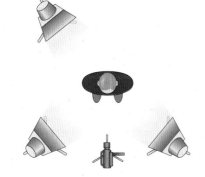

TECH TIP
Be careful with camera-mounted lights, as used in the filming of broadcast news. It is a quick way of shooting but offers no control over the light and produces ugly results. However, "light rings" (left) are available, which mount to the front of the camera, over the lens, and throw a nice, soft light.

ONE LIGHT
The main, or key, light has the highest wattage and is the most intense light. When using one light, the shadows on the wall become more noticeable as the angle between camera view and light direction grows. Normally shadows are avoided, but they can be used to great effect.

TWO LIGHTS
The fill is half the wattage of the key and is used to fill in some of the shadows created by the key light. When the key light is placed at 45 degrees to the camera view, and the fill light is placed close to the camera with a direction close to its viewpoint, extremes of light and darkness are avoided.

THREE LIGHTS
The third light is a backlight. It is the same wattage as the fill and is used to create some separation between the subject and the background. It can add a halo glow to the subject, and depth and dimension to a scene. There is a risk of flare, even when, as is usually the case, the light is positioned high up.

BACKLIGHT

Strong backlight is very difficult to work with and needs very careful calculation of the exposure, according to the effect you want to convey. Strong backlighting can be used, as in *A Nightmare on Elm Street*, shown here, to create the sense of a foreboding menace, with the actors appearing in silhouette. You must ask, how does this "look" serve your story?

DAYLIGHT

Light cloud cover will give very even light without much contrast, as in Alexander Payne's *The Descendents*, which is useful for creating an atmospheric mood. Use reflector boards or photo flex fill disks to capture and shape the light. Hard, direct sunlight, on the other hand, can be bounced or reflected as hard or soft to create the look you want. Again, how does the look of the light you are creating serve your story?

INTERIOR SETS

Studio shooting allows for complete control of your light sources as demonstrated in *Captain America: The First Avenger*. You can create backlight and soft or hard light in any manner you choose. The more creative lighting you want, the more money is needed to create the stylized look you are after. More lights is not necessarily better lighting. Finally, ask yourself the question: How does the look of the light you are creating serve your story?

EXTRA GEAR

Once you have chosen the camera that's right for your movie, you will still need some ancillary equipment to support it—literally. A host of devices are available to help you stabilize your camera, from tripods, to dollies and cranes, to a variety of Steadicam-type units. All come with a purpose and a price tag.

Support

The most useful provider of support has to be the tripod (legs). When it comes to video tripods, it is wise to spend a little bit more than you can really afford, and go for the best. As a rule of thumb, a decent fluid head tripod will cost at least $200. Many professional units are sold in two parts, legs and head, with the head being the more important and expensive. When shooting movies, you must have a fluid head. A normal camera tripod is adequate if you are using it just for static (locked-down) shots, but when it comes to movements such as panning (following action horizontally) or tilting (vertical movement), it will not be smooth enough, and your camerawork will be jerky, but without the rawness of being handheld.

Apart from the quality of movements possible with the more expensive fluid-head tripods, they usually come with options that make them easily adaptable to other supports, such as jibs and dollies. These will increase the professional look of your camera movements.

There are cheaper, consumer-level, fluid-head tripods that are useful, but if you are serious about making movies, then invest in a quality stand from a company such as Miller. It will last for years and won't suffer from obsolescence the way other technology does. The fact that a tripod is almost impossible to find secondhand really shows how valuable it is—and should you need to sell it, it won't lose its value.

The other type of support is a rig worn by an operator, which allows him or her to move around and follow the action. It incorporates mechanisms that absorb the jiggling movement of walking to give a smooth flow. These rigs are very expensive, but there are some cheaper alternatives designed for DV cameras, which also double as monopods.

Other hardware you may need includes lights (see pages 70–73) and sound recording equipment (see pages 90–93), depending on your shoot and camera. Apart from these, there are many other items to take with you on the shoot, not least of which is the clapperboard, or slate.

Making a clean slate

Your shoot must use a slate. You can make your own or purchase one from an equipment store. There are also digital versions that mark time code, but they are extremely expensive and are not necessary. There are two main purposes behind the slate: shot information and sound synchronization. The slate is used to clearly identify the scene being shot and record important information about the scene, which you will mark up before each take. Information such as scene number, tape number, take number, time code, sound, camera operator, and director is critical in enabling the editor to locate and identify each scene. This information will also line up with the completed shot sheet (camera report) to make the editing process easier.

If you are recording sound separately from the camera, as is the case with lower-end DSLR cameras without audio inputs, a slate is important for sound synchronization. The "clack" of the two slate sticks coming together acts as a visual and auditory marker for syncing dialogue or any sync sounds. The editor will then match picture and sound in postproduction.

Computer

You will need some sort of computer for a range of tasks, from budgeting, to scriptwriting, to picture and sound editing. As with cameras, get the best you can afford (though it will inevitably be superseded by a cheaper and better model just after you've bought it!). Whether you buy a Mac or a PC is irrelevant. Both platforms have digital video editing software available. For example, there is Final Cut Pro for the Mac and

Table fields shown on slate: TITLE, DIRECTOR, DOP, ROLL #, SCENE/SLATE, TAKE, TIMECODE, EXPOSURE, DATE

LOW-BUDGET TIP
You can make your own slate from a small dry-erase board. Draw it up, as shown left, with a permanent marker pen, and then use a dry-erase pen to write up each take.

Adobe Premiere for the PC. (For more on editing software, see page 105.)

If you have shot onto HD you will need a machine capable of handling the resulting heavy output. Be sure to get a machine capable of creating, authoring, and burning dual-layer DVDs.

Ready to shoot?

A camera, microphone, tripod (or some other sort of support), and computer are all the gear you need to start making your first short film. Be sure to have enough recordable media to shoot onto. Whether it is tape or memory cards, always have extras on hand. There are dozens of accessories you can add to these basics, and they will be mentioned later. The important thing is to get started and familiarize yourself with your equipment.

USE YOUR COMPUTER

Buy the best computer you can afford, as it will be useful in many areas, including editing. Computer-based digital non-linear editing is easily accessible and cheap.

KNOW YOUR TRIPODS

FLUID HEAD

Fluid-head tripods are essential for smooth movement when filming, which is even more important when using video. Get one to match your camera—neither too heavy nor too light. Make sure it is adjustable to a variety of heights and can also be adapted for use with dollies and jibs. This model is produced by Miller, which holds the first patent for fluid heads and makes a range of tripods and heads.

LIGHTWEIGHT TRIPOD COMPACTED

Ranging from 63 in. (160 cm), (see photo below right), to a compact 27 in. (69 cm), (below), this adjustable tripod can handle a camcorder up to 20 lb (9 kg).

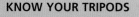

LIGHTWEIGHT TRIPOD

This tripod combines a 75 mm fluid pan-and-tilt ball head with a light, solid, spreaderless tripod. Features include a selectable counterbalance, bubble level, and a weight of 5½ lb (2.5 kg).

FLOWPOD

To smooth out the jolting of handheld camerawork, especially while walking or running, some sort of stabilizer is needed. Full Steadicam rigs cost thousands and usually require an experienced operator. Economical alternatives, such as the FlowPod, will do a good enough job, although they will never match a body-worn stabilizer.

SHOOTING BASICS

After all the preparation, and with the schedule planned out, you will be eager to get on with what most people would consider to be real filmmaking—the shoot. It is certainly the most intense part of the process and usually the shortest. If you have done all your preproduction correctly, that is how it should be.

You will now have other people involved in order to divide the workload, and if there is payment involved, you have a vested interest in getting the shoot done quickly. Even if the cast and crew are working for free, there is a limit to how much of their time you can take up, unless they are as committed to the project as you are.

For your first directorial shoots, you can surround yourself with people who know what they are doing and learn from their expertise. This can be a rather daunting experience, as you will have to face the fact that you know nothing when you are barraged with questions about what to do next or how you want it done. Alternatively, you can try to do everything yourself, and learn from your mistakes. Both approaches have their advantages and disadvantages, and your choice will be dictated by your personality and circumstances.

This section of the book covers some of the theory of practical filmmaking and provides advice on making the most of what you have to produce the best results. Of course, the only way to get results is to go out and do it, which is why theory is kept to a minimum.

Getting it right the first time

There are lots of things you can do in postproduction to recover from mistakes, but it is far better to avoid them in the first place, and this can be done simply by knowing your equipment. If you are not familiar with the functions and limitations of your camera, you are courting disaster.

With digital video there is no need to calculate all the permutations and combinations, as the variables will be dictated by the capabilities of your camera, including whether you shoot in widescreen or not (see pages 80–81). Although we are not living completely in an HD world, it is advisable to shoot 16:9 widescreen at a minimum, even if you are using an SD camera.

The holy grail of video is getting it to look like film. While the obvious solution is simply to use film, there are techniques that can alter the appearance of video to give it that "film look." A basic step to take is to treat your video shoot as though you were shooting film. This means proper lighting and carefully (manually) controlled exposure settings. These will improve the look of your shoot no matter which medium you are using.

But to achieve that film look you should also use

OBJECTIVES >>

■ **Write the big "to do" list**
■ **Discover how to make your digital video look like film**

DOES SIZE MATTER?
Shooting on a very large (far right) or very small (right) set should never force you away from the basics of shooting to get a great shot. All it means is that there is more or less of something that you would have to deal with no matter what. Remember that bigger is not necessarily better. Less can be more.

Wide-angle lens

Standard lens

Telephoto lens

MEASURE FOR MEASURE
To ensure accurate focus, a tape measure is used and the distance set on the lens focus ring. In digital filmmaking, you can use a tape measure for near and far focus positions only if you are using a DSLR camera with a stock lens.

something known as "Progressive Scan," which is available on some top-end DV cameras. Here comes the science... Most video cameras capture interlaced images, which simply means that two alternating images are captured and joined to create a single image. Progressive Scan captures a single image, similar to the way in which film is exposed one frame at a time. To further emulate film, 24 frames are captured per second. This is known as 24P video. The majority of HD cameras shoot 24P video, which is becoming standard. In the 24P world one needs to be careful. Some cameras shoot "true" 24P at 23.97 frames per second, whereas some will shoot it at 29.97 frames per second. You need to be sure of the actual frame rate your camera is recording at. You would need to make sure that the non-linear editing platform you use in postproduction is capable of handling "true" 24P at 23.97. In countries that use the NTSC video standard, which runs at 30 fps (frames per second), 24P makes a significant difference. PAL, the other major video format, runs at 25 fps, and cameras in PAL countries are generally 25P. More about video formats and film look is covered in the postproduction section (see pages 98–127), but if you want to achieve the look of film with video, you have to use Progressive Scan.

Cinematography is a technical pursuit. It has its creative side, but most importantly it is about getting the shots, and making sure they are properly exposed, correctly color-balanced, and in focus. It is also the responsibility of the director to ensure that enough coverage is shot. This will be done in consultation with the director of photography who, on a low-budget film, could also be the director.

SHOOTING ESSENTIALS
• Batteries (fully charged)
• Camera
• Changing bag for loading film
• Tapes
• Power supply and/or battery charger
• Lenses (if your camera takes changeable ones)
• Tape measure
• Lens hoods and "flags"
• Tripod and other supports
• Gaffer tape
• Reflectors
• Slate/clapperboard
• Notebooks, pens

FOCAL LENGTH
Camera lenses come in different focal lengths for different uses. A wide-angle lens will show a lot more foreground, but will make the background seem farther away, whereas a telephoto lens will bring distant objects closer, including the background, giving a compressed feeling. See "Zoom" on pages 86–87.

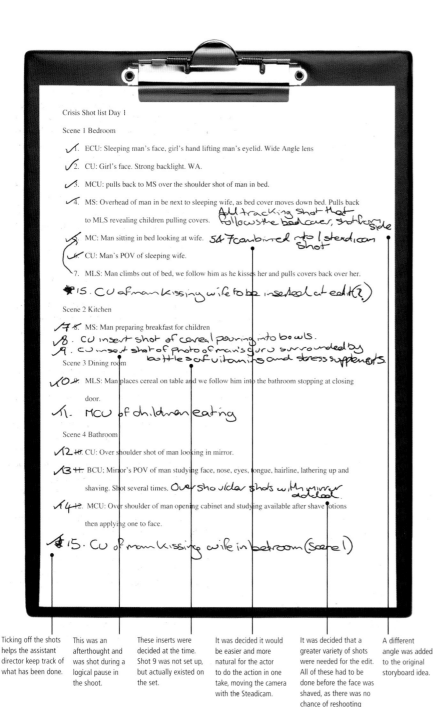

Crisis Shot list Day 1

Scene 1 Bedroom

1. ECU: Sleeping man's face, girl's hand lifting man's eyelid. Wide Angle lens

2. CU: Girl's face. Strong backlight. WA.

3. MCU: pulls back to MS over the shoulder shot of man in bed.

4. MS: Overhead of man in be next to sleeping wife, as bed cover moves down bed. Pulls back to MLS revealing children pulling covers. *Add tracking shot that follows the bedcover, shot from side*

5. MC: Man sitting in bed looking at wife. *5 & 7 combined into 1 steadican shot*

6. CU: Man's POV of sleeping wife.

7. MLS: Man climbs out of bed, we follow him as he kisses her and pulls covers back over her.

★ 15. *CU of man kissing wife to be inserted at edit (?)*

Scene 2 Kitchen

7 8. MS: Man preparing breakfast for children

8. CU insert shot of cereal pouring into bowls.

9. CU insert shot of photo of man's guru surrounded by bottles of vitamins and stress supplements.

Scene 3 Dining room

10. MLS: Man places cereal on table and we follow him into the bathroom stopping at closing door.

11. MCU of children eating

Scene 4 Bathroom

12. CU: Over shoulder shot of man looking in mirror.

13. BCU: Mirror's POV of man studying face, nose, eyes, tongue, hairline, lathering up and shaving. Shot several times. *Over shoulder shots with the mirror added.*

14. MCU: Over shoulder shot of man opening cabinet and studying available after shave lotions then applying one to face.

★ 15. *CU of man kissing wife in bathroom (scene 1)*

Ticking off the shots helps the assistant director keep track of what has been done.

This was an afterthought and was shot during a logical pause in the shoot.

These inserts were decided at the time. Shot 9 was not set up, but actually existed on the set.

It was decided it would be easier and more natural for the actor to do the action in one take, moving the camera with the Steadicam.

It was decided that a greater variety of shots were needed for the edit. All of these had to be done before the face was shaved, as there was no chance of reshooting after that.

A different angle was added to the original storyboard idea.

Coverage means getting a variety of shots for each scene. These can be: an establishing shot that is a wide angle of the whole scene; medium shots showing the main protagonists; and close-ups of each person talking—often done as over-the shoulder-shots (see page 83 for the problem of "crossing the line"). The other shots needed are cutaways—close-ups of hands, panoramas, POV (point of view) shots out of windows… These can directly relate to the immediate action, adding to dramatic detail or providing important story information, or may simply be a way to break up the monotony of talking heads. As a first-time filmmaker, you will probably shoot everything, and unless you have a very developed sense of how the scene will cut together, it is highly advisable to take the time to do this. If you are confident about how the shots will flow in the editing room, then you can only shoot the footage you know you will need; there is no need to get a wide, medium, or close-up shot of everything.

On feature films, the B unit—a separate crew that works independently, often after the main shooting is done—handles this. On low-budget films (or videos), the luxury of a separate B unit is out of reach, but for a small outlay (the price of a camera), you can increase your coverage while minimizing shooting time. A two-camera shoot can really save you a lot of time and gives you added editing options and the security of two takes for each setup.

Positioning the cameras is important, not only to ensure that they don't appear in the frame, but also to get the best possible angles. You may decide to keep one of the cameras static on a tripod (locked down) while the other moves, either handheld or on some sort of rig such as a dolly. Quality sound only needs to be recorded to one of the cameras, or a separate recorder, as dealing with two booms is asking for trouble. For a two-camera shoot to work, the most important thing is to use identical cameras and lenses. Ensure that they are properly white-balanced and calibrated (if possible). This will eliminate any inconsistencies in color and look, and will make any eventual grading much easier.

SHOT LIST WITH AMENDMENTS

During the shoot, shots are altered, joined, or added. Marking changes on the original shot list serves as a backup to the shot log and will help the editor. Get the assistant director or continuity person to write the changes.

SHOT SHEETS

SHEET 1

PRODUCTION NAME: VFS – FRIDAY NIGHT						
REEL #:			DIRECTOR: PREETI			Page #: 1
CAM #:			CAMERA: FLAVIO			/ OF 3

SCENE	TAKE	PICTURE	AUDIO	T/C IN	T/C OUT	T/C TOTAL
1A	1 G/NG	books – Insert	CH.1 MOS CH.2	00:00:00:00 H:M:S:F	00:00:23:00 H:M:S:F	H:M:S:F
1B	1 G/NG	books – Insert	CH.1 MOS CH.2	00:00:23:00 H:M:S:F	00:00:56:00 H:M:S:F	H:M:S:F
1B	2 G/NG	books – Insert	CH.1 MOS CH.2	00:00:56:00 H:M:S:F	00:01:32:00 H:M:S:F	H:M:S:F
1C	1 G/NG	Sleep apnea	CH.1 MOS CH.2	00:01:32:00 H:M:S:F	00:02:35:00 H:M:S:F	H:M:S:F
1D	1 G/NG	C.U – Sign	CH.1 MOS CH.2	00:02:35:00 H:M:S:F	00:03:20:00 H:M:S:F	H:M:S:F
1E	1 G/NG	M.S – "No dave puzzle"	CH.1 MOS CH.2	00:03:20:00 H:M:S:F	00:04:33:00 H:M:S:F	H:M:S:F
1E	2 G/NG	M.S – "No dave puzzle"	CH.1 MOS CH.2	00:04:33:00 H:M:S:F	00:05:51:00 H:M:S:F	H:M:S:F
1F	1 G/NG	C.U – "DAVE spilling beer"	CH.1 MOS CH.2	00:05:51:00 H:M:S:F	00:06:42:00 H:M:S:F	H:M:S:F
1F	2 G/NG	C.U – "DAVE spilling beer"	CH.1 MOS CH.2	00:06:42:00 H:M:S:F	00:07:32:00 H:M:S:F	H:M:S:F
1G	1 G/NG	Sleep apnea	CH.1 MOS CH.2	00:07:32:00 H:M:S:F	00:08:27:00 H:M:S:F	H:M:S:F
1G	2 G/NG	Sleep apnea	CH.1 MOS CH.2	00:08:27:00 H:M:S:F	00:09:21:00 H:M:S:F	H:M:S:F
2	1 G/NG	Dutch Shot	CH.1 MOS CH.2	00:09:21:00 H:M:S:F	00:10:20:00 H:M:S:F	H:M:S:F
2	2 G/NG	Dutch Shot	CH.1 MOS CH.2	00:10:20:00 H:M:S:F	00:11:31:00 H:M:S:F	H:M:S:F
2	3 G/NG	Dutch Shot	CH.1 MOS CH.2	00:11:31:00 H:M:S:F	00:12:25:00 H:M:S:F	H:M:S:F
2A	1 G/NG	Blury bottle	CH.1 MOS CH.2	00:12:25:00 H:M:S:F	00:13:04:00 H:M:S:F	H:M:S:F
2A	2 G/NG	Blury bottle	CH.1 MOS CH.2	00:13:04:00 H:M:S:F	00:13:36:00 H:M:S:F	H:M:S:F
2B	1 G/NG	Lying on the flow	CH.1 MOS CH.2	00:13:36:00 H:M:S:F	00:16:05:00 H:M:S:F	H:M:S:F
2B	2 G/NG	Lying on the flow	CH.1 MOS CH.2	00:16:05:00 H:M:S:F	00:18:47:00 H:M:S:F	H:M:S:F
2B	3 G/NG	Lying on the flow	CH.1 MOS CH.2	00:18:47:00 H:M:S:F	00:22:23:00 H:M:S:F	H:M:S:F
2C	1 G/NG	W.S – dead	CH.1 MOS CH.2	00:22:23:00 H:M:S:F	00:23:00:00 H:M:S:F	H:M:S:F
2C	2 G/NG	W.S – dead	CH.1 MOS CH.2	00:23:00:00 H:M:S:F	00:26:00:00 H:M:S:F	H:M:S:F
2D	1 G/NG	C.U – freaking out	CH.1 MOS CH.2	00:26:00:00 H:M:S:F	00:27:34:00 H:M:S:F	H:M:S:F

FRIDAY NIGHT

CAMERA REPORT
The assistant camera operator, or the camera operator on a small crew, marks down all the details of each shot as it is taken so the editor knows exactly what he or she has to work with.

Shot lists

The cinematographer/camera person needs two lists. The first is a list of shots to be done on the day (the shot list). This is usually drawn up during preproduction and/or the night before, with the director, the producer, and the director of photography. The second (called the shot log, shot sheet, or camera report), which is more important, is a list of every shot taken. This is invaluable for editing.

For video you will need to create a simple sheet that lists movie title, shooting date, roll (or tape) number, slate number, take, time code, shot description, and a tick box. You can add other data, such as lighting source and exposure settings, but these are not vital and will depend on whether you can actually adjust them on the camera.

Once you have created the sheet, it must be filled out before every shot. The roll or tape number—obviously starting at 1 (or 001 if you prefer)—is written on the tape and also on its storage case. How they are coded is entirely up to you, as long as you know in which order they are shot and the film's title.

The slate number is the same as the setup or shot number from the shooting schedule. The take number is the number of times each setup is shot. The time code is the running time of the tape shown as HH:MM:SS:FF (hours:minutes:seconds:frames) and is recorded onto a separate track on the tape that does not show up when played back, unless you want it to. This is different from the date and time, which many consumer cameras embed into the scene. Most decent miniDV cameras will record the time code, with pro cameras having manual adjust as well, so that each tape can be consecutively registered. Putting this on the sheet before each shot makes it easier to find when transferring to a computer.

The shot description should be basic—start with "Int" or "Ext," and include shot type (LS, MS, CU, etc. See pages 88–89). The tick box allows you to indicate whether the take was usable. The information on the sheet should match what you write on the clapperboard (see page 74).

Although this seems over-meticulous and time-consuming, it will eventually save you a lot of time. These are some of the important basics of cinematography. There are more details of other aspects on the following pages.

FRAMING

Now that you have familiarized yourself with some of the basics of shooting, you are ready to get going—but which format is the best? In this case, format refers to the shape or ratio of the medium, which is rather dictated by the type of camera you are using.

Screen formats

The two principal moviemaking formats are Academy (4:3) and widescreen (16:9). The Academy (as in the awards) ratio is derived from a single frame of 35 mm film. Standard televisions, however, are 4:3, as are computer monitors and the default settings on most video cameras.

Widescreen is the format of the latest televisions and has been adopted for HDTV (high-definition television). If you are serious about getting your work broadcast, this is the format you should be shooting in. HD cameras and most top-of-the-range professional DV cameras, and an increasing number of serious amateur cameras, will shoot in this format naturally, without resorting to digital trickery that can degrade picture quality. The technique, known as anamorphic compression, achieves the effect by compressing the width of the image in the camera, and decompressing it when played back on a widescreen television.

Faking it

If you can't shoot naturally in widescreen on your camera, an anamorphic lens can be placed in front of the main lens to compress the image.

With film, another lens would be placed on the projector to un-squash the image. This is how Cinemascope films are made, though they use the much wider ratio of 2.35:1. For video, it can be decompressed in postproduction.

If you want to shoot widescreen on a normal video camera, without resorting to squashing the picture, you can mask it. The widescreen (1.85:1) that you see in cinemas uses this method, so why shouldn't you? It is simply a matter of putting some gaffer tape over the monitor or your flip-out LCD screen as a guide. Some cameras have the mask built in as an option, often called "letterbox." Alternatively, instead of the very sticky gaffer tape, try using a couple of strips of colored cel (as you would use for lights), so you can see what is happening outside the masked area.

If you shoot very judiciously, keeping the boom out of both frames, you can have widescreen and Academy versions in the one shoot, leaving decisions on format to the editing stage. Of course, you can add an anamorphic lens to the front of your camera, but they

SAFE AREA
Editing software has "safe area" masks. Using a professional field monitor during the shoot will help to keep you from shooting outside that area.

are not cheap and the total cost could end up as high as that of buying a 16:9 camera.

As widescreen televisions become increasingly commonplace, it makes sense to start shooting everything in this format, no matter which method you choose to achieve it. While this book is all about using affordable equipment, if you can stretch your budget to buy a proper 16:9 camera, it will serve you better and for longer. And the new consumer HD cameras are offering even better options. Widescreen not only gives you a lot more area to work with; it will get you into the habit of working in a professional format and learning the best way to use the screen space.

One final thing to consider, regardless of format, is the safe area. This relates to the viewable area on a television. Many pro cameras have an option for showing this, and a field monitor will as well. However, make sure you don't shoot anything vital on the very edges of the frame. Most editing software has an option to show the safe area.

The most important thing is to get on and make your movie. Don't lose valuable time agonizing over which format to use and the best way to achieve it. If shooting 4:3 is going to be easiest, then shoot 4:3; you can concentrate on 16:9 for a future film.

HDV1080I

The latest HDV cameras offer high-resolution images in a native 16:9 widescreen format. For even reasonably serious moviemakers this is the format to use (1920 x 1080 pixels).

720P

A smaller HD format, still at a native 16:9 (1280 x 720 pixels). Most broadcasters (in North America) deploy at 720P.

PAL DV

PAL is the television standard for countries that don't use NTSC and offers a higher resolution that runs at 25 fps. When shooting in the 4:3 format you need to consider how the image is framed, depending on your lens. Always ensure that you shoot enough width to allow cropping for letterbox widescreen (768 x 576 pixels).

NTSC DV 4:3

The same crop as the PAL version but at NTSC resolution. The other main difference between PAL and NTSC is the frame rate and color fidelity (720 x 540 pixels).

NTSC DV ANAMORPHIC 16:9

The decompressed NTSC anamorphic widescreen frame (853 x 480 pixels).

PAL DV WIDESCREEN

The decompressed anamorphic PAL DV (1024 x 576 pixels).

PAL DV ANAMORPHIC

To achieve widescreen on DV cameras, anamorphic compression is used, either with an adapter lens or through the camera's electronics. It compresses the image horizontally (as shown) to fit into the camera's 4:3 frame, which is then decompressed when viewed on a widescreen TV or a projector (768 x 576 pixels).

PAL DV PAN AND SCAN

If you shoot anamorphic widescreen but need to reduce down to 4:3, you can lose some of the image, which is acceptable in this case, but with two actors facing each other it can be a disaster (768 x 576 pixels).

FRAME SIZES

When it comes to shooting digital video, there are different frame sizes and resolutions, depending on the camera's format and CCDs. Above you will see all the different varieties, from HDV to miniDV. It does not differentiate between Interlaced and Progressive Scan.

COMPOSITION

Composition—an artistic aspect of filmmaking that is hard to quantify—is the way the elements are placed within your frame, and their positioning and relationship to one another. A lot of it is subjective and will often occur intuitively and/or accidentally.

Studying still images, such as paintings and photographs, is one of the best ways to learn about composition. Of course, films have the added dimension of movement, which means that your composition is in a constant state of flux, whereas photographs capture a single moment.

While there are some basic "rules" of composition that are worth following, intuition plays a large part, as do "luck" and "accidents" (what photographer Henri Cartier-Bresson called "the decisive moment"), although the last two are less likely to occur in the controlled environment of a film set.

Third divisions

One of the principal guides for composition is the division of thirds. Divide your screen horizontally and vertically into three, and then place the actors, objects, or scenery into the nine subdivisions. You don't need to put the lines on the viewfinder, as approximation is fine. In the image below the gray horizontal lines show the division for the widescreen (16:9) version and the red horizontal lines show the division for the Academy (4:3) screen version (see pages 80–81). Notice how the characters' facial features remain within the central horizontal division in both formats. If you weren't aware of this, the next time you watch a film look at how the shots are framed and you will notice that the actors are usually placed at the edge of the screen.

As most movies are shot in widescreen, this presents problems when they are transferred to the "small screen" ratio of 4:3 using the "pan and scan" process, unless the letterbox format is used, which will tend to cut off one of the actors. The gray bands (top and bottom) show how a letterbox widescreen would look when shot on a 4:3 camera. Because the composition allows for both versions, it is more acceptable to cut off the tops of the heads than having to reduce the sides, leaving a large chasm on the screen.

Even if you are shooting in 4:3 format, you can still divide your screen into thirds, but the composition changes slightly and your actors will have to work much closer together. Placing an actor's face right in the center of the screen, with lots of space above it and around it, is a mistake often made by first-time filmmakers, but that does not mean it cannot be used to achieve a particular effect. It all depends on execution and intent.

Focus groups

Your composition will also be dictated by your choice of camera lens, position, and the mood or effect you want to achieve. For example, shooting an actor from a low position gives that person an air of authority, while shooting from above diminishes his or her power. By altering the camera position relative to the character as the story progresses, you can subtly enforce changes in

Bands show a letterbox widescreen shot on a 4:3 camera.

Gray divisions for widescreen (16:9) format

Characters' facial features remain in the central divisions.

Red divisions for Academy (4:3) format.

DIVISION OF THIRDS
Dividing your frame into thirds vertically and horizontally is a great aid to composition.

his or her role. A similar effect can be achieved by choosing a particular lens for a certain character's personality. A long lens will tend to isolate the actor from the background, which goes out of focus. This can be used both for people who are too self-important and for loners who feel they can't fit in. Equally, a wide-angle lens can be used to evoke a feeling of loneliness, as the character is not being differentiated from his or her surroundings.

Crossing the line of axis

Almost as complicated as the offside rule in soccer, the 180-degree rule, or "crossing the line," is one of the fundamentals that has to be understood in order to avoid disorienting the viewer. When filming two people facing each other, you have to keep the camera on the same side of an imaginary line drawn through the middle of them. Even though it would seem logical to

film both of them over the same shoulder, it does not work (see diagram and pictures below). And just like the offside rule, even professionals can get it wrong.

Eye line

A bad eye line is a much easier mistake to make than crossing the line. The eye line is where the actor looks when he or she is being filmed in a single shot. Looking directly into the camera is generally frowned upon, unless it is a talking-to-the-audience shot. Even for point-of-view shots, it is better if the actor can look away slightly. Most people never make real eye-to-eye contact in conversation but focus on another part of the face—the mouth or the eyebrows. Having another actor behind the camera will often help with this.

CHECK THESE OUT

- *Amélie* (Dir. Jean-Pierre Jeunet). Every shot is perfectly composed yet never superfluous to the story.

- Paintings by Edward Hopper. Striking and deceptively simple compositions that tell enigmatic stories.

- Photographs by Henri Cartier-Bresson. The master of black-and-white photojournalism who managed to capture the decisive moment, when action and composition were in harmony.

Over the shoulder

When shooting over the shoulder shots like this, you have to be very careful of not crossing the line (see above) when reversing the shot.

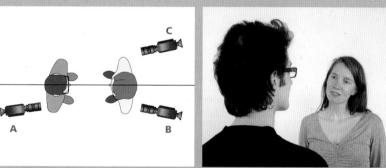

Camera A

The establishing shot of the sequence, taken with camera A. This can be over the shoulder, as shown, or simply with the facing character.

Camera B

The opposing shot, from camera B, either over the shoulder or solo character, when edited gives the impression that the two characters are facing each other as they appear on opposite sides of the screen.

Camera C

Although it would seem logical to shoot with camera C, over the same shoulder of the two characters, by doing this and crossing the line, it would disorient the viewer to have both characters appear on the same side of the screen during the intercuts.

CAMERA MOVEMENTS

Having looked at the composition of the images being created, you have to remember that you are working with moving images and that the composition is going to change, often rapidly.

OBJECTIVES >>

- **Choose your moves**
- **Understand basic movements**
- **Use handheld cameras**

CHECK THESE OUT

• www.homebuiltstabilizers.com. A great collection of homemade stabilizers and some instructions on how to build them.

• Storyboard software such as FrameForge (www.frameforge3d. com/Products) and Power Productions' three storyboard programs (Storyboard Quick, Storyboard Artist, and Storyboard Artist Pro, www.powerproductions. com) all allow you to experiment with camera moves. See pages 24–29.

Long static shots, such as Omar Sharif's arrival across the desert in *Lawrence of Arabia*, are the preserve of cinema epics or art house installations.

In short films you want to keep the on-screen action flowing, much of which will be achieved in the editing room. Modern audiences have become used to seeing almost continuous camera movement and may become unnerved by a static camera. On the other hand, putting camera movement in just for its own sake is not always advisable. It comes down to a creative decision that you, as the director, have to make. If you are in doubt and are working with an experienced DP, ask his or her advice. If not, go with your instincts—you can always shoot again if it doesn't work.

Any camera movements that you intend to use should be decided at the storyboard stage. Storyboard software, such as FrameForge, will allow you to try out different camera moves and create an animatic. Alternatively, you could use an inexpensive 3D program, like Daz 3D Studio or Poser, that will let you put 3D characters into a set and animate the camera. It is vital to have a clear idea of what you want to achieve before you start shooting so you can have all the right equipment on the set. Once there, you can change the shot or try other moves, but that is only possible if you have the right gear in the first place.

Making your move

The basic camera movements are pan, tilt, track, dolly, and crane. Anything else—such as aerial shots—are beyond the low-budget filmmaker, unless they have well-connected friends willing to do favors. Even cranes, tracks, and dollies come with a (rental) price tag, but inventive filmmakers can find ways of getting their shots without added expense.

Tracking and dolly shots are the most commonly used and, if well executed, they will give a professional look to your movie. Using a dolly on a track will ensure that movement is smooth, especially if done by an experienced grip, and can be accurately repeated. If you

CAMERA MOVES
The diagrams here show the main camera movements, which you can plan on storyboarding software. If you don't have access to special software, draw some rough sketches to plan your camera movements.

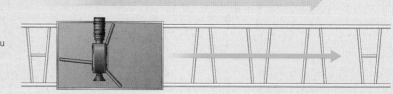

Track: Moving the camera on a wheeled platform, alongside the action.

Tilt: Following the action vertically from a fixed position.

Pan: Following the action horizontally from a fixed point.

are filming in an area with smooth, flat floors, any sort of wheeled conveyance will do the job.

A well-oiled wheelchair is one of the most popular low-budget solutions, as it allows the cameraman to sit comfortably and even to mount the camera on a tripod or a similar device. The weight of the wheelchair and the camera operator will help to ensure that movement is smooth and even. In fact any device with smooth, quiet wheels can act as a dolly; or even wheelchairs, roller skates or blades are good, too. Be sure that your camera person is experienced with this type of motion before you start.

For the low-budget filmmaker, handheld camerawork is a staple, if not stable, method of adding movement to films. Again, weight is an issue. Most miniDV cameras are extremely light, which does mean that carrying them around all day won't wear you out. However, developing a method of carrying one while shooting so that it doesn't record every jolt of your body movement takes lots of experimenting and practice. Up to a limit, the larger and heavier the camera, the more stable it is, especially if it can be mounted on the shoulder. Stabilizers and harnesses, such as Steadicams, will make movements much smoother by absorbing impact, but, like all equipment, they come at a price. Most consumer-level DV cameras come with some sort of image stabilizer, either digital or optical, that is designed

COMPLICATED MANEUVERS
The elaborate dolly setup shown here will add value to the look of the film. It is, however, the intricate dance, the blocking, between performer and camera, that will take some time to work out. Be careful if you are pressed for time, as a move like this will eat up time quickly.

USING A TRIPOD
The cardinal rule is to always use a tripod. No matter where you are or how difficult the terrain, using the stability of a tripod will help you to get the professional shot you want.

HANDHELD
Shoulder-mounted or handheld camera shots let you get right in among the action. The weight and size of the camera will have some influence over how you execute the shot.

to reduce visible camera shake. Switch it off! It will actually reduce the quality of your image during any controlled movements you make.

Cranes are used to get those shots that rise above people's heads, or swoop over a crowd. They are very complex pieces of gear, and if you need to retain complete control of your camera, to focus or to see what you are shooting, they have to be even more sophisticated. If you use a very wide-angle lens and/or autofocus, a much simpler rig can be used, or constructed, but any pan or tilt movements may have to be sacrificed, depending on the height of the jib. Even though a crane shot can look spectacular, you should ask yourself if it, or any other movement, is going to vastly improve the way your story is told.

Before you start planning the various camera movements and trick shots, ask yourself how they are going to improve the flow of the story. Stories are usually written in the third person ("the God view": he did this, he thought that) or the first person (I, me, mine). What narrative role is the camera playing? Whose point of view is it showing?

The narrative of your film will have some influence over your choice of camera angles and movements. For example, if you were making an urban thriller, incorporating a variety of overhead, pan, and tilt shots would add an air of credibility, imitating the ubiquitous surveillance and CCTV cameras in modern cities. You don't need any complex equipment for these shots, just a good, elevated vantage point, or a very stable ladder (see pages 88–89). You could even use the often-frowned-upon zoom to add authenticity.

Zoom

Most DV cameras offer both optical and digital zoom. While it may be tempting to use the 300x digital zoom, don't. If you have that function, switch it off, as it results in very poor-quality images. Only use the optical zoom, which will be in the range of 10x, and use that sparingly.

One of the disadvantages of using a zoom is the way it changes the background in relation to the main subject. This is caused by two factors—foreshortening and depth of field. Foreshortening is caused by the

USING A DOLLY AND TRACK

DOLLY AND TRACK
A lightweight, transportable track and dolly are ideal for shooting on location with DV and smaller-format (16 mm) film cameras, to ensure smooth, consistent shots.

CONSTRUCTING YOUR DOLLY
Precision is needed in the construction, so get help from someone who has a workshop and the right tools.

SUBSTITUTE DOLLY
A wheelchair or roller blades makes a good substitute dolly if you have a smooth surface to run it over.

effect of a telephoto lens making the background look closer, whereas a wide-angle lens makes everything look farther away. Depth of field is the amount of the image that is in focus on either side of the main point of focus and is influenced by the focal length and aperture of the lens. A wide-angle lens has a large depth of field that makes it ideal for handheld/Steadicam shots, as it is very forgiving, retaining focus and disguising camera shake. Long lenses, on the other hand, require very precise focusing. Even with a simple tripod-mounted pan shot, the focus has to be altered throughout the shot (this is known as "follow focus").

If you want to use a wide-to-telephoto zoom movement, you have to set your focus on the subject at the maximum length, then zoom it out to start the shot. Because of the depth of field, everything else will remain in focus during the zoom. Of course you will have the autofocus switched off.

The aperture controls the amount of light that passes through the lens onto the CCDs or film. Only the top range of DV cameras will allow manual control over this, although this feature exists on most film cameras. Without going into great detail about the physics involved, the smaller the aperture (which is the higher number, e.g., f/16), the greater the depth of field.

It is because of the optical effects of zooming that dollies are used when a wide-to-close-up shot is needed. Using a fixed-length lens and moving the camera results in a much more natural feel, as the relationship to the background remains constant. Of course this type of dolly shot requires a carefully rehearsed follow focus.

Watch these moves

Combining a dolly and zoom shot, so the head remains the same size and the background appears to be rushing toward the camera (see *Goodfellas*), has been done too many times and is best avoided, no matter how good you think it looks.

It is tempting to have a lot of camera moves to make your movie look "professional," which is not a good reason in itself. You will find out in the editing process that all those movements don't quite flow together and your professional look has gone. It is much easier to cut between two static shots than two dolly shots, or a dolly and a cutaway.

Another problem is that too much emphasis is placed on getting the technical part of the shot right and not

enough on capturing the actors' performances. Get a good variety of static shots, from different angles—using two cameras if necessary—and add movement in postproduction, or imply it with clever editing. Eliminating tracking shots will also save you a lot of time and money.

If you want to have realistic movement in your films, keep your camera on a Steadicam-type rig. Everything will be more human, there will be no chance of tracks appearing in a shot, and you will be able to get around locations a lot easier. It will even help overcome the potential legal problems of using a tripod in public places.

Using camera movements can add to your film's overall look; don't let them distract the viewer from the action.

STAYING STEADY

The use of a Steadicam-type camera support allows for more diverse and variable access to getting the shot down. It can still be a time-consuming process even though you are not on a fixed track system.

Shot types

When specifying camera moves for the camera operator, the type of shot can be described using shorthand. For example, "MS on actor push in to CU" means "start with a medium shot of the actor and track in for a close-up." Below are the main shot sizes and shot types:

1. Extreme long shot: This shot usually establishes the setting, such as a town or an island, to give an impression rather than specific detail.

2. Long shot: When filming a person, this shot shows the entire body and the setting. Also called a "wide shot."

3. Medium shot: This captures a person from the waist up, and is especially useful if the person gestures a lot. Also called a "mid-shot."

4. Close-up: Generally, this shot shows a person from the chest up and is particularly good for intimate interviews.

5. Extreme close-up: Shows specific detail and encompasses just the person's face, or perhaps just his or her hands.

6. Bird's-eye view: Useful when you want to depict the layout of a location, such as a railway track, or can show a person from above and a distance away, looking straight down on them from a stationary position.

7. High-angle shot: Not as high or as distant as the bird's-eye view, a high-angle shot looks slightly down at a subject. If this is a person, it usually signifies that he or she is feeling vulnerable and overwhelmed.

8. Low-angle shot: The low-angle shot looks at the subject from below and is used for interviews, especially with "experts," to make them seem powerful or in control.

9. Eye-level shot: The camera is at the same level as the subject, usually during an interview.

10. Canted/Keystone shot: Here, the camera is at an angle to the subject. If a person is shot this way, it's to signify uneasiness or tension.

11. Pan: The horizontal pivoting of the camera from a static position, right to left or left to right.

12. Dolly shot: This is a smooth, moving shot. The camera and tripod are usually set on a stand-alone rolling platform (doorway dolly) or a platform that uses tracks, like a miniature train.

13. Tilt: The vertical pivoting of the camera from a static position, up and down.

14. Crane shot: The camera is mounted at the end of a crane, which is controlled by a person at the other end. An example is beginning from a bird's-eye point of view, then moving down to eye level.

15. Aerial shot: Similar to the bird's-eye view, only moving; for example, a shot of a city, filmed from a helicopter.

16. POV (point-of-view shot): A shot that is seen from the point of view of a character within the scene. Point the camera in front of you, so we can see what he or she sees.

SOUND

Considering that film is usually thought of as a visual medium, sound plays an incredibly vital role. With the generally available technology, surround sound is the only affordable way of achieving an immersive movie experience. Bad sound can ruin a movie more surely than bad images; conversely, good sound can actually rescue a movie with bad photography.

Capturing quality sound for your movie is another craft (where technology meets art) that you will need to learn. If your film contains dialogue, you will have to record it so that the words and mouth movements match up. This is known as lip synchronization. At this early stage of your filmmaking career, foreign-language dubbing isn't going to be one of your considerations, but it is worth remembering that the actor's voices should be your primary audio interest, with as little ambient sound as possible. For this you will need the right sort of microphone (such as a Sennheiser 416 shotgun) and you must know how to use it properly. Just as the quality of the lens affects the picture, so the quality of your microphone will have a huge influence on sound quality.

The microphone has to be connected to a suitable recording device. With DV this is usually the camera itself. Sound is recorded digitally onto the same tape as the pictures, and as long as the microphone is pointed in the right direction, with the correct recording levels, you will get sound that is as good as that produced by most other portable recording devices, and it is guaranteed to be in sync. Pro and semi-pro cameras with XLR microphone inputs will not only allow you to use better microphones, but they are less susceptible to distortion. You should avoid using the camera's built-in microphone, unless it is a shotgun type, as it will pick up too much ambient sound, especially that close to the camera, such as the tape drive's motor, the cameraman's movements, or even his breathing. In certain documentary situations, using the onboard microphone may be unavoidable, but when working with actors, always keep the microphone away from the camera.

The disadvantage of DSLR cameras is that you need to ensure there is an audio input. If there isn't, you will need to record your sound as if you were shooting with film, using a separate sound recorder and a slate to sync the audio and visual aspects.

OBJECTIVES >>
- **Choose equipment for good-quality sound**
- **Understand dialogue and microphones**
- **Understand ambient sound**

HARD DISK
Hard disk recorders have become a viable option for filmmakers; small portable models incorporating mixing functions and connectability with computers are now very affordable.

ZOOM RECORDER
This sound recorder is designed to accurately capture stereo sound without the need for an elaborate mic, boom, pole, and recorder system.

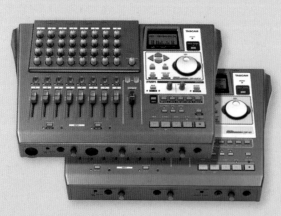
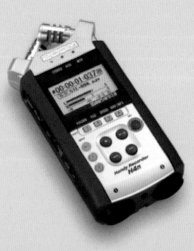

CLAPPERBOARD/SLATE MARK
Apart from giving a visual reference
with scene and take information,
the clapperboard or slate gives an
audible marker to synchronize sound
and pictures.

LOW-BUDGET TIP
Wireless microphones and receivers are expensive to
rent. The tried and true approach of a boom pole
mounted with a mic can be configured cheaply.

DAT
Portable Digital Audio Tape (DAT)
recorders have replaced the Nagra as the
preferred method of recording sound on
movies, especially among the smaller
independent filmmakers.

ADAPTER
Small, inexpensive audio interfaces, such
as the Tascam US-122, complete with
phantom power for XLR microphones,
can turn a laptop computer into a
convenient recording device.

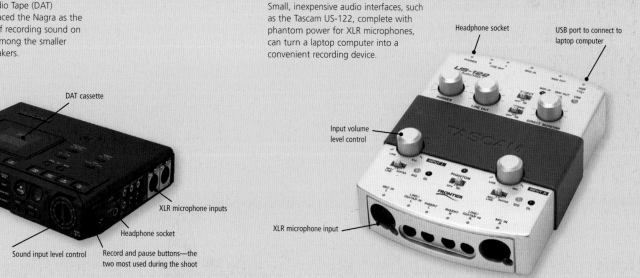

DAT cassette

Headphone socket

USB port to connect to
laptop computer

Input volume
level control

Tape counter and audio
level monitor

XLR microphone inputs

Headphone socket

Sound input level control

Record and pause buttons—the
two most used during the shoot

XLR microphone input

HEADPHONES
Quality headphones will block out external noise and allow you to clearly hear a full dynamic range of sounds. Try to match the quality of the headphones with that of your microphone.

PALMTOP RECORDER
Zoom Palm Studio is a small recording device that can be concealed on the actor and used with a small microphone, instead of a radio microphone.

TOP QUALITY
A high-quality microphone, such as this Sennheiser MKH 416, is expensive, but the superior sound it captures is worth the investment.

Stepping up to the microphone

Professional shotgun microphones are extremely sensitive and will pick up an incredible amount of ambient sound, despite their narrow recording field. To ensure that you capture only the actors' voices, you need to have the microphone as close to them as possible. For this you need to mount the microphone on a boom, a long pole that keeps it out of shot and pointed at the actors. The boom operator has to move the microphone during dialogue exchanges while keeping it out of shot—not as easy as it sounds.

This works fine if you are in an enclosed environment, but shooting your characters from a distance in a crowd can present different problems. Tiny clip-on (lavalier) radio microphones are often used, but they are susceptible to interference and are an additional expense. Portable recorders are one solution, although transferring the digital sound to a computer so that it remains digital is not as simple as it should be. Another small recording device is the Zoom Palm Studio. This miniature studio records onto a SmartMedia card that can simply be mounted on the computer using an inexpensive card reader, like those used for digital still cameras.

Apart from all the environmental sounds, shooting outdoors has the added problem of the elements, and wind in particular. This can be overcome by adding a windsock (one of those furry covers you've no doubt seen) to your microphone, which silences the noise of the wind blowing across it.

A good set of headphones (cans) is as vital a part of the sound recordist's equipment as the microphone and recorder. These should be the padded, sound-insulated

RADIO (RF) MICROPHONE
A tiny microphone is placed as close to the throat as possible, or sometimes hidden in the hair, and is attached to a small radio transmitter, which must be hidden out of camera view.

SOUND ON LOCATION
With lightweight recording devices it is possible for the sound recorder to double as the boom holder. Having control of the microphone makes it easier to ensure optimum sound, as the recorder has instant monitoring of the recording through the headphones.

ones favored by music buffs. Those from your portable music player just don't block out external noise. Although you will set the levels visually using peak meters, all those unwanted sounds can only be heard by listening.

Whatever equipment or method you choose to record the sound, getting the best voice recording is paramount, especially with dramatic dialogue. Even though it is possible to rescue disasters in postproduction, the actors will not always be able to recapture the intensity of the moment.

Ambient sound

Eliminating ambient sound from the voice recording starts with keeping people on the set quiet.

This is relatively easy, as they (should) understand the importance of a noise-free recording. All cell phones have to be switched off. Some people put theirs into silent mode, but if radio microphones are being used, the phones can still interfere with the signal (as can taxis and emergency vehicles, but there is nothing to be done about those). Unfortunately, the rest of the world won't come to a standstill while you record a take.

Apart from judicious placement of the microphone, there are measures you can take to eliminate any extraneous noise, and most of them involve common sense. For example, don't shoot your film under a flight path; next to a major road or highway; near emergency services, schools, or railroads—you get the idea. Cities are incredibly noisy places and unless you are after that continual urban hum, try to find places or times when it is at a minimum. Sundays and public holidays are good, and may be the only times you and your crew are free anyway.

Although you are making every effort to remove all extraneous sound, you are still going to need some, depending on your movie, of course. All those sound effects like footsteps, doors shutting, and car engines have to be included, as well as general noise. In our daily lives we don't usually notice these sounds, or simply shut them out—they become conspicuous only by their absence. A scene without any ambient noise would seem flat and unnatural, so it has to be recorded, preferably while on location. Use your standard sound-recording equipment, announcing what the sound is and for which scene/slate. Also keep a written note of what you have recorded.

If you are using a DV camera, the easiest method is to place the slate in front of the lens with a note of the sound you are recording. This can be imported into your editing software, along with the rest of your footage. Record everything you think you will need, as clearly as possible, but anything you miss can be added in postproduction (see pages 122–125).

Automated Dialogue Replacement (ADR)

In certain situations it is a waste of time to try to record good audio with actors, such as filming near an airport or in a busy city center. In these instances, record the sound on location for reference, then have your actors listen to the recordings in a quiet studio and repeat the lines they hear exactly as they said them the first time. They are just repeating so it will match up exactly.

AUTOMATED DIALOGUE REPLACEMENT
Sometimes it is impossible to record good-quality audio on location, so you will need to re-record the sound post-filming, ensuring that the new audio matches the original recording.

Slate	Take	Timecode	Description
	WT	00:11	Girl shouting "Dad"
	WT	01:25	Deep breathing for opening
1	1	03:12	Atmos
	2	03:32	
	3	03:53	
3	1	04:18	Atmos
	2	04:49	
	3	05:04	
	4	05:45	
2	1	06:33	Girl's breakfast dial
	WT	08:50	
4	1	10:07	Blanket and laughter
	2	10:47	
4a	1	11:29	
	2	12:14	
	WT	12:57	
5	1	14:09	Atmos + dial
	2	15:35	
	3	17:17	
	4	19:03	
	WT	20:38	
6	1	23:52	Atmos
7	1	25:25	Atmos + cereal in bowl
8	1	30:07	Cereal in bowl
	2	30:45	
	3	31:12	
	WT	31:37	

RECORDIST'S LOG
The sound recordist's log should contain similar information to that of the camera operator, except with additional wild track (WT) or atmosphere takes, causing the time code to differ slightly.

STUNTS AND SPECIAL EFFECTS

Stunts and special effects are the stock-in-trade of Hollywood movies, especially the "summer blockbusters." The makers of these mega-budget movies have access to all the professional expertise the industry has developed over the years.

Whether computer-generated (CG), stop-motion models, or huge sets with a cast of a 100 stunt artists, most special-effects techniques were developed from low-budget films. While most of these "low-budget" films had more money than you have (at the moment), they still depended on ingenuity and creative thinking to find the solutions that have evolved into the more sophisticated standards we are used to today.

Postproduction special effects such as CGI are covered later (see pages 114–117). This section is all about in-camera effects, those that have to be created and used during the shoot.

The effects you use will be dictated by the type of film you are making. A romantic comedy ("rom-com") is not usually going to place heavy demands on your "effects department," unless you are planning to use slapstick. For this it is probably worth casting someone who can make pratfalls. It certainly makes shooting easier and is one less extra mouth to feed. The other way is to create the effect by suggestion, using cutaways of reaction shots, or using POV (point of view) shots. This requires judicious planning, shooting, and editing, but it does mean you remove the risk of injuries.

Horror movies, one of the most popular genres with the lo-no budget filmmaker, create their best scares through suggestion, especially given modern audiences' immunity to in-your-face horror. While everybody talks about how gruesome the film *Se7en* is, in fact most of the crimes are not shown, but are either hinted at, described, or shown after the fact.

Blood on your hands

With horror, thriller, crime, and practically every other action-based genre, at some point you are going to need blood. Real blood, even from animals, is not a viable option, partly because it doesn't look "real,"

OBJECTIVES >>
- ☐ **Create in-camera effects**
- ☐ **Achieve effects by suggestion**
- ☐ **Fake blood and gore**

SMOKE MACHINE
A requirement in any action sequence or war film, such as Sam Mendes' *Jarhead* shown here, the smoke machine is a necessary accompaniment to any kind of explosion. Expensive to buy, they can usually be rented quite easily.

but also because it is too hard to work with. Theater blood (as in stage, not operating) can be bought, but a homemade solution is a lot more economical.

Blood is usually accompanied by guts, or their friend, gore. Dismembered limbs will usually require the expense of prosthetics to make them look real, but spilled guts can easily be created by a visit to the local butcher, with the added bonus that if you have pets, their dinners will be provided for the week.

Once you have made copious amounts of blood, you need to find convincing ways of spilling it. These usually involve acts of extreme violence. If you decide that the subtle cutaway-shot method does not give the impact you want, you are going to have to find ways of depicting grievous bodily harm without actually causing damage to your actors, or to the sets.

People seem to find an endless range of methods for harming each other, ranging from bare hands (martial arts) to glass bottles (use sugar glass), from knives and swords to firearms, and on to bombs and automobiles. Portraying any act of violence in a film requires huge amounts of preparation and rehearsal, hopefully aided by a trained, professional stunt coordinator. This will mean that the first thing that explodes is going to be your budget—not only for paying the stuntperson but also for the all-important insurance coverage.

The simplest thing is to eliminate any big stunts—car chases, explosions, and so on—and reduce any other stunts to the minimum the story needs. Although the general rule of movie storytelling is "show, don't tell," sometimes it is easier and more powerful to imply and not show.

Firearms and fight scences

Hong Kong-style martial arts seem to show up in every genre of movie, even when it doesn't make sense that the characters would have a knowledge of karate. Nobody seems simply to brawl any more. If you want to include hand-to-hand combat, check out your local karate (or other martial arts) club. Their training teaches members how to pull punches convincingly, and it shouldn't be too hard to convince some of them to be in a film.

The other popular agent of violence is the firearm. If your script calls for firearms, there are several important things to consider. There is a good chance that you can get away with using replicas and adding the sounds in postproduction. In some countries, even buying replica guns is restricted and requires registration, so it is advisable to look into it before you start. If you want to go for authenticity and use real guns, you are going to have to employ a licensed gun handler. He or she should supply all the guns you need, along with blanks (if required), and give the actors any necessary training. He or she should also be able to supply the squibs, the small explosives that create the blood-splattering effects of bullets entering the body.

Of course, low-budget ingenuity can overcome these perilous demands and create a decent effect with minimal danger to your actors. Exploding squibs always look impressive, if unreal, but are very dangerous. Instead of using explosives, a safer method is to use compressed air, plastic tubing, and the blood you prepared earlier. The compressed air can be either the canned variety (but this can get expensive) or one of

CHECK THIS OUT

The Francis Ford Coppola-directed *Dracula* starring Gary Oldman is a direct and intentional homage to the early magicians and special effects filmmakers. Every effect in the film was shot "in camera." Multiple exposures, duplicating black sets, etc. were all used to create a stunning visual masterpiece.

A lot of research went into effects and magic for the film and was then duplicated during the shooting process.

Q&A

MAKEUP ARTIST
Stevie Bettles

1. What is the biggest misconception about makeup for film and television?

The biggest and most common misconception I find within the industry is the amount of time and manpower it takes to create the makeups. People both inside and outside the industry think it is possible to produce anything with no more than ten-minutes warning. A lot of what we do can take days, weeks, or even months to create, with anything up to a dozen guys and girls working on it.

2. What is the best way to getting good makeup on a low budget?

When it comes to effects on a budget, being creative with your solutions is the key. This means not just how you make the effects but also how the director shoots them. It is a team effort. You can also look for the new, talented graduates from makeup colleges who are happy to work for very little money in order to express themselves creatively.

3. What should a first-time producer look for when hiring a makeup artist on a low budget?

Passion, enthusiasm for the work, dedication to the craft, raw talent, and patience, coupled with confidence without being overbearing.

4. What is the hardest part of a makeup artist's job?

The hardest part of being a makeup artist is striking a balance. Not only creating what you want to see but also what the performer and the director are looking for. It is a difficult balancing act that we do every day.

5. Is there a makeup artist whose work is particularly notable?

I have always been a fan of two makeup artists in particular. The first is Jack Pierce who created the original *Frankenstein* makeup for Universal Studios, and the second is the legendary makeup artist Dick Smith who created makeups in movies such as *Amadeus* and *The Exorcist*.

ALL IN THE DETAILS

From applying minute details, such as tattoos, that must remain consistent throughout the movie (right), to full face makeup such as the Avatar-style shown here (far right), a makeup artist's job can take large amounts of time to complete to perfection so you must factor this into your scheduling and budgeting.

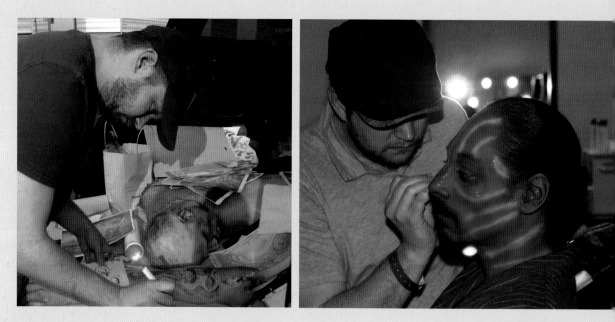

those hand-pumped insecticide sprayers (new, of course). These are cheap and reusable. A motorized compressor is too problematic and noisy to consider.

For a more natural—though less spectacular—look, a small, partially inflated water balloon or condom filled with blood can be burst by someone out of shot, or by the actor pulling a thin wire across it (although theoretically, condoms are designed not to burst, whereas water balloons are). Whatever method you use, it is vital that clothing is precut to let the blood seep out. Don't use your best shirt for this stunt, and keep an identical spare or two in case of retakes. It is actually a good idea to have multiple cameras at different angles for stunt shots so that they don't have to be repeated. This will also give you more coverage for the edit, which is where these effects are really made to work.

For anything involving guns, explosives, fire, or cars, always hire professional experts. Legality and safety should be your primary concerns, even if it is lo-no-budget filmmaking, and make sure you read your insurance policy properly. You're not going to finish your film if you are in prison (although it will give you plenty of time to polish your screenplay). There are a lot of things you can fake in movies, but safety and insurance aren't among them. A simple rule is: Don't ask anyone to do anything you wouldn't be prepared to do yourself.

ACTION SEQUENCES
Attempting to do stunts and live-action special effects has two main considerations.

Safety This kind of work should never be attempted by amateurs and rookies. Injury and even death will come knocking if you do not enlist the help of seasoned professionals.

Cost The costs associated can be astronomical because certified people must coordinate and participate in this kind of shooting. Obtaining insurance and location permits are also a major consideration.

Before you start, ask yourself if there is a more cost-effective and safe approach for getting your shot. For example, can the same thing be obtained by post effects?

4

Once everything is in the can, that is, when the shooting is finished, it is time to start putting all the pieces together. Remember, postproduction takes up 75 percent of the total time to complete your film. This seems like a lot, but this is ultimately the most rewarding part because everything comes together. During postproduction, everything you shot will be edited into a cohesive whole, sounds will be added and mixed with any music you want to include, and additional special effects can be inserted, as well as the all-important titles and credits. The process finishes with the final tweaks, such as color correction, before deploying the finished film.

POSTPRODUCTION

As with the shoot, proper planning and systematic working methods will make the process a lot easier without hindering the spontaneity of the creative process. Hopefully the rigors of preproduction and production haven't left you jaded, but it is still advisable to take a short break from the movie, even just a couple of days, before immersing yourself in postproduction. This will let you look at what you've shot with fresher eyes. Enlisting the help of someone experienced in the different fields, even in an advisory capacity, may help things run more smoothly and rapidly. As nearly all postproduction work is done digitally these days, this section concentrates on the type of workflow that uses the best and most affordable tools on the market. However, as in any creative pursuit, it is the skill of the craftsperson and not the tools that determines the quality of the work.

THE EDITING PROCESS

Once your story has been shot and is "in the can," you have to collect all the pieces together and put them into an order that is not only coherent but also has the necessary rhythm and pacing to captivate an audience. Bad editing can ruin your movie, just as good editing can sometimes rescue a bad shoot, but proper planning and organization should mean that neither situation occurs.

During the shoot, keep an accurate list of every shot, with reel number, time code, description, and an indication of the shot's usability. Logging all the shots means that you can practically do a paper edit without looking at a single image.

Paper edit

The initial stage of editing is known as the paper edit or paper cut. It is a simple workflow process that can go a long way in terms of saving time and money. You might also hear it called the edit decision list, or EDL. When the process of editing the picture is complete, the EDL is the locked reference to refer to for the rest of the postproduction process.

A paper edit is simply the process of taking all the logged information and putting it in the right order; when it comes to capturing the images from the tape to your computer, you will know exactly where to find them, and the order in which they need to be placed,

saving hours of searching through tapes looking for a shot. That does not mean you should ignore or disregard all the other footage. There may be a certain look or a phrase that the actor delivers in an otherwise rejected take that can be inserted.

Photocopy the script onto the largest sized paper you can find—11 x 17 in. (A3) is perfect. Sift through and view all of the footage to make choices about what

OBJECTIVES >>

- Learn the workflow of editing processes
- Understand the purposes of editing
- Know the importance of the shot log

PAPER EDIT
The paper edit, or paper cut, is the very first, rough assembly of your story. This step ultimately saves you time in the editing suite.

			CLIENT: Olde English Malt Beer		**DATE:** March 17, 1993			
			DIRECTOR: You		**PAGE:** 1 of 1			
			PROJECT: Queen Victoria Testimonial					
			VIDEO:		DUR:	RUN:	AUDIO:	
			1. **FADE UP FROM BLACK TO**					
Tape 2	in:	02:00:35:15	W.S. Port of Portsmouth		:02	:02	SFX of Docks	
	out:	02:00:37:15	docks with ships.				MUSIC UP:	
							CUT#1: L Guitars	
							MUSIC UNDER	
Tape 5	in:	05:15:20:00	2. **CUT TO** M.S. Pub of		:02	:04	ANNR.: VO	
	out:	05:15:22:00	Smith Bros.				IN 1882 THE	
							SMITH	
							BROTHERS OF	
							PORTSMOUTH	
							BREWED	
Tape 9	in:	09:08:31:15	3. **DISSOLVE TO C.U.** of		:03	:07	ANNR.: VO	
	out:	09:08:34:15	Pub sign with Royal				A FINE	
			Coat of Arms.				MALT BEER	
							FOR HER	
							MAJESTY	
							QUEEN	
							VICTORIA	
			///////////// CONTINUED /////////////					
Tape 11	in:	11:22:05:10	9. C.U. OF Beer Bottle		:05	:30	MUSIC UP	
	out:	11:22:10:10					MUSIC OUT	
			FADE TO BLACK					

shots to use to cover each scene of the script. Write down the time code for each shot picked. The beginning and ending of each shot is indicated with the T/C numbers to the left of the scene on the photocopied script page. If your camera doesn't have a time code, use the counter code information, indicated in minutes and seconds. When you've gone through the entire script and all of the time codes are written down, the paper cut is complete.

Offline—rough cut

The offline stage is the basic assembly. It is not pretty, but it gives initial life to the story. The first rough cut is when all the material from the shoot, visual and audio, is put together in a very loose format, based on the paper edit. You will be using a digital non-linear editor (NLE) such as Apple's Final Cut Pro, Adobe Premiere Pro, or Avid. Import, or digitize, your rushes into your edit suite. How you do this will depend on the equipment

that is available to you. Once the rushes are ingested into your choice of edit suite, the first assembly amounts to organizing the footage into "bins" in the software, and labeling everything so that it makes sense and can be put into an order that resembles the chronology of the script.

From this, a rough cut is made (see page 107). The material from the first assembly is put into an order that starts to resemble an actual movie. Even at this stage, a movie intended to be only 10 minutes long can run for 15 or 20 minutes, and a feature of 85 minutes can run for twice that length before it's whittled down—remember that rough cuts still have plenty of fat on them.

The editor will slice away at a rough cut until it is much closer to the final length, bringing in the director to give approval (assuming that these roles have been split). Many DVD re-releases are marketed as "director's cuts," but this first-cut stage is really the director's cut, as it is the one that is approved before being tweaked

Directors' cuts

The best example of a director's cut of a movie is Michael Cimino's *Heaven's Gate*. Producer Steven Bach wrote a book (*Final Cut*) about this film and its director. Cimino was fresh from winning the Oscar for *Deer Hunter* in 1978 when the studio handed him *Heaven's Gate*. There is a studio cut and director's cut. Check them out to see the glaring differences. Ridley Scott's *Blade Runner*, starring Harrison Ford, is another good example, see above.

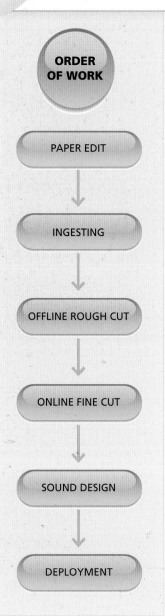

THE POSTPRODUCTION PROCESS

Getting your movie from the cutting room to the cinema.

ORDER OF WORK

PAPER EDIT

INGESTING

OFFLINE ROUGH CUT

ONLINE FINE CUT

SOUND DESIGN

DEPLOYMENT

and fine-tuned to the best of the editor's ability. Depending on the level of the director's involvement, even a rough cut could be called a director's cut. There may be two or three rough cuts, depending on how much time you want to spend getting the rough picture assembly close to the final lock.

Online—fine cut

Online is defined as the process that adds all of the final bells and whistles—sound, special effects, titles, and so on. Once the director and producer have approved the cut, it is up to the editor to tighten it. This involves shaving off excess seconds or minutes, tightening transitions, and establishing the film's rhythm. The shorter the film, the more difficult this can be. Each cut has to be tighter and tell more of the story. As a generation brought up on MTV, we are used to short, fast cuts in music videos and commercials, and to a certain extent these techniques can be transferred to narrative films. It's all about pacing. Action and thriller films will work better with quicker cuts, while moodier or romantic movies will work better with longer cuts. Either way, it is always best to avoid unnecessarily long shots and to reduce the overall length of your film in order to maintain the viewer's interest.

However you cut it, once everyone (editor, director, producer—who may all be you) is satisfied with the visuals, the titles, sound effects, and final music score can be added to give what is known as the fine cut. Editing software, such as Apple's Final Cut Pro, Adobe Premiere Pro, and Avid, will generate these automatically. Digital-video shoots, on the other hand, are ready for printing the fine cut back to a distribution tape or for burning onto a DVD.

The editor's role

Planning starts during preproduction. If you are going to bring in an experienced editor, get his or her input when you are writing up your shooting list. He will be able to tell you what sort of shots will be needed for the edit. If you intend to do your own editing, you will have to consider how much coverage you will need to shoot with establishing shots, close-ups, inserts, and cutaways.

Some of these you may not decide on until the day of the shoot, but bear in mind the importance of having a wide variety of shots and angles (see page 78). If possible, during the shoot the editor could even be on set and, using a laptop, start assembling a rough cut right away. Any inserts or pickups that need to be shot can be done immediately, rather than calling the actors back later. Whether you can convince an editor to do this is another matter. If you are directing and intend to edit as well, then working like that will be impractical, but as the director/editor you should be aware of exactly what you need.

Now you understand the stages involved in the editing process, but before you start, it is important to also understand some elemental philosophies about editing, which are outlined opposite.

THERE ARE FOUR BASIC REASONS FOR EDITING:

1. TO COMBINE:
- This is the simplest form of editing. It involves editing shots together in the proper sequence.
- This form is best when there is not enough time for extensive postproduction.

2. TO TRIM:
- This kind of editing is utilized constantly to cut down the length of a production to fit a specific length of time, e.g., a 30- or 60-second commercial or a 30-minute program.
- This process eliminates unnecessary material, which ends up "on the cutting room floor."

3. TO CORRECT:
- This type of editing is utilized to cut out bad portions of a scene or shot, to replace them with good alternatives.
- Correcting errors that occurred during the production can be complicated and difficult, as well as costly in terms of time.
- Only on rare occasions can the thinking "we'll fix it in editing" be applied. You must be very clear about the technical limitations of editing. Aim to fix it during the shooting process instead.

4. TO BUILD:
- This process involves taking many shots, which are taken out of sequence, picking the best takes, and placing them in the desired sequence.
- It is a long, involved process but ultimately the most rewarding.
- This is where it all "comes together" in a sometimes tedious but very purposeful manner.

WORKING TOGETHER
The director and editor must have a symbiotic relationship when cutting the film. A great editor is a both a great listener and a great technician.

THERE ARE THREE EDITING CONSIDERATIONS:

1. MECHANICAL:
- In editing, you need to be mindful of when to change the shot, or what is the best cutting point and why.
- How do you change the shot and how quickly? Consider the type of transition to be used. A hard cut, a wipe, a dissolve? How will the transition affect the flow and continuity of the piece?
- Be mindful of the order or sequence and duration of each shot. How will the cutting rhythm affect the piece?

2. PRACTICAL:
- You want to create a smooth flow of picture development.
- Omit errors and distractions.
- Shorten or lengthen your shot durations. Do you want to keep the shots all the same length or stagger the lengths?
- Using transitions will allow you to bridge the elements of space and time.

3. ARTISTIC:
- Editing can allow you to shift the center of interest by spending more time on one element over another.
- You can emphasize or hold back visual information.
- You can be highly selective in what the viewer is to see.
- You can create interrelationships and mood.

THERE ARE TWO STYLES, OR STRATEGIES, OF EDITING:

1. CONTINUITY:
- Create continuity through straightforward editing.
- Utilize unobtrusive transitions for a smooth flow.
- Show the viewer the action and nothing else.

2. RELATIONAL:
- By cutting together unrelated shots you can imply a relationship or mood. This is called intercutting.
- Intercutting must be carefully thought out. It should have a clear purpose in mind.
- It can be used to build the piece in terms of story and mood.

EDITING YOUR MOVIE

Now that you have gone through the painstaking task of preproducing and shooting your film, the real work begins. At this stage only 25 percent of your film is complete. That's right, only 25 percent! That number alone should tell you that not only does a lot of work remain, but it is the most important and critical stage thus far.

CHECK THESE OUT

- www.apple.com—Final Cut Pro and iMovie
- www.adobe.com/motion—Adobe Creative Suite Production Premium
- www.avid.com—The full range of Avid software for Mac and PC

Never attempt to take shortcuts in the shooting just to get to the editing. You, or anyone along the way, should never utter the old adage, "fix it in post." It will only create mistakes and headaches along the way.

The role of the director (you) and editor (probably you) needs to be synchronistic in every way. This is where the director can really begin to see his or her vision come together in a finite way. A good editor is critical to this process as he or she is there to serve the story in every way. He or she is an advisor and even life saver. But, the editing can only be good if the right footage, and enough of it, exists. Limiting the editor with less than what is needed will kill the story and make the film inconsistent. The three most widely used non-linear editing packages (NLEs) are Adobe's Premiere Pro, Apple's Final Cut Pro, and Avid. Over the next eight pages, we will take a look at the key processes that take place in the editing suite and will examine what your role as the director is and how you can work effectively with your editor and with your software. Each of the steps has been demonstrated on Final Cut Pro, but on the opposite page there is a comparison of the three packages.

The director's involvement

While shooting a picture, the director will, from time to time, confer with the editor about the manner in which the project should be treated in the editing room. Usually the director will attend the rushes in the evening after the day's shooting and view the shots filmed from the previous day. The director will make suggestions to the editor, explaining what he or she had in mind on the set, for while shooting, the director must, at all times, visualize how the various shots will go together.

The director's work is far from finished when he or she has photographed and canned the last take of the picture. Then starts the sometimes long and arduous editorial process, which includes the selection of the best takes and angles, the forming of the first rough cut, the trimming and tightening of the picture to improve the pace and tempo, the addition of sound effects, musical score, optical effects and titles, and the final dubbing that transfers as many as ten soundtracks as one. Then the picture is ready for the preview—an event in which the director is hugely interested.

The director's store of knowledge pertaining to the many facets of film production should include a thorough background in the techniques of editing. Cutting is just another extension of the director's ability to tell a story well. There have been directors who practically "cut in the camera." They shoot so that the editor has a minimum of editorial freedom.

John Ford was a pioneer in this respect. Those that choose this style of shooting had better be right, for many errors in shooting can be fixed in the editing room, provided there is sufficient film shot and enough angles to enable some editorial latitude. In the hectic pace of television production, the director seldom sees a rough cut, if at all. He or she is usually engaged on the next show at another studio, often in another city.

However, as the director of your own show you can be assured of the opportunity to follow through in the various phases of editing.

Helping the editor

As the director you should understand thoroughly the problems that can arise in the editing room. You should learn at once the fact that a smooth cut is achieved by cutting on movement. This means that, other things being equal, you as the editor would cut two takes somewhere during the actor's action of taking out a cigarette and lighting it. Or you would cut on the actor's movement as he or she rises, turns, or in some way causes movement. The director who wishes to win the respect of his or her editor will always overlap his or her action from one camera angle to the next.

This means the director will have an actor perform exactly the same movement in each angle he takes, from exactly the same place in the action.

This allows the editor to find a common spot in cutting a wide shot to a close-up in the scene.

The pickup

Sometimes a director will turn to the script supervisor after a take and say, "All right, print that—and we'll pick it up." What the director is saying, in effect, is that the scene was good to a point and that only the balance of the action needs be done again. The actors return to their positions, and the director tells them from what point in the dialogue or action they will start. But herein

Why invest?

When you consider that only 25% of your movie is complete when you finish shooting, postproduction takes on a very important role.

It is wise to invest in a non-linear editing (NLE) platform that fits comfortably into the longest part of the moviemaking process. You no longer have to spend tons of money to achieve a professionally cut film.

Here are some questions to ask yourself:
1. Does it fall within my budget?
2. Simplicity of navigation—Does the interface seem friendly and easy to learn?
3. Technical ease—CODECs—Does it handle different video formats and CODECs?
4. Technical ease—tool sets—Does it have what I need? For example, title generator, color correction?
5. Technical support—updates and fixes—Does this platform have a reputation of being stable? Does the support offered appear to be fast?

Remember that resident platforms such as iMovie or Movie Maker do not offer the kind of tool set sophistication you will need to give your film a polished, professional look. They can be useful for completing a rough picture assembly prior to moving into the final cut stage of your film, but that's about it.

No matter what platform you choose, it all comes down to whether it serves the story well. Professional editors understand this and are able to adapt and comfortably use whichever platform works best.

A cumbersome work flow that is full of technical glitches will only get in the way. It is easy to spend too much time figuring out these problems.

Non-linear editing software

Comparing the three main editing platforms essentially comes down to your own preference and what you have access to. They all do the same thing.

AVID

Avid is an industry-standard NLE. It comes in a diverse range from a free, cut-down DV version up to systems dedicated to working with full feature films and episodic production.

PREMIERE PRO

Adobe's Premiere Pro represents great value as part of the Creative Suite bundle. It has been around for a long time and has a dedicated following. It integrates with the rest of the Adobe Creative Suite software packages.

FINAL CUT PRO

Apple's editing software, Final Cut Pro, has not been around as long as others but has placed itself firmly into the world of professional editing. For those who prefer working on a Mac, this is the logical choice.

Q&A

OFFLINE FILM EDITOR
Joe Wilby

1. For the beginner, do you recommend Final Cut Pro X, Adobe Premiere, or Avid, and why?
It doesn't really make a lot of difference; you'd have to be lucky as a beginner to even get a choice. Just use whatever you can get your hands on to get some experience of editing. Does it matter whether you drive a BMW or a VW or is it more important to consider your destination and the route you are going to take.

2. Discuss the importance of being consistent with video formats and codecs through acquisition, post and deployment.
It's really important to know what format the material will be shot on and what format you will be delivering so you can plan your post process in advance.

3. As a beginner editor, what do you suggest one should look for in an NLE platform? For example, ease of navigation, tool sets?
It's not about the tools that you choose to use, it's more about how you approach the problem that you have in front of you, and how you navigate from the chaos of the rushes into the final completed puzzle, well, as complete as they will ever be. There is a saying that "No films are ever finished, they are merely abandoned."

4. Aside from software bundles, what are the key components with respect to hardware? Graphics card, RAM, CPU?
Hardware? A really good chair, a plentiful supply of tea (or coffee if you prefer), glasses (if you don't need them now you will after ten years of editing!), and maybe a window in your edit suite would be nice. A wise man once said, "The more money you spend, a better system you will get, and the amount you can expect to be able to accomplish in time will also increase."

5. What is the main job of the editor?
I would say it's cutting out the bad bits and keeping the good bits.

6. Any tips for a beginner?
Don't become too precious about what you've already cut, don't be afraid to rip it up and start again. As you are reviewing, take notes of passing thoughts as these may well be the same thoughts that a viewer will have. Your thoughts from the first viewing of the rushes are the most potent; pause it, make notes, they will possibly be the same as your audience. Don't be afraid to say what you think; a director has to be able to trust your honest opinion especially when he or she is clinging onto his or her "rubber shark."

7. What do you mean by "rubber shark?"
Legend has it that when editing *Jaws*, Steven Spielberg and his editor Verna Fields had frequent battles about how much rubber shark should be in the film. The editor having "fresh eyes" could see that having more rubber shark risked the viewer seeing it for what it was. Spielberg on the other hand had invested so much time and effort in obtaining the shots of the rubber shark in difficult conditions that he wanted to use more, though it risked ruining the film. It is not uncommon or immoral for an editor to shave a few frames off here and there when the director isn't looking; that is all part of the job. I have often told directors who are getting hung up on a shot or sequence that they have invested a lot in, and which isn't giving a lot of benefit to their film, that it is their "rubber shark," to the point that now when I work with them they say to me, "Is this my rubber shark?" It has become a very useful term.

8. What is the most ridiculous comment a director has made to you?
"We need to make it faster or slower, or a bit of both."

AN EDITOR AT WORK
Film editor Joe Wilby in his editing suite.

lies a danger, lurking silently, only to show itself later in the cutting room, unless the director remains alert. There are only two ways in which a scene can be picked up and expected to cut in with a previous take. First, the director must provide a shot that will bridge the action, such as a close-up to be inserted between the last part of the preceding take and the first part of the succeeding take.

Second, the director must change the camera angle or picture size (framing) on the pickup shot to allow the editor to cut it to the preceding take in case there is no logical bridge shot. This follows the rule that no two shots made from the same identical point of view should be cut together, commonly known as the jump cut. Many times a scene plays perfectly in "one"; in other words, the movement of actors and camera around the set makes unnecessary the insertion of close-ups. The problem arises, then, of how to make a pickup and properly bridge the parts of two different takes. A simple solution is to first determine at what point the two takes should be cut together.

If at this point the preceding scene is in a medium shot, all that is necessary is to move the camera into a close-up of one of the actors, then as the succeeding scene gets under way, dolly back to the medium shot and resume.

If, in the preceding scene, the camera was in a close-up of one of the actors, the succeeding scene should start either in a close-up of the other actor, or in a medium shot of both.

Keeping covered
The director must fully visualize the proper sequencing of all the shots as he or she makes them, particularly in the matter of camera movement. He or she must decide where effective camera work should be utilized, and confine it to scenes that do not call for cutting away to other shots. The director should literally "cut in the camera" in relation to camera movement as he or she builds the scenes one by one throughout the shooting process, but he or she should not fail to cover himself or herself, that is, to provide the editor with more than one take of each scene. This is a protection of which every professional director avails himself or herself, for many

Offline editing process

The sequence here and on the following pages shows the offline editing process from start to finish for the multiple international award-winning film *The Be All And End All* (2009). This micro-budget independently funded British feature film was shot on Super 16 mm film telecined to PAL videotape and offlined using Final Cut Pro Ver 6, but the process will be similar whichever NLE you are using.

things can go wrong between an okayed take on the set and the assembling of the paper cut and rough cut.

Get creative

How you edit your movie is dictated not only by what you have shot but also by how you use it. Working with a digital NLE (non-linear editing) package, you get lots of video and audio tracks so you can layer all your shots. And it is easy to experiment with different cuts because the editing is non-destructive. Shots can be lengthened and shortened at will, and played back immediately.

When Robert Rodriguez made *El Mariachi* (1992), he shot all the action on a 16 mm camera without sync sound. He recorded the dialogue immediately after the shoot on a portable cassette recorder. When it came to editing, as soon as the dialogue started going out of sync, he inserted another shot—either a reaction shot, a close-up, or a cutaway, anything that allowed him to get the sound and picture back together. The editing was done out of necessity, a creative solution to a technical problem, but it gave the picture added pace and tension.

Fades and effects

Editing software comes with many different transitions and effects built in. There is always a temptation to use them—because they are there—but they may not be the best things for your movie. All the tricky transitions should definitely be avoided and even subtler ones, such as dissolves, should be used sparingly and with discretion. Filters are not all for special effects; they also include things like color correction and balance, although a professional broadcast monitor is really needed to do this successfully. There are also third-party filters that can facilitate a lot of editing effects jobs, such as creating film looks or adding "scratches."

Although these effects can improve the look of your movie, if they are not used carefully they will make it look amateurish, and they will never make a badly scripted, shot, or edited film look good.

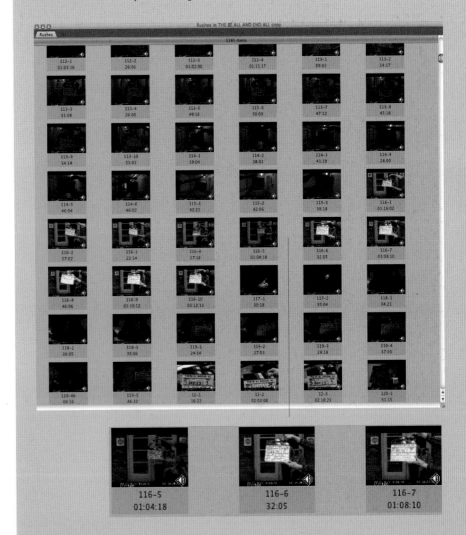

1 IMPORT OR DIGITIZE THE RUSHES
If your source is already digital, then you only need to import these into your project. If your source is on tape it will need to be digitized by connecting a tape deck to your edit suite.

Audio in THE BE ALL AND END ALL copy

Name	Media Start	Media End	Duration	In
BAAEAs154_003.wav	00:41:14:18	00:42:56:12	00:01:41:20	Not Set
BAAEAs154_004.wav	00:42:56:13	00:44:25:23	00:01:29:11	Not Set
BAAEAs154_005.wav	00:44:25:24	00:44:53:11	00:00:27:13	Not Set
BAAEAs154_006.wav	00:44:53:12	00:46:22:03	00:01:28:17	Not Set
BAAEAs154_007.wav	00:46:22:03	00:47:49:09	00:01:27:07	Not Set
BAAEAs154_008.wav	00:47:49:10	00:49:29:15	00:01:40:06	Not Set
BAAEAs155_001.wav	00:49:29:16	00:50:20:22	00:00:51:07	Not Set
BAAEAs155_002.wav	00:50:20:22	00:50:52:08	00:00:31:12	Not Set
BAAEAs155_003.wav	00:50:52:09	00:51:21:06	00:00:28:23	Not Set
Disk 2 of 3				
BAAEAs156_001.wav	00:51:21:07	00:52:57:05	00:01:35:24	Not Set

2 IMPORT SEPARATELY RECORDED AUDIO

Commonly the audio will be recorded separately as WAV files. These may have multiple channels for the boom and various radio mics.

Synched Rushes in THE BE ALL AND END ALL copy

Name	Duration	In	Out	Media Start
Scene 150				
Scene 151				
Scene 152				
Scene 153				
Scene 154				
Scene 155				
192-1	00:00:36:12	15:19:05:04	15:19:41:15	15:19:05:04
192-2	00:00:11:10	15:20:14:13	15:20:25:22	15:19:42:11
192-3	00:00:09:10	15:21:27:06	15:21:36:15	15:20:35:03
193-1	00:00:11:21	15:21:49:02	15:21:58:10	15:21:42:12

4 ORGANIZE THE CLIPS

Organize the merged clips into suitable bins. In this instance each scene gets its own bin. It's worth using time to get organized at the start.

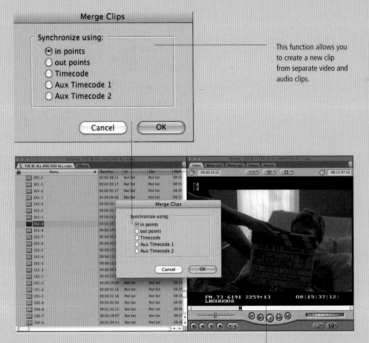

Merge Clips

Synchronize using:
- ● in points
- ○ out points
- ○ Timecode
- ○ Aux Timecode 1
- ○ Aux Timecode 2

[Cancel]   [OK]

This function allows you to create a new clip from separate video and audio clips.

5 MAKE AN ASSEMBLY EDIT OF A SCENE

Add shots to the timeline, in sequence, and see how things are working in a loose form to get an idea of the best way to portray the scene.

You'll notice that in this case the audio has also been sped up by 4%; this is because the film was shot at 24 fps but is being edited in a 25 fps environment (which is 4% quicker).

3 SYNC THE AUDIO

Sync the audio with the picture rushes using the timecode or the clapper board. If a Sync Slate was used on set then the timecode on the slate should (closely) match the timecode on your WAV files. If not then you can use the clapper board as a sync point (see page 74).

In this instance there was no Sync Slate, so an in-point is marked on the clap in both the video and audio clips.

6 WORK THE SCENE INTO A ROUGH CUT

By now you will have established the grammar of your edit sequence. You may like to replace some takes, and tighten or loosen certain areas.

Adding keyframes allows a quick way of adjusting your audio levels.

7 MUSIC AND SOUND EFFECTS

Add some music and sound effects if required. Often the audio recorded on-set needs a little help to enhance the scene. Sound effects help to enhance and highlight actions that occur on and off screen. Music has many uses such as enhancing emotion.

8 ADJUST AUDIO LEVELS

Make sure the spoken word in your film can be heard, that the music rises and falls where required, and that your sound effects sit at a natural level.

The two channels on a music track will be panned to the left and right to maintain their stereo relationship. Most dialogue will be in mono (or panned to the center).

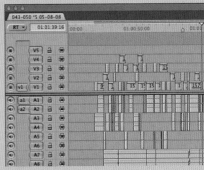

9 RUN ROUGH-CUT SCENES

Having got to this point with a few scenes, assemble a few rough-cut scenes together and see how they run. You may find that the pacing of a scene needs to be adjusted now that you are seeing it in sequence.

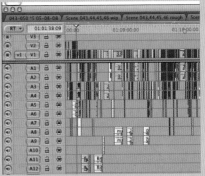

10 ASSEMBLE YOUR FILM

Assemble the whole film and see how it runs, making adjustments until you are happy with the offline edit. You may completely lose some scenes, rearrange scenes in a different order, or possibly intercut scenes.

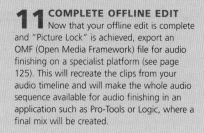

11 COMPLETE OFFLINE EDIT

Now that your offline edit is complete and "Picture Lock" is achieved, export an OMF (Open Media Framework) file for audio finishing on a specialist platform (see page 125). This will recreate the clips from your audio timeline and will make the whole audio sequence available for audio finishing in an application such as Pro-Tools or Logic, where a final mix will be created.

You can give each clip "handles" so that the audio mixer has access to a little bit more material; in this instance there is an extra second at either end of each clip.

12 EXPORT EDIT DECISION LIST (EDL)

Export an EDL (Edit Decision List) for picture grade and visual finishing. This is a list of all the timecode ins and outs of the clips that you have used and it relates back to the original film rolls. The selected parts of the original film rushes can then be color-graded to give the whole film the required look. Later on in the postproduction process, the graded picture and final mixed audio will be reunited.

In this instance a CMX 3600 EDL is required; commonly an XML is also used and carries more information.

TECHNICAL STUFF

Before one frame of your film is cut, there are some key technical setups and decisions to be made. It is important that you know the technical statistics about the footage you acquired: its frame rate, resolution, and compression qualities. This will and must remain consistent across all software platforms used in the editing and manipulation of your footage.

If the technical aspects of your footage do not remain consistent, you will face a host of technical issues, such as interlacing and compression downgrading. At the point of shooting, the camera report, shot sheet, or shot log should contain this information. This technical stuff gets transcribed into the postproduction environment and is written down and tracked by the editor. In the case of your first film, that would most likely be you. This simple act of knowing what the footage contains technically will allow you to focus on the wonderful creativity of editing.

Conform

Due to the electronic inaccuracies of the common video signal, a system is in place to monitor and adjust video and audio signals. In North America it is the NTSC (National Television Standards Committee) deployment standard. It is the worst quality of all systems in the world, as compared to other world deployment environments, PAL and SECAM. Therefore, a conform, a measurement of picture (color bars) and sound (1khz tone), is used to check against program material coming in for distribution. In adherence to the strict deployment standards required by broadcast networks and festivals, it is important that you set up your conform prior to cutting. This allows for technicians to check the final file for any irregularities or problems. The image below shows the information a typical conform layout must contain.

CODECs

CODEC stands for compressor/decompressor. This relates to how a computer software platform and its components handle the input and throughput of a data stream. For our purposes we relate this to the recording and playback of video and audio signals. Some data streams are larger than others; for example, an HD (High Definition) video signal is much larger than SD (Standard Definition). All computers need assistance, or an interface so to speak, to get these signals in, working, and then out of the machine. Throughput is also very dependent on hardware. RAM (Random Access Memory) and your CPU are the work horses. There needs to be a lot of horsepower when dealing with large data streams such as special effects or HD.

A TYPICAL CONFORM

This is a typical conform. You can see on the timeline the various elements that should be included.

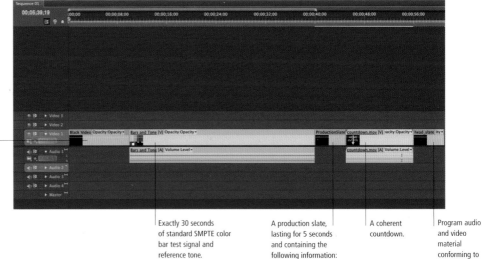

At least 10 seconds of coherent black recorded prior to the beginning of the reference test signals (color bars/tone). There should also be 60 seconds of coherent black following the end of the program material.

Exactly 30 seconds of standard SMPTE color bar test signal and reference tone.

A production slate, lasting for 5 seconds and containing the following information:
• show title
• duration
• date
• director.

A coherent countdown.

Program audio and video material conforming to project specifications.

Due to the wide range of deployment situations and camera encoding, the world of CODECs can and will be a mystery. The best advice is to know what your particular camera encodes the footage to and use that CODEC with your NLE software.

Overall, H.264 is probably the best of all worlds, but it will depend on your captured material. Try different ones, but always be clear about what your final deployment is to be. If it is the Internet, a broadcast system, or a projection system, you must know and understand the differences of each. You can only do this by rendering small tests to see how each one performs.

There are many CODECs and therefore much debate on which is the best to use. In 2007, one of the pioneers of HD deployment over the Internet, the video-sharing website Vimeo, offered consumer HD support by deploying 720p playback. What follows is a very good guide to CODEC selection as advised by Vimeo:

CODEC—H.264
A CODEC is the format in which your video will be encoded. Different CODECs have different features and varying quality. For best results, we recommend using H.264 (sometimes referred to as MP4).

Frame rate—24, 25, or 30 fps
If you know at which frame rate you shot, it is best to encode at that same frame rate. However, if it exceeds 30 fps, you should encode your video at half that frame rate. For example, if you shot 60 fps, you should encode at 30 fps. If you're uncertain what frame rate you shot at, set it to either "current" or 30 fps. If there is an option for key frames, use the same value you used for frame rate.

Data rate—2000 kbps (SD), 5000 kbps (HD)
This setting controls both the visual quality of the video and the file size. In most video editors, this is done in terms of kilobits per second (kbps). Use 2000 kbps for standard-definition video and 5000 kbps for high-definition video.

Resolution—640 x 480 (SD), 1280 x 720 (HD)
640 x 480 for 4:3 SD video, 640 x 360 for 16:9 SD video, and 1280 x 720 or 1920 x 1080 for HD. If you have the option to control the pixel aspect ratio (not the display aspect ratio) make sure it's set to "1:1" or "1.00," sometimes referred to as "square pixels."

Deinterlacing—maybe
If you are shooting on an older camera, enable this option. Otherwise, you may get weird-looking horizontal lines in your video. With newer camera models this won't matter, so you can leave this option unchecked.

CODEC—AAC (advanced audio CODEC)
For best results, we recommend using AAC for the audio CODEC.

CODEC SETTINGS
When selecting the settings for postproduction editing, you must know what your camera recorded with. You must clearly understand that staying consistent between cameras and post platforms bears no room for error. Above you can see the H.264 CODEC is selected. It is also important to note how many other CODECs there are in the world! The same goes with the playback CODEC. NTSC DV (see below) is the standard by which most cameras record in North America. Familiarize yourself with the camera you shoot with to be certain. Never make assumptions.

POSTPRODUCTION SPECIAL EFFECTS

With so many films filled with CGI special effects (SFX) on release, it can be very tempting for low-budget filmmakers to want to add some to their films. Technologically, effects have come a long way from Ray Harryhausen's hand-built, stop-motion puppets, shot frame by frame in front of a back-projected film in his garage.

With the incredible processing power of home computers and the low cost of the necessary software, there really is not a lot to stop filmmakers from trying to emulate the efforts of ILM (Industrial Light & Magic), not even pride or good taste. Yet with all the expertise that Hollywood studios can buy, they don't always achieve convincing results. Although Harryhausen's animations may not match modern CGI for realism, in terms of sheer craftsmanship they remain incomparable.

Modern special effects still use the same basic principle—animation mixed with live action—but instead of it being done frame by frame, it is now composited together on a computer. Horror, fantasy, and sci-fi, the main users of SFX, also happen to be very popular genres with low-budget moviemakers.

Using CGI

To make the most of CGI you need to start with a good 3-D modeler and animator. The right talent will be able to produce stunning animation even with budget-priced software. Try to keep the animation simple and restricted to non-organic objects—spacecraft, robots, or buildings—so there is less chance of it looking unrealistic. Keep your use of CGI to a minimum, or use it where it doesn't have to be integrated with the live-action footage.

If you want to put actors into a scene created with 3-D animations, you have to shoot them on a chroma key (green or blue screen) background. For best results, you need to shoot on a high-resolution digital format that doesn't employ high compression. Also, lighting your green screen set is critically important. See the notes and diagram on the following page. Besides a good camera, you will need either lots of blue or green chroma key paint or a backdrop cloth in the appropriate color.

It is best to use a large studio space where there is plenty of room in which to set up the backgrounds and light them properly—you need to use strong, even lighting that doesn't cast shadows. The foreground action has to be lit to match the CGI elements. Filming in a large studio makes it possible to separate the background and foreground lighting, and it provides enough space to shoot with a longer lens that will both bring the background closer and throw it out of focus.

OBJECTIVES >>
- **Understand CGI effects**
- **Know about useful software**
- **Explore filters and other effects**

STOP-MOTION ANIMATION
Stop-motion animation using models was the primary method of making special effects before the advent of CGI. The detail in Ray Harryhausen's monsters is still impressive, even by today's standards.

Chroma key (green or blue screen) lighting

There are two different types of keying available:

- Luminance key: Either white or black is removed and replaced with another video source. This can be tricky because of the amount of brightness and darkness associated with any given frame of video. Although not impossible, it may require a lot of adjustment of tolerances to get the proper keying effect.
- Chroma key: The video signal is made up of three basic components: red, green, and blue (RGB). You remove either the green or the blue and replace it with another video source. This system is easier because you are targeting a very specific element of a video signal. Be mindful, though, that your subject does not contain blue or green within the range of chroma key green or blue. In other words, a dark blue can work.

There are a few considerations when contemplating chroma key lighting:

- The size of the blue screen. This will dictate the number and intensity of instruments.
- Distance from the blue screen to the subject. If the space is small, placing the subject close to the blue screen can create shadows and cause a high level of blue reflectance.
- The luminosity of your blue screen should be equal to or higher than the brightest object in the scene, but no more than two to three f-stops higher than the subject's hot spots.
- Is the studio big enough for full shots?
- Do you have enough lighting? High-key chroma key setups need a lot of light.

Summary

Green is revered as the best color choice for shooting on DV formats simply because in the world of DV and its 4:1:1 color space, the green channel is where the luma values are drawn from and it is sampled more than blue, and therefore has more data to work with in postproduction. The blue channel in DV is sampled far less and is usually a poorer choice to use for keying purposes. Compared to blue, red and green do not suffer from this perceptual anomaly quite so easily— again, this refers to the DV 4:1:1 color space. You will get smoother edges when you key out the color in

Blue or green?

The term "blue screen" will usually be used to refer to any colored backdrop used for keying. But which should you choose?

- Blue generally gives better results when working with skin tones, but green is better for bringing out shadows in low-light situations and is easier to work with digitally.
- It is generally easier to get an even, solid coat with blue paint; the green paints tend to require repeated applications for an even coat, and touch-ups don't blend in as well.
- Some software, such as Ultimatte, works best with a very specific blue screen color.
- Make sure that your blue screen color doesn't appear in any of the foreground subjects. Make sure that the costume, makeup, and set design people understand the color issues as early as possible.

GREEN SCREEN
Green screen is not just the preserve of Hollywood blockbusters. It lets low-budget filmmakers create huge set pieces without the need of a construction crew and massive sound stage. In his homage to sci-fi B-movies *Captain Eager and the Mark of Voth*, director Simon Davison shot his actors against green screens, then added backgrounds that were either 3-D CGI created on computer or cardboard models. These were all composited together using Adobe After Effects on a standard desktop computer (see www.captaineager.com).

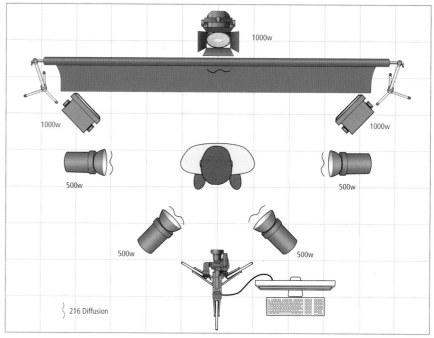

EFFECTIVE USE OF GREEN SCREEN
The secret to getting good results with green screen is lighting and the positioning of the camera, actors, and backdrop.

LIGHTING FOR GREEN OR BLUE SCREEN
This illustration clearly shows the importance of lighting for your green or blue screen. The sidelights, fill light, and backlight not only illuminate the subject but also serve to push back the reflectance of green or blue that falls onto the subject. It creates the clean edges that are fundamentally important for a good effect.

postproduction if you use a green screen at the shooting stage. Remember, there are just three things you need to get right for a decent key: lighting, lighting, and lighting. Good luck!

Going the other way, dropping 3-D CGI characters into the live-action footage, you can create alpha masks that will be exported with the character to isolate it from its background. The CGI footage and the chroma key footage are combined using compositing software such as Adobe After Effects or Autodesk. Most editing programs, such as Final Cut and Premiere, can also handle chroma keying, although compositing software will give you more complex tools for 2-D and 3-D effects.

Screen paint
Apart from straightforward chroma key/CGI, all kinds of effects can be achieved using filters or other effects programs. These are usually the preserve of pop videos or dream sequences and can easily stray toward the cheesy if not used with discretion. Using image-altering effects to compensate for bad shooting does not work.

However, if you decide that your story needs the actors to turn into cartoon characters, or fall into the world of a Van Gogh painting or an early silent movie, these effects are quite easily achievable, given the right software.

Not all effects have to be spectacular or fantastic. There are also little things that you might need to add to your film to give a touch of realism, such as a sign placed on a shop window, or the flash from the end of a prop gun when it is fired.

Although almost every feature film has some sort of postproduction special effect, and some comprise only special effects, it is far more important to concentrate on producing a good story with believable characters than to try to emulate Hollywood. If using SFX is necessary to tell or enhance the story, do it sparingly, but remember that the breakthrough films of most independent directors were simple narratives, well told.

Q&A

MD, LONDON VISUAL EFFECTS STUDIO, GLOWFROG
Nigel Hunt

1. Why is principal photography so important to making good effects?
Principal photography is the backbone to the shot. Having great photographic plates to work from ensures that the quality and composition are carried through into the final composited VFX shot.

2. What is the difference between a good effects shot and a great effects shot?
Care and consideration going into planning the lighting and composition. Planning and discussing the VFX before and during the shoot, between the director, DP, and VFX supervisor can result in savings later on in the process by ironing out unforeseen obstacles to the shot such as changing weather!

3. What are some rules to making great effects shots?
Planning and discussion as mentioned above. The use of computer-generated animatics helps clarify to the production team the final shot and what potentially is involved. Gathering reference material on shoot day such as lighting, location, and set/location photographs for textures.

4. Do you need tons of money to make effects shots? What advice could you offer to low-budget film makers?
Not anymore. With off-the-shelf hardware and software it's possible to create feature film effects on your laptop.

5. How should an effects shot fit into the storytelling?
That depends on what you consider an effects shot. In modern production this could be simply removing a street sign or on the opposite scale producing a vast establishing shot of a city. The effects shots should be driven by the narrative and always complement the storytelling.

FILLING IN THE BACKGROUND
In this still from *Bloody Tales of the Tower*, created for the National Geographic Channel you can see the setup of the scene against the green screen and the final shot, once the VFX background has been added in.

FROM SMALL SCALE TO LARGE SCALE
In this shot from *What's the Earth Worth?*, for the History Channel, you can see an ambient occlusion pass of a 3-D model of New York City (top). The picture below shows the final VFX depicting the "real" New York skyline.

TITLES AND CREDITS

Titles are an important part of your film. Not only will they impart necessary information to the viewer, they will also help to set the mood before the narrative starts to unfold.

When you design titles for your project, you must always keep in mind that your film will ultimately be deployed to some kind of broadcast system. This is critical, so as to prevent cutoff and misalignment of your text.

ACTION AND TITLE SAFE AREAS
This illustration clearly shows the safe title and safe action areas. Working within these will prevent your graphics and titles from being cut off.

The simplest static letters can work to form exciting and attractive titles, but putting in that little bit of extra effort will demonstrate a professional attitude toward the whole filmmaking process. To create dynamic titles, you need to start considering their design as early as possible so that they can become part of the look of the production and promotion package (see pages 130–133).

When preparing titles graphics, give close attention to the following:
- aspect ratio
- scanning and essential areas
- readability
- color and color compatibility
- grayscale
- style

Aspect ratio
Aspect ratio means the relationship between height and width—the shape of the picture-frame rectangle. The proportions of the television screen are 3:4, 3 units high and 4 units wide, or 16:9 for HD. All graphic information must be contained within this aspect ratio. All graphics are prepared in aspect ratio.

Scanning and essential areas
As mentioned earlier, your film will eventually be seen via a broadcast transmission system. With this in mind, even when graphic material is in aspect ratio, part of it still may not reach the home screen. Within the aspect ratio, there is a peripheral loss of picture area.

The amount of picture loss depends on transmission factors, and the masking and alignment (or rather the misalignment) of the home receiver. In order to make sure all of the information contained on a graphic shows up, you must include the scanning and essential areas. The essential area, sometimes called the critical area or safe title area, is centered within the scanning area. It is the portion seen by the home viewer.

Readability
This means that the viewer should be able to read the words that appear on the screen. There are five rules of thumb when designing text graphics:
- Keep all written information (text) within the essential area.

- Use relatively large letters with a bold, clean contour. The limited resolution of the television image does not reproduce thin-line letters very well for credits. Use fonts with an edge and drop shadow for optimal readability.
- Limit the amount of information. Less information makes it easier for the viewer to comprehend.
- When placing text over a background, keep the background simple and not busy.
- Watch the color and contrast relationship between the lettering and the background. Besides different hues, there should be a considerable brightness contrast between the letters and the background.

Color and color compatibility
When building graphics, do pay attention to color harmony and color balance. When deciding which colors go with which other colors, classify them into the following two groups: high-energy colors and low-energy colors (see right).

Grayscale
The digital video system is not capable of reproducing pure white (100 percent reflectance) or pure black (0 percent reflectance). At best, video reproduction of white is about 60 percent reflectance for white and 3 percent reflectance for black. These brightness extremes are called "TV white" and "TV black" (see right).

Style
Style, like language, is a living thing. It changes according to the specific aesthetic demands of the audience at a given location and time. To ignore it means to communicate less effectively.

You learn style not from a book, but primarily through being sensitive to your environment. Some people not only sense the general style that prevails at a given time but manage to enhance it with a personal, distinctive mark.

Always keep your approach to style simple. Do not go overboard on style and identify your guest from China with a super in Chinese lettering, or your news story about the downtown fire with flaming letters. Do not abandon good taste for effect.

HIGH AND LOW ENERGY COLORS

When choosing colors for titles and credits you are aiming for a balanced color scheme that is legible.

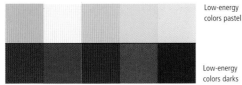

High-energy colors

The high-energy group includes basic, bright, highly saturated hues, such as red, yellow, orange, green, and warm blue.

Low-energy colors pastel

Low-energy colors darks

The low-energy group contains subtle hues with a low degree of saturation, such as pastel colors, browns, dark greens, purples, and grays.

To achieve balance, you can set a high-energy color against another high-energy color so that they achieve equal graphic weight, for example yellow against red.

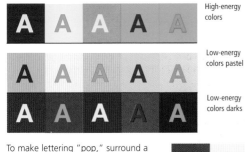

High-energy colors

Low-energy colors pastel

Low-energy colors darks

To make lettering "pop," surround a high-energy color with a larger area of low-energy color, such as a red on a dark gray background or a blue on pastel yellow.

GRAYSCALE

When designing graphics you must think about whether or not the colors differ enough in brightness or light to dark values. By dividing the brightness range between "TV white" and "TV black" into distinct steps, you have the video grayscale. The most common number of brightness steps in a grayscale is ten. Digital video can reproduce all ten steps under the most ideal conditions. The average reproduction range is five steps. In all areas of graphic design, a two-step difference between two colors (such as the background color and the foreground color), when properly lit, is considered a minimum spread. You need to imagine the value of the colors you are using to check there is enough difference.

Plot the value of the color you are using to a matching point on the grayscale (above). A high energy yellow will be lighter in value than a high energy red. To achieve the best legibility/readability, choose type and background with the most value difference; the minimum would be a two-step difference.

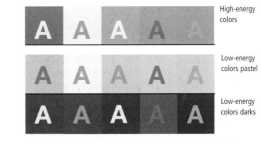

High-energy colors

Low-energy colors pastel

Low-energy colors darks

The colors used far left are shown converted into monochrome (left). The translation of color into grays is called color compatibility. Even if you select colors that have various degrees of brightness, intense light levels may wash out all but the most extreme brightness contrasts. The best way to determine if there is enough brightness contrast—that is, whether a color scheme is compatible—look at the graphic or scene in the camera viewfinder or monochrome (black and white) monitor. If the picture looks sharp, the colors are all right.

CHECK THESE OUT

Listed here are some good examples of how title design works to augment and strengthen the overall visual design of a film.

- *Se7en* (Dir. David Fincher)
- *Catch Me If You Can* (Dir. Steven Spielberg)
- *Conspiracy Theory* (Dir. Richard Donner)
- *eXisTenz* (Dir. David Cronenberg)
- *Ghost in the Shell* (Anime, Dir. Mamoru Oshî)
- *Naked Lunch* (Dir. David Cronenberg)

Titles software
- www.adobe.com/products/ aftereffects.html—AfterEffects
- www.apple.com—LiveType and Motion
- www.discreet.com
- www.macromedia.com—Flash

Free typefaces
- www.acidfonts.com
- www.chank.com
- www.fonthead.com
- www.girlswhowearglasses.com
- www.houseind.com
- www.typodermicfonts.com

ENGAGING TITLES

The title sequence for *Gulliver's Travels* is a great example of how titles can set the visual tone for a film. The credits appear in different fonts and positioned within various perspective control shots of New York cityscapes.

RIGHT TYPE

Choosing an appropriate typeface will help to convey the mood of a film.

Bembo—classic, neutral font

Wilhelm Klingspor Gotisch—old-fashioned and gothic font

Movie making

Helvetica Neue—professional, discreet font

Mister Frisky—quirky, fun font

Casting type

The best place to start is with the selection of a typeface. Try to avoid the generic faces that come with your computer. Times New Roman or Bembo are classic and, used discreetly, can look impressive, but from the thousands of typefaces available, you should be able to select something that exemplifies your movie's story or theme. If graphic design isn't one of your strengths, find someone who has a good eye for it and get him or her on the team, because you are going to need his or her skills throughout the production.

Once you have chosen a typeface or two (keep it simple), you and/or the designer can start working on concept ideas for titles and other material, such as posters. Because short films are just that, short, you need to keep the titles brief and possibly integrate them into the film itself—sometimes called TV titles. Chances are you won't have well-known actors, so you don't need to start with their names. Credits are best left to the end and made as concise as possible.

Motion graphics

Most editing software comes with title/credit creation functions that cater to most needs. They usually have a range of preset effects that can be customized, but more often than not, these have a generic look that lacks the spark of originality. To create something unique you will need to use dedicated software such as Adobe After Effects or Autodesk products. Not exactly low-budget items, they are very powerful and versatile. Users of Apple's Final Cut editing programs get LiveType included in the package. This will create dynamic, animated type for use with the editing software, as will Motion, another motion-graphics editor from Apple.

Another all-around tool, Adobe Flash, is not cheap, but it is capable of producing everything from animated type to websites and interactive content. One of Flash's advantages is its small file sizes, for use on websites, but the .swf format will also integrate with video-editing software. For quick, inexpensive text effects for Flash, Wildform's WildFX Pro is a perfect solution, although some of the effects are a bit cheesy.

Not all film titles have to be computer-generated. Invention is what low-budget moviemaking is all about. Use stop-motion animation techniques and collage; draw titles by hand and film them, or use a scanner and import the image files; or film the title written, painted, or printed onto a surface and integrate it into the scene. Whatever technique you choose to use, remember the maxim of good design: "Less is more."

Credits where credit's due

The closing credits, when most people leave the theater, are mainly for the benefit of those whose names appear there. It is therefore important to include everyone who worked on or appeared in the movie, and to credit them properly. If they are working for nothing to gain experience, having their name at the end of the movie will help them to get more work. You will also need to thank everyone who donated services or locations, and include copyright and disclaimer information. Whatever style you use (rolling or static) the credits need to be on-screen long enough to be read, but not so long that they impinge on the running time. A good rule of thumb for the length of time that the credits should appear on-screen is that you should have time to read the text comfortably twice. So, the more text you want to have on-screen, the longer your credits will have to run for.

Given the general public's aversion to watching credits, filmmakers have tried enhancing them with outtakes (examples include the movies of Jackie Chan and Pixar). Others have put additional scenes after the credits, while some use a popular tune (see pages 126–127 for why you won't be doing this). Despite all these efforts, Joe Public still won't read the credits. The important thing is that they are there, and hopefully they will be read by the right people.

DYNAMIC TITLES

The titles generator in Final Cut Pro is a simple way of producing dynamic, animated titles, when used with discretion.

TITLES SOFTWARE

Resident text generators are usually pretty good at doing the basics you will need for opening titles and closing credits. Adobe After Effects will give you the ability to add motion and dimension to your text. Always keep it simple and readable.

POSTPRODUCTION SOUND

The importance of getting good sound has been covered on pages 90–93, but it is during postproduction that you can really elevate it to new realms. Audio is the second stage of postproduction and is done after the fine cut or online picture cut is completed.

OBJECTIVES >>
- **Know when to hire an expert**
- **Edit and add sound**
- **Find out about the dialogue track**

The original sound is examined for flaws, and then it is cleaned up or manipulated to create a clean final soundtrack. There are limitations to the cleanup of very poor source recordings, so the original dialogue must be recorded as cleanly as possible. The individual responsible for this intricate work is called the mix-down engineer or sound designer.

There are essentially five stages of sound postproduction for a picture:

1. Spotting—where the sound designer and producer or director sit down with a dub of the final picture with time code burn-in. They decide on the logical placement of dialogue, sound effects (SFX), and music within the overall soundtrack. In and out points are logged in order to build an edit decision list (EDL), and trouble spots are noted; all the requirements for the final audio are dealt with in these sessions.

2. Laydown—this is the process of transferring synchronized source audio tracks from the picture and laying them down digitally using Pro Tools or a similar postproduction sound software bundle. The time code

from the picture master is also laid in; this ensures sync when laying back to the picture master.

3. Sweetening—this is the process by which the sound designer builds all of the necessary sound elements required for the picture. Additional audio beyond the source tapes is recorded. This stage also involves adding the necessary processing effects such as noise gate, compression, and delay.

Generally speaking, an "M&E" is defined as the music and (sound) effects track. Additional information is needed to accurately define which track best serves your purpose. These are the typical headings and groupings:

I. Dialogue (D)
A. Production dialogue
B. Looped (replaced) dialogue—also called ADR (automated dialogue replacement)
C. Added dialogue
1. Specific English-language voices
a. Hospital pages, TV, or radio announcers
b. Specific dialogue from crowds or on- or off-camera actors

II. Narration (N)—often called VO or voice-over
A. Any scripted or non-scripted narrative dialogue, spoken by an off-camera personality

III. Translations (T)
A. English translations of on-camera characters in a language other than English

IV. Music (M)
A. Scoring
B. Source music (music that takes place at the location), such as a jukebox, or radio playing music
C. Performance music (live)

DIALOGUE REPLACEMENT
Sometimes the dialogue is not very clear during the shoot and must be re-recorded in a studio, preferably using the same recording equipment used during the shoot. (See page 93.)

V. Effects (E)
A. Hard effects (specific sound effects such as a door slamming, phone ringing, car driving by, etc.)
B. Background effects (atmospheric and ambient effects, such as wind, rain, traffic, crowds, etc.)
C. Foley (effects performed to picture such as footsteps, clothes rustling, handling noises, etc.)
D. Production effects (sound effects recorded at the time of the production dialogue, which are separated, by editing, from the dialogue)

4. Mixdown—most audio for video mixes are made up of more than one sound element. The various sound elements can be grouped (see above list) into categories and subcategories, each with a descriptive title that identifies its contents.

The similar audio elements from each category are usually combined and recorded as sub-mixes or "stems." The "full" or "final" mix includes all of the stems, and therefore all of the audio elements, at the appropriate level. This is the mix the audience will hear. Variations on the full mix can be achieved by using various combinations of the stems.

A frequently used term for describing alternative mixes is "mix-minus." This defines a mix that does not contain one or more of the sub-mix/stem tracks.

For instance, a "mix-minus narration" track would be a mix made up of all the stems except the narration. Another way to communicate the variations of mixes is by way of the initials of the stems. An "M, D & E mix" would signify a music, dialogue, and effects mix.

5. Layback—once the mix is completed, it is transferred back onto the picture master. The original time code is used to maintain the necessary sync.

Sound advice
One of the best things you can do is find yourself a good studio-based audio person. These are usually people who like playing around with audio waveforms on computers. Alternatively, find a technology-savvy musician, who comes with the bonus of being able to help compose the soundtrack. Whoever you choose, getting the optimum final sound is vital to your movie's presentation.

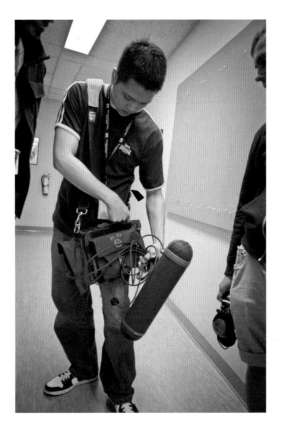

TIME TO PREPARE
Be sure to give your sound person enough time to set levels in order to capture the sound correctly. Too often the sound department is forgotten and this can lead to costly fixes in postproduction sound.

Foley and sound effects
All your dialogue and wild-track recordings from the shoot should already be digitized and stored on the computer, either in your editing software or in a separate sound-editing program, such as Pro Tools. Depending on your software, you should allocate a separate track for each sound. An affordable video editor, such as Apple Final Cut Express, allows 99 audio tracks, and although it doesn't have the same level of control that the pro version or Adobe Premiere offers, it is more than capable of producing a well-balanced, in-sync soundtrack. For a more complex sound mix, try a dedicated audio program such as Pro Tools or MOTU Digital Performer. These are music-recording/mixing programs, incorporating film-scoring facilities, favored by professional musicians. They are sophisticated and require an experienced user, but the results are excellent.

Any sounds that weren't captured during the shoot are added at the postproduction stage. Work on sounds

LOW-BUDGET TIP
If you cannot afford to purchase a postproduction sound package such as Pro Tools, then utilizing your non-linear editing bundle, such as Final Cut Pro, will serve you well.

Q&A

FOLEY ARTIST
Philip Rodrigues Singer

1. Why is location sound recording so important to a sound mix?
The primary goal of a location sound recordist is to capture the actors' dialogue. Practically everything related to film sound can be later recreated in a studio with sound FX, but the dialogue is unique to the live performance of the actor. Dialogue is routinely replaced in the postproduction studio (a process called ADR). The original recording, made by the location recordist, is often called a "guide track" because it also serves as a basis for sync and sound for the final soundtrack.

2. What is the difference between a good mix and a great mix?
If you notice that a film has a good sound mix, then it's simply a "good mix." If you fail to notice the actual soundtrack because you were so involved in the film then it's a great mix! The film *Dead Man Walking* was almost entirely ADR'd, which means almost every single line of dialogue in the film was recreated, and yet the film is utterly seamless, though it was not the original soundtrack. This is an example of a mix that is so realistic it can fool an audience—this is a great mix.

3. What are some rules to getting a good final mix?
Balance and subtlety are key to good mix. Nothing should stand out and yet every sound should be clearly heard in detail. The three

CUSTOM SOUNDS
To achieve the best quality, most of the original sound in a film is either enhanced or replaced. A foley artist (seen here) can recreate almost any naturally occurring sound effect while sound FX editors replace mechanical and ambient sounds such as cars, explosions, and background noises.

elements of dialogue, music, and sound FX have to blend together without conflict, and yet each element has to have its influence on the overall sound. Balance should occur not only within the elements of a mix but also across media platforms. Basic broadcast releases and complex theatrical 5.1 surround soundtracks have to be accommodated in a single mix; therefore, getting a balance between media formats is an important aspect of sound mixing.

4. Do you need tons of money to record and mix sound?
Technology has made it possible to record and mix on very inexpensive equipment. A laptop and some external midi equipment can turn virtually anyone into a film sound editor and mixer. The craft of film has never been about money, equipment, or technology. It's always been about creativity and the mastery of the surrounding technology. Using off-the-shelf equipment and software, a filmmaker can produce amazing results if they possess experience and skill.

5. How should sound design fit into the storytelling?
Sound should create reality that is on and off camera. Sound and picture are two sides of the same coin of storytelling. Sound is therefore woven into the story just as any image, music cue, or dialogue line.

6. What tips or advice could you offer to a beginner, low-budget filmmaker?
Take the time to learn your craft from the ground up. Experience and hands-on training cannot be entirely taught or bought in a tech store. The best way to learn the craft of filmmaking is to make films. It doesn't really matter what equipment you use or what software you buy, but rather how well you use the tools at hand; this can only come from honest practice. Given the boost technology has provided the film and television industry, the barrier to entry into the art of filmmaking has never been lower, so get out there and start making films.

FOLEY TOOLKIT
This handy collection of tools is used by foley artists and sound FX editors to create sounds for theater, radio, and cinema. Such tools and props are different in shape, dimension, and material, and can be "played" individually or in combination to produce a wide range of rich and subtle sounds which add depth and character to the finished soundtrack.

Using a variety of built-in audio editing tools, one can cut, copy, paste, and massage the audio effortlessly.

Pro Tools can support many tracks simultaneously, combining audio, instrument, and midi data together, allowing for virtually unlimited recording capability.

Pro Tools locks to SMPTE Timecode allowing synchronization between the audio and picture. Familiar "tape deck" controls allow easy record, play and search capabilities.

AVID PRO TOOLS

The Avid Pro Tools software and hardware family allows professionals to compose, record, edit, and mix high-quality music or sound for picture. Available on Mac or PC, Pro Tools is the industry's standard audio production platform and features a wide variety of audio plug-ins.

that need enhancing—footsteps, doors creaking, and so on—is usually done by foley artists. They create and record all manner of sounds and noises in a studio using their own favored props.

Hiring a good foley artist is going to be expensive, so you may have to settle for the cheaper option of pre-recorded sound effects. These are available on CDs or as downloads from websites, and the quality varies. Free downloads are available, but you get what you pay for. Commercial sites offer superior search facilities and previews, so you can be sure of exactly what you are acquiring. There are pitfalls to buying CDs: you don't know what you are getting in advance, and you have to pay for a disk full of sounds you don't need, for the sake of one effect. This makes downloading individual sounds an attractive option.

ADR and voiceover (VO)

What happens when something goes wrong with the all-important dialogue track? Providing the visuals are okay, you can simply re-record the actors in a recording studio or any place you can keep soundproof. Known as ADR (automatic dialogue replacement), it isn't going to be quite as automatic as it would be in a professional

studio, but it is possible. Apart from a place to record, you will need a television or screen for the actors to watch to get the lip-sync correct, and headphones so that they can try to match the original feeling. It is then just a matter of recording onto DAT, HD recorder, or straight into a computer.

You can change dialogue, if necessary, by editing the visuals so the new lines are spoken off-screen, providing you shot enough coverage in the first place. Tweak the freshly recorded voices using filters to match them to the rest of the scene. Any voiceovers are done in the same way and mixed into the soundtrack.

Mix and match

On feature films, sound engineers use huge multitrack mixing desks and the highest-quality monitor speakers to ensure that the audio is well balanced and that what needs to be heard is audible. While you may only have access to a software mixer, you should make sure that you have good speakers, or at least top-quality headphones, that will allow you to hear the full dynamic range of the sounds; once you start incorporating music, this will be even more important.

CHECK THESE OUT

- www.bias-inc.com—Peak and Deck, sound-recording/editing software.
- www.motu.com—Digital Performer, recording and sequencing software.
- www.avid.com—ProTools, highly respected sound-editing software, integrates with Avid Xpress Pro editing software.

Sound-effects libraries:
- www.sonymediasoftware.com/default.asp
- www.powerfx.com
- www.sound-effects-library.com
- www.soundoftheweb.net

MUSIC

Once you have all the dialogue and sound effects in place, you will probably want to add music. Of course, you should have (ideally) brought the score composer on board at the preproduction stage to give him or her a chance to start working on themes and motifs for the movie.

OBJECTIVES >>
- ■ **Know about copyright**
- ■ **Be able to enhance mood**
- ■ **Try sound mixing**

Oscar-winning scores

The following movies won the Oscar for best musical score. Check them out to see the power music can have in your film:

- *The Artist*, Ludovic Bource, 2011
- *The Lord of the Rings: The Return of the King*, Howard Shore, 2003
- *Titanic*, James Horner, 1997
- *Dances With Wolves*, John Barry, 1990
- *The Way We Were*, Marvin Hamlisch, 1973

BIG BUDGET, BIG BAND
Scoring music for a production, as shown here, is only an option for big budget pictures that can afford this approach. With today's technology you can have access to this kind of orchestra within a digital box since software such as GarageBand and Reason put a world of music at your fingertips.

You are probably wondering where you are going to find a composer for an original soundtrack and how you are going to pay them, when it would be easier just to use something from your CD collection.

As you must no doubt be aware, the music industry (not necessarily the musicians) is very strict on the enforcement of its rights. If you use an existing track, you will have to pay for it, and you will also have to deal with all sorts of contracts. If you are going to use music, do not use existing music, unless it is royalty-free and properly licensed. There is a lot of library music available, of varying quality and price, but whether it exactly fits your film can be a matter of luck.

Knowing the score

Music in film helps to establish themes or to create mood. The style of the music will depend on the type of film and the idea you are trying to convey. It will also be influenced by your taste, and by your budget. Whatever genre of music you want to use, it is best to make sure that it is original. If you are not a musician or don't know one, or, worse, know one who isn't very good but insists on helping, what can you do? If you use any of Apple's video-editing software (Final Cut Pro, or Express, or even iMovie), you will also have access to music software designed for people not very adept with musical instruments. GarageBand and Soundtrack use prerecorded loops of real musical instruments that can be sequenced and layered to create a rich, original soundtrack. The Soundtrack program is designed for use with video so that all the sound can be cued properly.

These programs cannot fully replace a talented composer who is trained to understand how to evoke emotions through music, but they will do a more than satisfactory job.

Being able to create the music is not enough, though; to get maximum impact it is vital to know when and where to use it. Study a wide range of films to learn what works best in particular situations. The most successful scores are those you don't notice but that still manage to enhance the visuals or the mood. In fact, we have become so used to music in films (as in our everyday lives with the ubiquity of portable music players) that its absence becomes unsettling—something worth considering when designing the soundtrack.

Once your musical score is completed, it has to be mixed in with the rest of the sound.

Stereo sound is standard, and for early films this should be more than sufficient for most viewing situations. If you really want to enhance the aural experience with surround sound (5.1), you will have to use specialized software such as Bias Deck, Pro Tools, Nuendo, or Adobe Soundbooth. Some of these are quite affordable, and if they are used properly, they will certainly give your film a professional sound.

Soundbooth has a limited but powerful set of audio tools enabling detailed editing of the waveforms.

Tasks such as changing "Pitch and Timing" as well as "Loops" are available in the sidebar menu. In addition, Soundbooth has a variety of built-in effects options for reverb and equalization.

The editing interface allows the sound designer to see the waveform and manipulate it directly on screen.

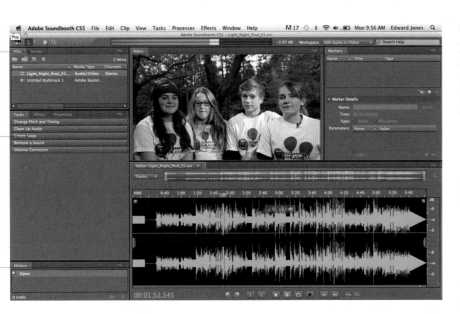

DIVERSE TOOLS

Adobe Soundbooth (top) or Apple's GarageBand (below) are good examples of programs that combine both a music-looping interface and a sound editor. These diverse programs can be an effective alternative to Pro Tools for creating music and a mix for your film.

CHECK THESE OUT

- *Complete Guide to Film Scoring* by Richard Davis (Berklee Press Publications, 2000)
- *From Score to Screen* by Sonny Kompanek (Schirmer Trade Books, 2004)
- *On Track: A Guide to Contemporary Film Scoring* by Fred Karlin and Rayburn Wright (Routledge [2nd ed.], 2004)
- *The Reel World: Scoring for Pictures* by Jeff Rona (Backbeat Books, 2000)
- www.adobe.com/products/audition—audition audio software to integrate with Premiere for Windows
- www.apple.com/ilife/garageband/—GarageBand, Soundtrack, and Logic audio software
- www.bias-inc.com—Peak and Deck sound-recording and editing software
- www.groovemaker.com—loop editor for Windows and Mac
- www.sonycreativesoftware.com/products/—SoundForge and other audio programs
- www.motu.com—Digital Performer recording and sequencing software
- www.steinberg.net—Cubase and Nuendo software for music and media production

Each sample on a track can be easily edited and rearranged in this highly visual interface. Samples can be clipped or looped to produce perfect results.

GarageBand features a wide range of virtual instruments, such as piano, drums, and strings. Using a Midi keyboard, one can create an entire orchestra in minutes—talent not included.

Familiar "tape deck" controls allow quick and simple playback and record capabilities.

Individual tracks can be further manipulated within the waveform editor in the lower panel.

5

One of the biggest parts of a Hollywood movie budget is dedicated to marketing and distribution. Having spent millions on getting the film made, the studios need people to see it to recoup their costs. Low-budget filmmakers can't match the resources (financial or otherwise) of the big studios, but they do have assets that the studios often lack—imagination, originality, and the freedom that comes from having nothing to lose.

DEPLOYMENT

Of course, you want people to see your film—that is, after all, why you made it—but your target audience isn't going to be the Saturday-night popcorn crowd. If your ambition is to be a filmmaker, you need people with lots of money to see your movie, to see your capabilities, and to give you the financial backing to work on bigger projects. This section covers some of the ways you can get your films out to the toughest audience—the jaded industry people who have seen it all and usually know it all. But as William Goldman keeps asserting, in Hollywood "nobody knows anything." And that goes pretty much for the entire international film industry.

MARKETING

Just being a good cook isn't enough; presentation is a big part of a chef's success. And so it is with filmmaking. Although talent will usually shine through, it is the presentation of your work that will get it noticed. The following pages will give you some ideas using readily accessible methods, including festivals and the Internet, that won't cause you to go deeply into debt.

The whole marketing machine is a complex one, made up of focus groups, advertising specialists, and media experts. They use every method at their disposal to entice the public to part with their money at the local movie theater, no matter how good or bad the film is. One of the big problems with short films is the lack of a lucrative market. Short films used to be shown in movie theaters before the main features, but nowadays only advertisements and trailers are shown. The following pages suggest some places to get your movie seen, but first you will need to create an attractive package, giving it a chance by providing an edge over the competition.

Press gang

Your most important marketing tool is the press kit. This has to be multipurpose, serving the media, potential buyers/distributors, and festival organizers. No matter what design or packaging you choose, it has to contain: a copy of the film, a trailer for the film, a written synopsis of the film, bios of the key cast and crew members, and photos. You should also include some posters or flyers. If the package is going to the media (radio, TV, newspapers), include a sheet of ten frequently asked questions (FAQs) with the answers.

Package breakdown

The design of your package creates the all-important first impression. You are never going to be able to compete with the majors, but try to be creative; go beyond using a standard folder of loose pages with a DVD or videotape tacked on. Make the overall design consistent with any graphics used in the movie. Try to keep all the written info bound together, so individual sheets don't get lost. Make sure the package is robust enough to withstand handling. There is no point in creating something that is stunning but disintegrates as soon as it is touched. With the low price and high quality of digital printing, you should be able to do

CREATING OPPORTUNITIES
March!, directed by Damon Cardasis, was conceived and created in six months, from concept to wrap. The idea came from an article in the NY Press about a landlord kicking out his tenants in order to take over the building for himself, and the film is a mockumentary centered around this story. The budget for the film was a little under $10,000, raised through family and friends, and through kickstarter.com. Given that the budget was so low, there was no money for a real marketing campaign. The filmmakers' goal was to complete the film and send it off to film festivals. Through this process the filmmakers established the LES film festival (see page 136). Their experiences made them realize that there were other low-budget filmmakers out there, without massive marketing resources, looking for opportunities to show and share their material.

something impressive without breaking the bank.

Include the finished film. Technology changes quickly, but DVD is your best option. Almost everyone has a player, and a computer can also play DVDs. If you are concentrating just on the local market, you don't have to worry about format (PAL/NTSC). If you are going for international distribution, you will have to create both versions and make sure there is no region encoding. Include a trailer for the film on the DVD and make sure the disk is easy to navigate. Your DVD will have lots of free space, so you can also include a digital version of the press kit. Use formats such as PDF or RTF, because not everyone uses Microsoft Office. More importantly, make sure both Mac and Windows computers can read the disk. Besides a DVD, you may want to include a CD that contains all the digital files (photos, synopsis, etc.), and a version of the film as a QuickTime movie that can be seen on non-DVD equipped computers. You have to cover every eventuality.

PRESS KIT

In addition to a copy of your film, posters (above), flyers, and postcards (right) are great items to include in your press kit to market your film. A synopsis and any press clippings you have (below) provide the recipient with further information about your film.

KEEP YOUR BUDGET IN MIND

When planning your movie, always remember your budget and make decisions accordingly. Given the extremely limited budget on *March!*, the filmmakers' decision to use SAG actors, so they could be confident in getting the best possible performances, meant that they had to complete the shoot in a very limited time in order to make their money last.

What to include in your press pack

- Labels design
- Application
- Manuscript of film information
- Technical information
- Credit list
- Contact information
- DVD
- Mailing list (who you are sending it to)
- Locations for distribution of promotional material
- Multiple copies of your film in different formats or file types

Short synopsis.

Crisis? What crisis?

Matt is entering middle age.

His arrival in the parking lot of a well-known furniture superstore sparks an existential crisis that will deeply affect him.

SYNOPSIS

The length of the synopsis will be dictated by the length of the movie. Make the short one intriguing, with the longer ones revealing more of the story but never giving everything away. After all, you want people to watch it!

Medium synopsis

Crisis? What crisis?

Matt's fortieth birthday is approaching fast. He has a loving wife, two beautiful children, and a comfortable domestic existence. Life doesn't place too many demands on him, but there are some he'd rather avoid and today he is faced with one he can no longer put off. In the parking lot of a well-known furniture superstore he suffers an existential crisis that will deeply affect him and those he loves.

Long synopsis

Crisis? What crisis?

Matt's 40th birthday is approaching fast. He has a loving wife, two beautiful children, and a comfortable domestic existence. Life doesn't place too many demands on him, but there are some he'd rather avoid and today he must fulfill a promise he made to his wife and accept the inevitable. After surviving a journey from hell, he arrives at his destination (the parking lot of a well-known furniture superstore), where he has to face his demons, only to suffer an existential crisis that will deeply affect him and those who love him.

Written material needs to include a synopsis of the film, although three would be better—long, medium, and short. The short one can be as few as 50–75 words, while the long one can be as much as a page. The actual length will be partly dictated by your film. Write simply and concisely, avoiding too many superlatives. You are writing an outline of the story, not a review. If you don't feel confident, find a copywriter to do it for you. They should also be able to use correct grammar and spelling, both of which are important if you want to appear professional. Cast and crew bios may require even more creativity if you are relatively unknown or inexperienced.

Don't lie or exaggerate, but find ways to make the most of what you have. "First-time filmmaker" and "untrained actors" will both attract the right attention if the film is good.

FAQs with answers will make it easier for journalists to write an informed piece without having to leave their desks. It also ensures that they have the right information. You will need photos of the principal cast and crew, and a selection of production shots. These can include behind-the-scenes shots and photos of the actors taken during rehearsals. A good digital camera should do the job. You can take prints from it, and magazines will need the images digitized for laying out anyway. These can go on the CD or DVD.

Always go for quality over quantity in all the material in your presentation. You are dealing with busy people who won't take the time to sift through a mountain of pages and pictures to find something worth using. In the end it is the film that counts, no matter how slick your presentation may be.

Publicity

Publicity has to start before you begin filming. Local newspapers need to fill their pages with articles other than domestic disputes. Let them know you are shooting a film, especially if there is a human-interest angle to it: "Local people aiming for Cannes." You can even supply them with the photos and copy. If they publish it, you will have a clipping for the press kit.

Q&A

LES FILM FESTIVAL FOUNDER
Damon Cardis

1. How important are marketing and publicity in gathering an audience for your film?
Extremely important. Probably the most important—how else will people know to come!

2. What approach to marketing could a low-budget filmmaker take, which would be effective but not break the bank? What should they prioritize?
We believe that there is a multitude of ways to market your film, with the film festival being the most obvious. Film festivals help you to reach a larger audience than you normally would, while at the same time have someone else help you with the marketing of it. On top of this you should work very hard to market your own work. Don't just rely on other people to do it for you. Social networking is one of the most obvious and easy ways, as well as blogs and posting. Also, get creative; flyer your entire neighborhood, write on the sidewalks with chalk, ask local businesses if they can get involved or want to advertise your movie. Put it in a church bulletin! Do whatever you can to get the work out. If you don't do it, no one will.

3. What innovative or exciting marketing techniques have you seen recently?
I think that "guerrilla marketing" is always more interesting. There are millions of adverts everywhere and it's hard to capture people's attention. Do everything from writing on the sidewalks to streaking to get people to stand up and take notice. Humor helps a lot too!

FESTIVAL FOUNDERS
Damon Cardasis, Shannon Walker, Tony Castle, and Roxy Hunt worked together to create the LES Film Festival to give low-budget filmmakers the opportunity to have their films seen.

4. How can filmmakers utilize festivals and competitions to get their movies seen?
A film festival is a great way for people to come see your movie. The festival takes care of the venue and its own marketing, which will inadvertently lead to pushing your film, but goes above and beyond as well. Use the recognition of the film festival to show that your work is worth seeing.

5. At what point in the process of making a film can the branding, marketing, and publicity begin?
Branding, marketing, and publicity should begin on your film before you even start shooting. Get the word out! Build buzz. Update people on the status. Blast photos of stills from set. Get people excited to see it before it's even ready! There should be a massive push once the film is close to completion but get them eager to see it beforehand.

6. How has marketing of films changed over the years and how has technology been an influence on that process?
Technology has changed how everything is done. Whether through Facebook, Twitter, Instagram, or any other social media, getting a subject to trend can make your movie a massive success! The good thing is that the power is back in people's hands, but it's important to figure out how best to use this medium. Especially if you don't have money to buy advertising space.

7. Is there a particular genre of film that is easier to market than others?
Not particularly. People love great comedies, but also love talking about horror films that haven't allowed them to sleep for the past week. I think the key is to market your film the best you possibly can within its own genre. If it's a comedy, have the marketing material help convey that. Don't have a comedic poster of a horror film, unless that is the intent of your film.

SPREAD THE WORD
Film festivals, such as LES (far left), are great ways of gathering an audience for your film and you can utilize their marketing resources. You can also spread the word about your film through street-level marketing, such as flyers, posters (left), and social networks, which can be really effective and needn't break the bank.

YOUR CALLING CARD

Some people spend their whole career making short films because they enjoy the format and find it the best medium in which to express their ideas. Most filmmakers, however, use them as a training ground and a calling card before working on larger projects.

The *modus operandi* is much like that for marketing, described on the previous pages, but the focus is slightly different. Instead of the movie and its story being the most important element of the package, it has to concentrate on you and your talent. This does not lessen the value of the movie in any way, because ultimately that is what you will be judged on, but you are selling yourself and not the film. You are also targeting different people. Instead of trying to impress distributors or festival organizers, you want the movie to be seen by producers or financiers.

In reality, your first short film is not likely to be good enough to convince a major producer or studio to give you enough to make a feature. It is more likely to show your potential to backers for another short. These could be equipment-rental companies, labs, effects houses—the places that can help you to create a more professional-looking film. You can go to them and say, "Look, this is what I did on a miniDV with no crew. Imagine what I could do with your cameras/film/processing." Facilities houses are always on the lookout for hot new talent to which they can attach their names; they figure that if they look after you, if or when you make it big you will remember their help and give them more substantial business.

This sort of sponsorship is not the only way to get another movie made. There are all sorts of arts grants available, and having some previous work to show will definitely help your case. However, grants do come with all sorts of conditions attached, so they may not be something you want to pursue. It is also worth contacting your local arts council, as they usually have film and video funding. See page 161 for a list of international art grants available.

Show reel

If you really want to go for the big producers, you will need more than one short film, unless it is the greatest thing since *Citizen Kane*. You need a show reel. This is like a trailer for all your work, showing cleverly edited excerpts of the best pieces of directing, camerawork, or sound design. A show reel for directing would focus on directing style and film quality; screenwriters' show reels focus on highlights of the actual script and the relevant scene; editors focus on the pacing of cuts/transitions, and so on. With DVD-authoring software, a show reel can include not only the standard edited-highlights version, but also the full-length versions of your movies. That way, if the viewer's interest is aroused, he or she can choose whether or not to watch more.

WHAT MAKES A GOOD SHOW REEL?

Some students cut together several films into a show reel to show a range of genres, but this can make for an uncomfortable mix. Here, Richard Hibbert has condensed a longer movie into three minutes to showcase his skills.

What to include: the best parts—that is, good imagery, cut together to suggest a narrative flow. The style here is dreamlike; the camera floats around capturing characters at different moments. It's a slow and atmospheric journey through the city. Richard shows that he can light actors and interiors, and there are good images of panoramic cityscapes; clips that go in tight on actors' faces; and good framing and compositional devices. There isn't loads of manic cutting nor any use of cross fades.

15 SECS
At the start include your name and contribution. Avoid a long credit sequence; these opening credits are on screen for five seconds only.

Note the title and Richard's credits are on-screen throughout the short sequence.

28 SECS
Meet the protagonist. Characters are introduced with in-tight camerawork. This is a trademark style used here. If you do have a style that is used to unify a film, it's good to try to convey it in the reel.

43 SECS
Meet the enigmatic guy (he has no backstory and appears periodically, waiting for something). The actor is bathed in different colored neon lights, which is a chance to show off some lighting skills. Here, they feel part of the story.

Even the best show reel in the world is not going to help if you can't get the right people to see it. Ingenuity and persistence are two prerequisites, as is a thick skin to counter constant rejection. So how do you get your work to producers? Cold calling and unsolicited mailings do not work—you have more of a chance of winning a lottery.

Because the movie community is relatively small, networking is an excellent way to start meeting people. Joining an independent filmmaking organization or society gives you a chance to meet like-minded people. Once you start to become familiar with other filmmakers, there is a chance that you will be introduced to someone who is genuinely interested in what you are doing. "Who you know and not what you know" will get you a long way. Just remember to stay enthusiastic and passionate, and carry a DVD or two with you at all times.

Whatever method you want to use to get your film in front of a producer, from networking to stealth, you have to make sure you have something worth showing, which is where competitions and festivals come in handy.

Building a show reel

• Know what you want to show about yourself and your work. Is it your style or atmosphere, or are you particularly proud of your snappy dialogue and set pieces? Make sure they feature. Your show reel is like a more interactive or visual business card: it's about presenting yourself to employers or backers, and giving them an insight into your work. So be confident and showcase your strengths—show them the good stuff!

• Pace your work the way you want. People often tell you to keep your show reel as short as possible, and obviously a five-minute epic wouldn't really be appreciated and will largely get skipped—but don't be afraid to pass the two-minute mark.

• Keep it crisp and clear—always give your shots room to breathe in the edit. Don't be afraid to filter out anything you don't think is necessary: a clean and paced piece is much better than a crowded show reel with rushed shots.

• Music can enhance your images, but if you are considering putting music over the top, then aim for something that suits the content of your work, rather than something from your personal collection.

1.14 SECS
Nicely composed, panoramic night scene; the first of a couple such scenes to show off camerawork.

1.27 SECS
Character illuminated by firelight. Here, shadow and lighting are used to build atmosphere. Even in a short show reel, the aim should be to capture and convey the essence of the genre you are working in.

2.02 SECS
Graphic framing and composition. Here, whether intuitive or planned, a director's eye is revealed in the use of a color palette.

2.57 SECS
Closing credits, including contact details.

FESTIVALS

Festivals and competitions probably provide the best opportunities to have your film seen and gain some sort of recognition for all your hard work. These range from high-profile events like Sundance to small local ones. Naturally, you'd like to be seen at Sundance or Cannes, but then so does everyone. Picking a smaller, local festival or competition is a better place to start.

OBJECTIVES >>

■ **Learn to utilize festivals and competitions to get your film seen**

Given the sheer number of festivals and competitions, it is a good idea to do some market research before you start. Entering your movie into a festival or competition and having it rejected without explanation can feel like a personal slight, but it may have been simply because you didn't read the entry requirements. With hundreds or even thousands of movies being entered into events, you are not likely to receive an explanation or personal reply, if you get any reply at all. If you receive any feedback beyond acknowledgment of receipt, you are doing well.

To begin you will need a list of festivals. A good place to start is www.filmfestivals.com, as it lets you search for festivals by area and/or date, then gives you all the information you need or links to where you can get it (see page 171).

Look at the entry requirements and at the types of films that have been entered or shown on previous occasions. Although festivals may call themselves "open," they usually have a preference for particular types of films, while others are genre festivals. If your movie is sci-fi, it makes sense to look for sci-fi festivals, but if its themes are broader and less obviously sci-fi, you may be able to cross it over into other genres.

The other thing to look for is deployment format. Festivals are accepting movies on DV and HD. Some will want tape, DVD, or a data file such as a Quicktime file. Be sure to carefully check the deployment requirements, as they can vary from venue to venue.

Many festivals ask for an entry fee for your film. At this stage you need to make a decision about whether you want to part with your cash and take a chance. The bigger the festival, the higher the fee, with no guarantee that your movie will even be looked at when it is submitted. You also need to see what the fee entitles you to. At the very minimum you should get tickets to the showing. Also be aware that there are some unscrupulous people out there running festivals that don't ever happen, or promise more than the fee merits—research is vital.

Competitions

Most festivals will run some sort of competition in conjunction with the main event, although not all competitions are linked to festivals. Competitions are

LES FILM FESTIVAL
The Lower East Side (LES) Film Festival was started in 2011 by Damon Cardasis and Shannon Walker, along with Tony Castle and Roxy Hunt of BFD Productions. It is aimed at featuring the work of talented budget filmmakers, and showcasing those films in intimate settings in the heart of Manhattan.

often theme- or genre-based, like the festivals, so it is important to find one that is suitable. If you are a procrastinator, like most novice filmmakers, competitions are great motivators. Deadlines are a great way to get those creative juices flowing and help make you more decisive.

As with festivals, before you fork out any money for a competition (some do charge), look at what they are offering for the fee. See if there is any history behind the competition or its organizers. Filmmaking is a small community, and a bad reputation soon becomes general knowledge. Always read the terms and conditions before submitting your film to make sure you aren't signing away all the rights to your work.

If possible, have a look at previous winners. This will give you an idea not only of what the judges are looking for, but also of the level of competition, which may help you decide whether it is worth entering or not. The important thing is to get the film made in the first place.

If you can't find a reasonably local competition, where you can actually talk to organizers and see the finished movies, there are plenty of competitions online.

Every film festival has slightly different entry requirements, so read the submission information carefully. At the right is an edited example of the requirements of the Raindance Film Festival. All festival submission forms require a similar amount of information. Legal requirements may differ from country to country, so it is best to ensure that you have everything concerning rights in order.

1. The format the movie was shot on. This can be taken into consideration when it comes to final selection, for projection reasons.

2. These are the highest-quality standard formats available in most cinemas, although an increasing number have digital projectors that will show DVDs.

3. Some festivals specialize in specific genres (e.g., horror, sci-fi), but some categories are more open.

4. Take this from your already prepared press kit (see pages 130–132).

5. Listing your name can look either impressive or amateurish. It worked for Robert Rodriguez.

6. For your first efforts you will probably not be able to complete this, but if your film is shown at the festival, there is a chance someone will approach you.

7. Some festivals demand exclusives, while others want quality. Don't lie, as filmmaking is a very small world.

8. This is not a Faustian deal, so you are not signing your life away, but make sure you read all the terms and conditions carefully, and get advice if you have any doubts.

Festival entry requirements

Submission form
[requires the following information]:

1 • Film details
   • Originating format
2 • Festival screening format
   • Optical sound format
   • Aspect ratio
3 • Genre
4 • Short synopsis
   • Submitting party contact information:
   • Print source
5 • Credits
6 • Available rights
7 • Screening history
8 • Submission fees and agreement with the terms of the Raindance Festival

Submission deadline
• Films will be accepted from 9 March [of the year of the Festival] and no later than 1 July of that year

Submission format
• Films must be submitted on DVD only
• The title, screening format, and running time must be clearly labeled on the cover
• Submitted copies will not be returned but may be collected from Raindance after the festival

Submission eligibility
• All submissions must have been completed after 1 September [of the previous year]
• Films must not have been released in the UK on any format
• Submission packages must include a preview copy, a completed Raindance Festival submission form, the correct submission fee, and a press kit containing a 200-word synopsis, full cast and crew credits, a director's biography, and a CD with a director's photograph and two production stills
• All films in a language other than English must be subtitled in English
• Exploitation and pornography genres are not eligible

Selection of films
Submissions are reviewed and selected under the following criteria:

• Quality of narrative and production values
• Independent nature of the production
• Limitations and availability of screening slots
• Availability of film rights for distribution

Raindance endeavors to complete all selection procedures by 1 September [of that year] and inform all Submitting Parties, in writing, if their film has been successful or not at that time. Successful submissions will receive correspondence that will include important information on shipping the print or tape to the festival, press and publicity, guest accreditation, contact information, and how to make the most of participating in the festival. A selected print or tape must be received at Raindance no later than five days prior to its scheduled screening date.

THE INTERNET

If the vicarious thrills of the competition circuit aren't for you, one of the easiest ways to get your film seen is to put it on the Internet. You can send your movie to one of the many existing websites, or you can go completely independent and run your own site.

OBJECTIVES >>
■ Use established sites
■ Set up your own site
■ Generate traffic

Well-established sites, such as triggerstreet.com, have a huge audience, mostly of other filmmakers, improving the chances of your movie being seen by the right people. This is especially true for triggerstreet, as all newly posted films get a chance to be reviewed by other filmmakers as part of the conditions of posting to the site. Getting feedback from your peers is a useful way to find out if what you have done is any good, with the added bonus that you won't be humiliated in person.

Of course, if you are shying away from the competition and festival circuit, these sites may not be of much interest to you. Unfortunately, timidity is not a good quality in a filmmaker. The whole point of making a movie is for it to be seen, and anyone who tells you otherwise is either trying to fool you or is fooling himself.

Going indie

Remaining independent, with your own website, has its own range of pros and cons beyond independence. Before diving in and making your own site, you should consider some of the following points, most of which may seem obvious or commonsense.

Do you have a domain name? Most of the good .com names have already been registered. Look at some of the other possibilities; .tv is a good one for movies. Don't make the name too long or too difficult to remember: it's going to be tricky enough getting traffic to your site without making it difficult to type the name correctly.

This brings up the problem of getting people to your site. With billions of websites on the net, getting people to see your film requires ingenuity and a certain amount of luck. Meta tags are your first line of attack: with the right words placed there, search engines will find you, but your position in the search list will rely on the number of hits the site has had, so you end up in a kind of Catch-22 situation. The best way to generate traffic is to get a buzz going and let word of mouth (or email) do it for you. It does help if you have something worth showing, but hype worked for *The Blair Witch Project*. Emailing everyone you know and getting them to tell everyone they know will soon spread the word, and while this method is sometimes frowned on, if the message is just sent to people with whom you are

TRIGGER STREET LABS
Trigger Street Labs offers a home-grown feel to its visitors. You will get a sense that they really support the independent filmmaker. A disadvatntage is that they are not as well known or as often visited as YouTube or Vimeo.

acquainted, it shouldn't cause too much harm. Just don't inadvertently attach a virus.

A good website

Three important aspects of a website, often overlooked, are content, navigation, and speed. This book isn't about how to create websites, but ensure that the content is easy to find, easy to access, and worth watching in the first place. Make sure pages load quickly. Don't make them too graphics-intensive, which is advisable from the design aspect anyway. Macromedia Flash makes very interesting interactive sites, but they can be slow to display. Always make two versions of your film available—one for broadband and one for HD broadband—and make sure they are in a format that everyone can view; QuickTime is best for this, as it does

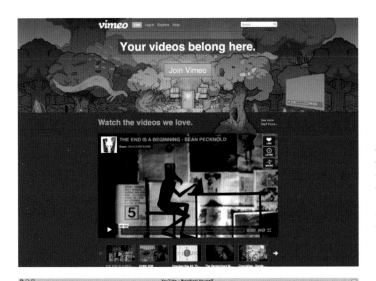

VIMEO

The advantage of using Vimeo is that they have been streaming high-definition videos for some time. The site is easy to navigate and they are well-established and more well-known than Trigger Street.

Get your film seen on the Internet

1. Write a brilliant script and make the movie, bearing in mind that shorter is better.

2. Find a site that caters to your genre of film.

3. Follow all the submission guidelines. Pay particular attention to the rules regarding rights and clearance.

4. Get all your friends, and their friends, to watch and vote for it.

5. Set up your own website to host your films.

6. Save the file in a suitable streaming format (QuickTime, Real, Windows Media). Don't make the files too big or offer two different-sized versions. Remember that QuickTime is free.

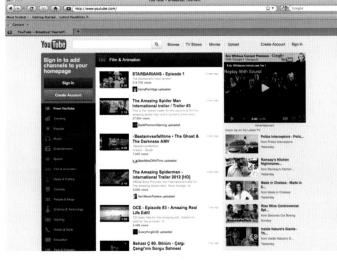

YOUTUBE

YouTube is by far the best known of the sites discussed here. Navigation is tricky and there is a real chance that you won't get many hits unless you obtain your own channel and really promote yourself. The YouTube hit is a rarity.

not need any special server software and the viewer is free to download.

An important aspect to consider when creating your website is its purpose. Is it going to serve as an online showcase, or are you going to use it as a commercial venture? Initially it is probably best to keep it as a showcase until the quality of your work, or your reputation, makes revenue a possibility. This can range from pay-for-view to selling DVDs, but take it one step at a time, and start by getting a finished film online.

CHECK THESE OUT

- www.apple.com/quicktime—QuickTime is the underlying technology for digital video on computers and the Internet
- www.macromedia.com—Web-creation software
- www.microsoft.com—Windows Media Player and server media software
- www.real.com—Real provides media streaming
- www.wildform.com—Convert standard video to the Flash format
- www.amazefilms.com—Internet film distribution
- www.triggerstreet.com—Kevin Spacey's online film community

RIGHTS

In simple terms, you own the copyright to any original work that you create, unless and until you sign those rights over to another person or organization. It's then that the whole issue of rights becomes murky and filled with lots of legalities and jargon that seem mainly to benefit the lawyers.

OBJECTIVES >>

- **Register your script**
- **Stay within the law**
- **Consider product placement**

You may not need to prove or defend the originality of your work while it remains in the nonprofit realm of private showings, but the sooner you learn to protect yourself, the better. This starts at the script-writing stage and usually involves registering your script with an organization such as the Writers Guild of America (WGA; www.wga.org) or a similar local organization. There is usually a fee for this, and it can be done on the Internet. The chance that a story similar to your own brilliantly original idea already exists is high, but having your screenplay registered is still your best protection.

Of course, if your screenplay is for your own episode of *Star Wars*, you may have trouble registering it. That doesn't stop you from making it as a fan film; you just can't sell it or make money from it—unless of course, George Lucas gives his permission and blessing.

Material protected under copyright can go beyond identifiable characters to include any recognizable product, work of art, or piece of music. Different countries have different rules, but it is best to abide by international copyright law, just to be on the safe side. We live in extremely litigious times, and a slight oversight in getting proper clearances could stymie the release of your breakout film for years, with the lawyers being the only ones making money. If you are going to have well-known products in your shots, get permission from the copyright owners or the manufacturers before you start shooting.

If you are clever, you should be able to turn it to your advantage, particularly if there is another major competitive brand. If your star needs to drink a can of cola, you can approach your preferred brand and ask them to supply not only the permission but also all the cans necessary for the shoot. Product placement is big business, so why not get a slice of that action and cover yourself at the same time?

Being careful

The use of music has been covered on pages 126–127, but be aware that any song playing on a radio or stereo in the scene is still classified as a performance, so it will need (expensive) clearance. By now you will know not to have such electronic devices on during filming anyway, simply as a continuity issue; they are added in postproduction.

For your first attempts at making films, it is probably best not to worry too much about eliminating all branding from the shoot, as it is unlikely to be seen by the general public. However, if your talent and/or ambition are so great that you are confident of the work being shown in public, then it is best to do the right thing from the start. You might be able to claim "fair usage," especially on not-for-profit (as opposed to not profitable) movies, in the sense that the items are in common use in everyday life, and provided they are not an integral part of the story, you will probably be safe, although restricted in where you can show the finished film.

The whole subject of copyright is huge and complex and fills many large and very dull books. If you have doubts, seek legal advice; it may save you a lot of money and aggravation in the long run. That goes for any contracts or agreements you are asked to sign as well. Distributors are out to make money above anything else, and even if you assign all the rights to them, you can be pretty sure that if litigation results from your oversight, they will send the lawyers to you. Bear that in mind before you sign away the rights to your work. Always err on the side of caution, and remember that even if it is a lo-no budget film, the law does not look on poverty as a defense.

CHECK THESE OUT

- www.marklitwak.com—Entertainment lawyer
- www.raindance.co.uk—Home of the Raindance Festival and courses and services for filmmakers, including script registration
- www.wga.org—Writers Guild of America for registering screenplays
- *Clearance and Copyright* by Michael C. Donaldson (Silman-James Press, 2nd ed., 2003)
- *Getting Permission: How to License and Clear Copyrighted Materials Online and Off* by Richard Stim (Nolo Press, 2000)
- *Rights Clearances for Film and Television Productions* by Stephen Edwards (available from www.pact.co.uk)

FESTIVAL CONTRACT

Here is a typical example of a screening contract for a festival. If in doubt, always consult an entertainment lawyer or a colleague with experience in dealing with contracts and disclosures.

Typical contract (for festival entrance)

By submitting an Entry, you hereby (a) represent that you are the sole author and owner of your Entry and your Entry is under no restriction, contractual or otherwise, which will prevent The Festival's use of it or you from meeting your obligations; (b) agree that the Entry shall be free of all liens, encumbrances, and claims of third parties; (c) acknowledge and agree that nothing in your Entry infringes on any copyrights or trademarks, or violates any person's rights of privacy or publicity and that you have obtained all necessary releases and permissions; and (d) agree to comply with these official rules and the terms of service.

Entries determined by The Festival to infringe on any intellectual property rights, or other rights, will be disqualified and no refunds will be given. All materials submitted become property of The Festival (but not the intellectual property rights, as described below).

RIGHTS: As part of the entry process, you must execute the official Submission Agreement. Please review this Submission Agreement carefully!

By executing the Submission Agreement, you will be, among other things, promising that you have obtained all necessary rights and clearances in connection with your film.

If your film is chosen as a finalist, The Festival will have the non-exclusive right to exploit your film in any way, in its sole discretion (but not the obligation to exploit your film in any way).

In addition, derivative rights to your film will be licensed to The Festival for a minimum period of two years, as set forth in the Submission Agreement.

If you do not obtain all rights and fully complete the Submission Agreement, your film will not be considered for entry.

This refers to the physical medium the film was sent on, not the movie itself.

Read the small print

"I hereby irrevocably and unconditionally waive any so-called 'moral rights of authors' in the Programs and such rights under section 77 and section 80 of the Copyright Designs and Patents Act 1988 as I now have or hereafter acquire in relation to the Programs." This simply means you are signing your work away, so you'd better hope they are paying you well.

"Non-exclusive" is a very important term, as it allows you to show it at other places.

Two years is a fairly standard length of time for a festival to use your work, although it doesn't state a maximum period. Remember, if you are at this stage, your work is being promoted at no expense to yourself—so it is a small price to pay.

6

This section provides six projects to inspire you to put this book away and start practicing your craft. The projects included here are all short films. The beauty of the short format is that it allows you to make any type of film, free from the constraints imposed by features and television shows. Short films can run from 30 seconds to 30 minutes, although some lengths are more commercially viable than others, and all the projects here run to a maximum of ten minutes.

PROJECTS

The projects are not straightforward narrative films. They represent a variety of genres and styles, including interviews and a music video. There is also advice on some well-established competition formats that will test your imagination and ingenuity to their limits. Explore all the projects and even mix them together. Let serendipity be your guide. The important thing is to start making movies and discover what you can create.

15-SECOND FILM

In the time it takes the average person to read the title and this sentence, you will have told your story and the film will be over. Count the seconds on your watch. Despite the brevity, there are television commercials that take that much (or that little) time to sell you an entire lifestyle concept.

Admittedly, the 15-second commercial is an edited version of a longer spot, usually inserted at the end of a commercial break to reinforce the message, so it does not have to convey a complete idea. But what about a stand-alone, ultra-short movie? What is its purpose?

The idea was dreamed up by advertising and marketing people, to whom the 15-second concept was already familiar, as a way of promoting the new generation of video cell phones. The limit was set partly because of the restrictions of the technology, and partly as a challenge to filmmakers. Outside of the original Nokia competition, there is an increasing demand for content from the phone networks as they try to offer more variety to customers.

Little ideas

Like all films, a 15-second opus needs an idea; in fact, the whole film will be the expression of that basic idea, so the simpler it is, the better. There is no time for complex character development or establishing a backstory. You have to set up the concept and get straight to the punch line, which probably represents one of the best devices to make it entertaining. In this

type of movie, the punch line provides the surprise, and sometimes the shock ending. Try not to make it too gruesome, upsetting, or offensive to viewers. It is always better to use humor, even if it is a bit sinister. You must ensure that the idea is resolved, avoiding the impression of incompletion. If you are using actors, find people who have very expressive faces.

Quick shots

Once you have your basic idea, you have to shoot it. It is best shot on at least a miniDV camera. If you have a suitably high-resolution camera built into your cell phone, then you can use this. Bear in mind, though, that it is much easier to reduce the resolution of a movie than to increase what wasn't there in the first place. Even though the final movie will be only 15 seconds long, you need to make sure you shoot enough footage. The shooting ratio will be much greater than it would be for, say, a feature, or even for a 10-minute short.

Of course, you don't have to create a complex, multiple-shot extravaganza. There is nothing to stop you from doing it all in a single take, if the idea works—and in 15 seconds, there is no reason why it shouldn't.

Assignment

Aim:

Create a 15-second movie, with or without sound, to show on a cell phone.

Crew:

Director

Camera operator

Editor

Equipment:

DSLR, DV, or cell phone camera

Tripod

HAVE I PASSED?
INT. CAR—DAY
A nervous **STUDENT DRIVER** sits beside a weary **EXAMINER**.
EXAMINER (consulting clipboard)
Parallel parking, turns, emergency stop. All excellent.

STUDENT DRIVER
So?

Shaving cuts

The longest part of the project will be the editing. Your first rough cut could be anywhere from 30 to 60 seconds. Now you have to start shaving away the seconds, and making decisions about how much and what parts of the shot best convey the idea. The only way to do this is to keep playing it over and over until it reduces to the required length. As a learning exercise, editing a 15-second film will teach you a lot about the economy of shot usage, and this will be invaluable when you come to make longer short films.

If you can make a 15-second film successfully, anything longer should be just that much easier.

SHOT LIST
The shot list for "Have I Passed?", a 15-second film, stills of which can be seen below.

HAVE I PASSED?

	SECONDS
Black, cut to	
"HAVE I PASSED" in large font on screen, single line, cut to...	2
CU: A pen scribbles on a pad, on a page headed "Driving Exam," checking boxes. Another sheet is being held up. MUSIC plays in the background. THE EXAMINER mumbles to herself, "emergency stop," etc.	2
MID: (Behind STUDENT, high, on Examiner, framed by Student seat), lowers sheet. Concludes "all fine."	2
MID: (Behind Examiner, high, on Student, framed by Examiner seat), Student leaning into window, hand on wheel asks "So?", confident.	2
BACK ON EXAMINER, who turns off music, shows clipboard. Carry "But you still haven't passed" over into, and match action into...	3
LOW: (From Examiner seat, clipboard into shot top right, Student on right too), Student looks down, clipboard flies up. Looks down from clipboard briefly on noise of door shutting.	3
WIDE: Over the car, Examiner turns from car with raised brows, taking deep breath, walks off.	1
Credits 1	2.5
Credits 2	2.5

EXAMINER
But you still haven't passed.

The **EXAMINER** shifts to climb out, placing clipboard and pen on the dash. The clipboard and pen fly upward.

EXT. CAR—CONTINUOUS
The **EXAMINER** clambers out of the **UPSIDE-DOWN** car, watched by the frustrated **STUDENT DRIVER** and an incredulous **PASSERBY**

FIVE-MINUTE DOCUMENTARY

There has been a significant rise in the popularity of the documentary in recent years, thanks in part to Michael Moore and his international successes. Check out Project 6, "Shooting an Interview," as it goes hand in hand with this one.

Anti-establishment and political documentary features were big back in 2004, and they overshadowed the thousands of other documentaries shot throughout that and every other year. Television still shows a lot of non-fiction programs that aren't "reality" or game shows. Nature and wildlife programs, travel programs, educational shows—the list is endless, and if you want your film to be on that list, you need a subject you are passionate about and want to share with others.

Most television programming is divided into 30- and 60-minute slots, but some broadcasters have five- and ten-minute slots they want to fill, often with something quirky that isn't a narrative. These short spots need to be informative, entertaining, and visually captivating, offering a little-seen window on the world.

If this sort of filmmaking appeals to you, and you want to be broadcast, you have to use the right equipment. Broadcast quality usually means shooting on the expensive DigiBeta format, but the arrival of HDV has opened up new possibilities for the low-budget filmmaker, especially for documentaries. At a stretch, it is possible to shoot on miniDV or DVCAM,

although the better the quality of the image, the better the chances of it being aired.

Digital video, in any of its flavors, is a great boon to the documentary filmmaker. Documentaries usually require hours of footage that have to be whittled down to something succinct, and the low cost of tape makes this possible. It is also easier to log and edit. The cameras are lighter and less intrusive, making the whole shoot easier.

Equipment aside, as with any movie, it is content that is most important. How you approach, interpret, and present your subject is what matters. Although there is a certain unknown quantity to the shoot that comes from filming real life, you still need to start with a clear concept of what you want to achieve. This may change during, or after, the shoot, but without an original plan you will be, as it were, shooting in the dark.

For your first documentary, don't be too ambitious. Pick a subject you are passionate about. It doesn't have to be political; it could be a sport, music, cooking, or trains. It's your enthusiasm for the topic that counts—and your ability to find a unique way of showing it.

Assignment

Aim:

Produce a five-minute documentary on a subject of your choice using digital video.

Crew:

Director

Camera operator

Sound recorder

Equipment:

DSLR or DV camera

Microphone

Camera support

UP CLOSE AND PERSONAL
Documentaries invariably require the camera to get close to the action. Wide-angle lenses are important for this, as is some knowledge and experience of the subject, especially if there is some danger involved or a chance of unexpected action.

INCLUDING INTERVIEWS
How much of your documentary you script beforehand will depend on the type of film you are making. If you are including interviews, some questions can be prepared ahead of time and then the cameras left rolling to capture candid and honest responses. A voiceover script can be written once editing is complete.

For example, do you like comics and know a comic-book artist? Why not film the creation of a page from concept to sketches to inks and colors? Film the studio, with different shots of the drawing process and coloring techniques. Interview the artist and film him or her doing something other than drawing. Try to incorporate some of the comic into the film's narrative. Shoot every stage of drawing and shoot lots, and from as many different angles as possible. Get close-ups of hands, face, eyes, mouth. Shoot over the shoulder, long shots, medium shots. Remember that tape is cheap and you rarely get a second chance to go back and shoot again. Sometimes you can mock up insert shots, especially with interviews, but in this example, reshooting a drawing, while not impossible, is best avoided—and remember continuity.

Editing all the footage together needs a slightly different approach from the standard narrative movie because faster cuts can be used without worrying about disturbing the story's flow. It can be tied much more closely to the soundtrack, and even cut to an existing (original) score. The important thing is to establish a good rhythm in the editing.

Of course, there is another type of documentary that can serve the novice filmmaker twofold—the behind-the-scenes-making-of-DVD-extras type. If you can find someone who is making a movie, offer to go and shoot all the behind-the-scenes stuff. Tell them you are learning about filmmaking and want to practice by making a documentary. Offer to share the results, but make it clear there are no guarantees if it is one of your first efforts. You will learn not only while you are shooting, but also from watching more experienced filmmakers at work.

These are just a couple of suggestions but, as with any genre, you have to get out and do it.

POSSIBLE SUBJECTS

Your documentary will be that much more interesting if the subject is something you are passionate about. Here are some ideas to get you thinking:

- extreme sports: skateboarding, BMX riding, surfing, hang gliding …
- preparing a traditional meal
- commuting on public transportation
- making a comic book
- making articles of clothing, for example, a handmade suit
- body piercing
- obsessive collecting
- a day in the life of a dollar bill

SKILL
For action sports, the cameraperson needs to be able to keep up with the action, to follow focus accurately, to pan and tilt, at the same time holding a good composition. A good tripod and familiarity with the equipment are vital.

POSITIONING
Finding the best position for a shot can mean being positioned well away from your subject. Walkie-talkies are an invaluable way to stay in contact. There are rarely chances for a retake, so you don't want the subject moving before the camera is ready. It takes a lot of organization to make it all look spontaneous.

MUSIC VIDEO

The music video, the pop promo, whatever you want to call it, is an ideal medium for any filmmaker to experiment with because there are no rules as such. There are also hundreds of bands and performers needing short films to promote their songs.

OBJECTIVES >>
- **Find a subject**
- **Sell the artist**
- **Decide which medium to use**

Assignment

Aim:

Produce a three-and-a-half-minute promo in one day with a small budget.

Crew:

Director

Director of photography

Assistant director

Camera assistant/focus puller

Lighting

Makeup artist

Runner

Equipment:

DSLR or DV camera

Assorted lights

Locked playback for lip sync

Locations:

Internal and external

Favors and freebies:

All you can get!

At the top end of the music video spectrum you can be dealing with budgets bigger than most independent features; at the bottom are the lo-no-budget shoots with which you are more likely to be involved.

Because of the creative freedom that music video offers, there are just as many filmmakers looking for artists as there are musicians looking for filmmakers, so if you want to break into this field it won't hurt to do a little market research first. The best place to start is with yourself. What type of music do you like? What style or genre of films do you like or want to make? Do the two complement each other?

Go to see as many local bands performing as you can. Talk to the band or their manager to find out what their ambitions and prospects are. Let them know you are a filmmaker looking for a band to shoot, but don't be too quick to offer your services. Choose an artist or band that you want to film, and whose music and performance you like.

If you find a band with a recording contract, or one good enough to be signed, they are going to need a video. A band is generally expected to have a completed package before a record company will sign them; that means a finished EP or album and at least one video. By offering to work for a deferred payment, and by clever negotiation, you may be able to get yourself a good deal. Many bands don't realize that the cost of making their expensive video comes out of their advance/royalties and is not met by the record company. This knowledge should help you to sell your services. If you give them a carefully budgeted schedule and explain that they will be paying for the video themselves, as the record company is only providing a loan, you will immediately gain their confidence. After that, it is up to you to produce the goods.

What to shoot

What you shoot for the music video is something you'll have to discuss with the band. If you can approach them with an original concept, rather than letting them come up with an idea, it is going to be more enjoyable for you. The film you make is going to be very important to you. It will go on your show reel, and your next job could depend on it.

IN MAKEUP
The makeup artist is often overlooked on the music video shoot, but is an essential member of the team—especially when working in close-up or effects makeup.

CREATING ATMOSPHERE
A smoke machine is used here to give atmosphere to the setting.

REHEARSALS
Rehearsals are vital in saving you time and money later, particularly if your shoot involves any stunts or combat. The vocalists will sing along to a recording for lip-syncing at the postproduction stage, but no live sound is being recorded on the shoot.

Creating a story based around the song, or the mood it evokes, is often a good approach. However, making something that is overly arty or conceptual could work against you. The film has to sell the band/artist as well as the song, so they will have to make an appearance in it somewhere. On the other hand, try to avoid a straight performance film; they can be a little dull after repeat viewing, even if record companies like this style for new artists. However, they are quick and easy to shoot, and in the end it is all about image and marketing the artist.

The arrival of the music DVD has opened a whole new range of opportunities for the music video maker. Previously, only singles releases were turned into videos, but now whole albums are given the visual treatment. As nearly all music videos are destined for the small screen, you can shoot in almost any medium without having to resort to 35 mm film. Most semi-pro and pro DV cameras are more than adequate for the job, but better still are the new HDV cameras. On a lo-no-budget route, DV is really your only option. With the right lighting and cameraman, the results will be perfect for its intended end use.

Try to make something that isn't going to date as fast as the music; avoid excessive flashy special effects. The average viewer may be impressed, but other filmmakers will instantly recognize that new software plug-in. Using some traditional animation might be more interesting.

Whatever you envisage and shoot, it has to fit with the music, not only in temperament but also in tempo. You should give great consideration to rhythm in any filmmaking project, especially at the editing stage, but it is the driving force behind a music video.

Whatever you want to do with the music video, be original but stay faithful to the music, and don't allow yourself to be ripped off.

DOUBLE-CHECKS BEFORE FILMING
A good crew is invaluable during a shoot, and experienced operators make sure everything runs smoothly. Here the assistant director (AD) and assistant cameraman double-check the equipment before the shoot.

RAIN STOPS PLAY
Filming on a rooftop, overlooking the city, was delayed by rain and strong wind but went ahead because of time constraints with the borrowed equipment and "volunteer" crew.

AND MORE REHEARSALS
Most musicians are confident performers in front of audiences and cameras. In performance-based videos they will need minimal direction, but rehearsal before shooting is still vital.

CHECK THESE OUT

- MTV or any other music channel
- Directors Label DVD series from Palm Pictures—Highlights the work of some of the best music video directors over the last decade
- www.shootingpeople.org—An online network of filmmakers
- www.musicvideoinsider.com—An e-zine and online community for music video directors
- www.mvwire.com—An online resource for the music video industry with news, interviews, and educational content

48-HOUR FILM

One of the biggest hurdles facing new filmmakers is actually getting started. There is always something preventing the movie from being made—no script, no camera, no actors, no idea, or no time.
In response to this dilemma, the 48-hour film challenge was devised to encourage filmmaking without excuses.

OBJECTIVES >>
■ **Take up the challenge**
■ **Work with a team**
■ **Plan your time**

Assignment
Aim:

Produce a five-minute movie on digital video within 48 hours, without knowing the genre or title until the beginning of the time limit.

Crew:

Director

Camera operator

Sound recorder

Makeup artist

Equipment:

DV camera

Microphone

Camera support

Props

Like all good ideas, there is some debate about who thought of it first, but versions appeared in the U.S., Canada, and the U.K., all around the same time. The premise behind the challenge has regional variations but is basically the same: shoot a five-minute film on miniDV within 48 hours. Although this is a challenge in itself, there is an added factor that makes it all the more interesting: It can't be planned ahead because the title and genre are not given until the beginning of the time limit. In its simplest form, contestants select a genre and a title from a hat, then go off and make their film. To complicate matters further, or simply to circumvent any possible pre-planning, additional elements are thrown into the mix, such as including a specific object, a certain location, or a designated line of dialogue.

Another variation has each team create a package containing a sound, a photograph, a location idea, and a prop. The packages are then mixed up and distributed among the other teams. Other restrictions include such things as limiting the size of the team, setting a minimum number of actors, and giving a specific running time for the finished movie. By setting a "no shorter/longer than" time limit, the competition becomes more egalitarian.

Be prepared
There is no surefire way to prepare for such an event, as the parameters will be changed with each competition.

However, you can take some steps to make things run more smoothly, and they all hinge around your team.

Making a short movie from start to finish in 48 hours is a very intense experience. Creative differences and lack of sleep can produce very volatile situations, so the most important thing is to have a clearly defined leader (not necessarily the director). There are two possible approaches to recruiting team members. One is to gather a team of professional or highly experienced specialists who don't know each other. Given that familiarity breeds contempt, by the time your team actually gets to know each other, the shoot will be over. Also, being specialists, they only need to be around to fulfill their appointed tasks. Finding such a team and convincing them to be part of such a folly, especially for a novice, will not be easy.

The alternative is to get a group of your friends, with whom you've been through thick and thin; just go for it and have fun. If you approach it without taking it too seriously—that is, with no expectation of winning—it is still possible to create something worthwhile. As the leader, you may decide to take on a lot of the technical/creative roles yourself (directing, camera, editing) and leave your friends to act, hold booms, and make coffee.

Whatever the creative conditions of the challenge are, the process to be followed is the same as with any other short film project, but compressed into a

READY OR NOT
Several of the park scenes in *Busted* are shot "handheld" to give a war-zone documentary feel, especially while the boys are chasing each other through the woods.

DISCUSSING IDEAS
Most of the action of the game in scene 5 (see opposite) is improvised, but in order for the director to know what to do with the camera, he runs through the young actors' ideas with them.

weekend. The preproduction will be long. Devising a
story to fit the genre/title, props, etc., is always time-
consuming, requiring brainstorming and openness to
other people's ideas. It seems to be inevitable that if
there is a genre your team particularly does not like,
that will be the one you get. The story has to be devised
within the limitations of your props, locations, and
actors, whether these limitations are imposed by the
organizers or by your team's dynamics.

Starting to film

Once a story has been fleshed out, start filming as soon
as possible. There will not be a lot of time for rehearsals,
so shoot right away; if you can get two cameras, that's
even better. Film all the rehearsals, and keep an accurate
shot log to make it easier to find the best takes when it
comes to editing. The more you shoot, the better your
choice will be.

Get all the shots you need but don't spend too much
time doing it, as you will need at least 12 hours to edit
and add sound. You also need to factor in time for the
unforeseen—such as equipment failure.

Adding a soundtrack

Make your rough cut as quickly as possible to give your
composer time to create the soundtrack. Musicians will
often have a supply of musical motifs they can access—
ideas they have been tinkering with but have never
completed—and that can be easily adapted, especially
if they are digital recordings. Once the final cut of the
visuals has been made, the soundtrack can be adjusted
to fit.

When your film is edited and the soundtrack is mixed
and synced, it is just a matter of transferring it from your
computer to the specified medium and returning to the
place from which you started.

Completing one of these 48-hour challenges will
probably change the way you approach filmmaking for
a long time. Watching crews agonizing for hours over a
20-second shot will be just that, agonizing. If there is no
organized 48-hour challenge in your area, you can still
do it yourself, or with some friends.

BUSTED

1. Day—Int: Suburban home
ALEX is ready for school. His backpack is full as we
see him disappear out the front door. His MOTHER comes
down the stairs, calling out to the shutting door as
she spies his English folder lying on the floor. She
picks it up and opens the door.

2. Day—Ext: Suburban street
Alex's mother calls down the street after Alex to
give him his folder. Alex runs back, kisses his
mother, and runs down the street, disappearing around
a corner.

3. Day—Ext: Another suburban street (cont.)
Alex throws the folder under a bush, out of sight,
and continues his journey.

4. Day—Ext: Outside school gates (cont.)
Alex runs past the school gates and finds his friend,
DAVID, waiting for him.

5. Day—Ext: Tree-covered park
From their backpacks the boys pull out camouflage
jackets, balaclavas, and toy guns. They change from
school uniform to army uniform. David faces a tree and
starts counting to himself as Alex runs off into the
woods. David pursues him. The boys play hunter and
hunted all day until one of them is finally "killed."

6. Day—Ext: Suburban home
Alex arrives home as his mother is taking the
garbage out. He is tired but greets his mother
enthusiastically. As he goes toward the door
his mother instinctively picks something from his
hair. She looks at it and does a slow double-take as
her son enters the house.

Fade out
Credits

CHECK THESE OUT

www.48hourfilm.com—A national film challenge in the U.S.
www.dvmission.ning.com—U.K. and European film-challenge site
www.seventhsanctum.com—A genre and title generator site

THE ONE-PIECE FILM

The one-piece film is a new form of short filmmaking that originated in Japan. It is one shot to capture one story.

In the 1990s, small groups of filmmakers and actors in Japan began using consumer-level video cameras and improvising short narratives for these films. Often, a general idea for a narrative was set up and actors had a concept of the basic story but were allowed to improvise around that story. Humor and irony are prevalent in most one-pieces, but the content and execution is open to the filmmaker.

SETTING UP
It is vital that you take time to position your camera carefully as you will not be able to move it, or zoom in on the action.

THE RULES

1. The camera is not allowed to move in any way. No pans, tilts, or handheld movement of any kind. It is critically important that you pick your camera position and pick it well.
2. Each film consists of a single unedited shot. It is a one-take story, so there is no need to keep several takes. If a mistake is made during the recording, record over the flubbed take.
3. Props and special lighting are not allowed. Challenge yourself and utilize the things in the location that you find. Try not to bring in things external to the location you shoot in.
4. No postproduction. There isn't the need to add music or effects because your story will stand on its own.
5. The one-piece is no longer than two minutes long.

POWERFUL PERFORMANCES
With no props, special effects, or fancy editing permitted, you must rely on the acting sills of your cast and the strength of your story to captivate you audience.

OBJECTIVES >>

- Shoot a one-piece story
- Generate a story idea
- Choose the location
- Plan the shot

Assignment

Aim:
Produce a story without anything but actors.

Crew:
Director

Camera operator

Sound recorder

Equipment:
DV camera

Camera tripod

PLAN, BUT BE FLEXIBLE
With only two minutes to tell your story, planning is key. However, allowing your actors to improvise around a basic story line can take your film in interesting directions.

SHOOTING AN INTERVIEW

Shoot a two-minute documentary-style interview. Shooting interviews is the basis from which to practice fundamental lighting and camera techniques.

OBJECTIVES >>
- **Light the subject**
- **Learn about camera framing**
- **Appreciate the steps to a successful interview shoot**

GETTING A RESPONSE
Try to conduct the interview in a setting where your subject will be comfortable, as they will feel more at ease and speak more candidly.

The objective
Shoot a two-minute sit-down interview concerning any subject or subject matter of your choice. Refer to Project 2 for story ideas (see page 146). Through your interview, try to reveal the true nature or identity of the subject or subject matter.

The challenge
Tell the story or reveal the reality and truth of a subject or subject matter by intercutting your interview with a series of interesting B-roll shots. Attempt to compose all of your shots in clear but interesting ways that may strengthen the idea or understanding of the truth of your topic. Make pretty pictures!

The rules
Your interview should be based in realism. Your framing should be clearly thought out, focused, and properly lit and exposed. Your interview should not exceed two minutes in length.

The interview
The objective of the interview is to direct a conversation that will stand without the interviewer's questions, to evoke memories and feelings in an interviewee, to provoke them into self-examination, and to take the interviewee over some personal threshold of realization that requires effort and courage on both parts.

To achieve this, consider:
- Telling the interviewee in advance that you only want to ask about an event that has been pivotal in their lives.
- A pre-interview so you can determine what is at stake and what is involved.

Concentrate on the responses of the subject and determine the underlying issues, but be sure not to ask any deeply probing questions until the filmed interview.

Ease your subject into the interview
If your interviewee is nervous, there are a few things you can do to create calm. Before beginning an interview, tell the subject:
- Not to worry about the recording, as anything can be edited out later; these are technical concerns for the crew.
- That you may interrupt if they get away from the subject or if you want more information.
- That you want the question reiterated in the answer so that you can later cut out your questions.

Provide a seat that does not spin or rotate. Anxious interviewees will drive you crazy with nervous rotations.

Conducting the interview
Try to set up the interview in the subject's own environment, such as a place of work, a kitchen, study, or whatever else seems appropriate. Try to make the setting comment on the individual. Consider visiting the site where an event occurred to ignite the feelings of the subject.

You as interviewer must listen very closely, not just for what you expect but also for the utterly unexpected subtext. Most missed opportunities happen when the

CONTROL YOUR ENVIRONMENT

Shooting an interview in a natural environment looks great but can be tricky. Be sure to have complete control over the room before committing to use it. Power, sound, and the ability to lock the room down are critical considerations.

---

interviewee was given a general question rather than asked something specific. Before leaving an interview, prepare the ground for a return visit in case you discover afterward that essential information is missing.

At the end of the interview, review the footage and establish that:
- The interviewee was at ease and spoke interestingly and freely.
- They supplied relevant facts about the subject matter.
- They supplied relevant facts about themselves.
- They gave an emotional perspective—how they felt, what the subject means in personal terms.
- They revealed their own change and development.
- They explained how they faced the substantial issue or implication for the first time.
- No questions or narration are necessary to make sense of the answers.

Assignment

Aim:

Create an interview that could fit into Project 2 (see page 146).

Crew:

Director

Camera

Sound recorder

Equipment:

DSLR or DV camera

Editing software

Five steps to shooting a successful interview:

1. Find a suitable location
- Make sure there is little distraction.
- Be sure that the location is quiet.
- If the location is in a building, get permission to be there, and request a private room.

2. Shoot the interview
- Shoot a wide establishing shot.
- Shoot the interviewee first.
- Re-frame after the answer for a more visually interesting interview.
- If possible, shoot the interview sitting down.
- Keep the interview short and to the point.
- If re-asks aren't needed, have the answers phrased so as to contain the question.

3. Shoot the re-asks
- Shoot the questions that had the best answers.
- If the interviewee leaves, frame the interviewer to appear looking at the interviewee.
- The interviewer performs reactions to the questions.

4. Shoot the B-roll
- B-roll is shot to enhance and embellish the story you are telling.
- This footage can be cut over top of the answer being given.
- B-roll is generally shot at other locations.

5. Gather stock footage
- Stock footage is previously recorded material.
- It is also known as file footage, found footage, or archive footage.
- This footage is gathered from other sources, such as production houses, television stations, etc.

- The interview was structured as a story with a beginning, middle, and end.
- The climactic moment is well placed.
- Nowhere did the interviewer overlap the interviewee.
- The sound quality was clear and intimate.
- The visuals had high impact.

Two-person point-of-view interview

There are several objectives here, but the main one is to find, manage, and present human conflict. Use your ingenuity to film a conversation with conflicting viewpoints that appears spontaneous.

First, locate and pre-interview two people, being careful at this stage to be non-directive. Pick a shared event in their lives about which each feels very differently and for which there are photos, movie or video footage, or other visual documentation on which they can concentrate. Note in advance what their cutaway images might support, so you can direct subject matter where visual support exists.

Make sure they cover everything you thought significant during your research phase. Aim to shoot a 10-minute interaction. You should:

- Do/say whatever is necessary so their exchange becomes natural.
- Make sure known differences of emotion and perception emerge strongly, and be ready to intercede if they do not.
- Get them to talk to each other rather than the camera.
- Contrive the setting so that the frame is packed and interesting and so that subject placement does not force awkward camera movements.
- Shoot from one camera position only, or use multiple cameras.
- Use zoom to shoot different-sized images of each person.
- Make sure the camera follows the scene's psychological focus.
- Shoot tons of reaction shots from each person.

Streeters

"Streeters" are interviews shot on the street with random participants. When shooting streeters, remember to stay informal and really listen to the subtext of the responses.

Four questioning techniques:

1. Closed-ended:
A question leading to an abrupt answer, usually a yes or no answer. This is ideal for interviewing subjects who cannot necessarily speak about specifics due to a legal situation.

2. Open-ended:
A question that encourages conversation and gives the interviewee wide latitude in their response. Think of using the five "W"s in your questions: who, what, where, when, and why. This will engage the interviewee in conversation.

3. Reflective:
Encourages conversation, allowing the interviewer and subject to bounce off each other's comments. This approach requires that you have done your homework—your research into the person and their history.

4. Directive:
Guides interviewee to your desired response. This type of interview is often very well rehearsed and planned out. It has to be if a clear and precise message is to be delivered. This technique is typical of "call to action" type of documentaries where it is hoped that the audience will "take up arms" or seek to act on a topic or issue.

7

By now you have a lot to think about. Making a film is a long and arduous process that is full of ups and downs. The last remaining pages of this book are dedicated to providing you with some further useful information about resources—specifically, what you can do to work in the movie industry.

THE INDUSTRY

If you are already or have now been bitten by the filmmaking bug, this book will hopefully be an ongoing resource guide for you. Working within the industry is a great way to continue the process of learning how to make a film. Whether it is a large or small show you will always come away having learned something new by watching others make their film. That is the beauty of this filmmaking industry; you will always experience challenges and subsequent growth by being in it in various capacities. Stepping back and being a crew member without the heavy responsibilities of producing or directing can be a real joy and a way to refresh your perspective as a filmmaker. Coming up with new ways to tell stories is what it is all about, and taking on new horizons helps us to be better storytellers.

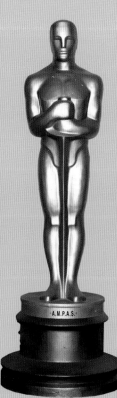

WORKING IN THE ENTERTAINMENT ARTS INDUSTRY

This is not as easy as it sounds: The entertainment arts industry is one of the more difficult industries to get into, the most difficult to work within, and yet ultimately the most rewarding.

So many artists take the time in between shows to make their own projects. They get involved in the local community and make short films and videos. It is a creative outlet that allows for creative freedom. This is where you, as someone wanting to get a start working on the big shows, can start. Make yourself available and get involved in your local filmmaking community. This is where you will be able to help out and network with established industry workers. They are the ones who can ultimately get you started in the industry.

Before you go running off to get involved there are some key things to know, understand, and live with. There are certain industry expectations that seem simple in theory but deep and serious in practice.

Industry expectations
There are three simple points to ponder and take to heart.

1. Be engaged
This is the cornerstone of success in the industry. It is something that a book, school, or individual CANNOT teach you. You must be deeply honest with yourself as you determine whether you have the level of commitment this industry demands of you. You will likely face 18-hour days, six days a week, for several weeks on end. It will wear you down and take you to a place that will force you to question why you ever wanted to work in entertainment to begin with. All the while your supervisors are watching you, and making judgments on how you deal with stress, boredom, and countless hours doing a seemingly mundane task over and over again. Ask yourself:

Can I take direction? Everyone wants to be a director, but the industry looks for those who can take direction. This is how you learn to be a good director.

Do I speak when spoken to? There is no argument or discussion at first; just do as you're told.

Can I be the consummate professional even when I am brutally tired and just want to go and sleep? Somehow you must summon up more energy to go on another minute, hour, and day.

2. Be trainable
Just when you thought reading books, going to school, and actually making short films was enough, you are faced with this statement. It is not about getting more formal education. It is about more than that—the balance between being "book smart" and "street smart." To be street smart you need to fully understand, live, and breathe the following statements:
- Hurry up and wait!
- Think on your feet!
- Do it this way!

If you are simply "book smart" there is the risk of becoming rigid. Everyone has their own way of doing things and it is up to you to be able to adapt to those ways and means. For example, if you get a job at Pixar, you more than likely will not be using the software that you learned with in school. The software at Pixar is proprietary, and you will have to adapt to it and learn it fast. This is the crux of being trainable. Again, take direction and do it without a word.

3. Have a portfolio
This is not a ton of your work that you think the industry should and must see. This is a body of your work that the industry has said you must have and present. Industry people do not have time to look at work that is irrelevant. It is up to you to find out what they want and provide it. A good example of this is an animation house: They will want to see a 30-second, fully rendered bouncing ball. Nothing else. This is their benchmark for assessing whether you have the right abilities. Make sure that, whoever you are meeting, you meet their criteria.

The reality of working in entertainment arts
You need to be very clear about what you want to work at now, not ten years from now. It is good to have a long-term career goal, but for now just simply getting a job, no matter what it is, should be your focus. You will not necessarily get your dream job right away, but so what? Take the gig and do your very best—as if it is the best job you will ever have. You will have plenty of time

MAKING YOURSELF USEFUL
Working in the film and television industry is complicated, but common sense on set will prevent you from making errors that could hurt your integrity. Always look for something to do, but know when to ask about doing it.

later to move forward from where you are now and head in the direction you really want. A lot of workers in the industry got their first job in a department not of their choosing; most ended up where they wanted to be in the end.

You have to get to know those who do the hiring and firing: NOT by making phone calls or busting in on a film set, though. Networking takes on different forms but is essentially a matter of being in the right place at the right time. No one has a crystal ball to predict when and where the right place is, but you can increase the odds:

- Get involved with local filmmaking communities. These are typically not-for-profit centers. Industry people love to hang out there because they can make their own films how they want. They are places that see a lot of independent short films being made. You can volunteer on productions and get some real set experience and get to know working industry pros.
- Attend conferences and festivals in your area. If you are really into filmmaking, this is a great opportunity to introduce yourself and get to know local industry people.

Unions

Virtually every film and television production doing business is operating within union collective bargaining agreements. Even low-budget productions ($10 million or less) have special agreements in order to get their show shot.

It is in your best interests to gain membership in the union of your choice. The reason is simple: You'll gain knowledge and experience that you can use in your own filmmaking efforts. It also helps you pay the bills and carve out a career at the same time.

Do your homework before joining, though. Each union has very specific requirements for membership. There are a lot of very specific tasks and items you will need to complete as part of the process. These processes are meant to include individuals who are serious about working in a very tough industry. Those who are not passionate and committed will never be able to endure the intensity of the industry's demands.

Here are the unions that typically represent specific trades:

I.A.T.S.E. (International Alliance of Theatrical Stage Employees)

This technical union contains groups such as the camera departments, art departments, and so on. Each department has very specific requirements in order to gain permit status. Search out the local chapter in your area for more information.

10 golden rules for getting your film seen

1. Have a great screenplay.

2. Have a really great screenplay.

3. Use the best equipment you can.

4. Use the best talent you can.

5. Have perfect sound on the film.

6. Have the film in a format that can be shown in a movie theater.

7. Follow all the submission guidelines for the festivals you enter.

8. Network and meet as many industry people as possible.

9. Be passionate and enthusiastic, but thick-skinned.

10. Make sure your screenplay is THE BEST.

CHECK THESE OUT

- *The Guerrilla Film Makers' Movie Blueprint,* Chris Jones (Continuum International Publishing Group, 2003)
- *Raindance Producers' Lab Lo-To-No Budget Filmmaking,* Elliot Grove (Focal Press, 2004)
- *Make Your Own Damn Movie,* Lloyd Kaufman (L.A. Weekly Books, 2003)
- *Rebel Without a Crew,* Robert Rodriguez (Plume Books, 1996)
- *Making Movies,* Sidney Lumet (Vintage (reprint ed.), 1996)
- *Shot by Shot: A Practical Guide to Filmmaking,* John Cantine and Susan Howard (Pittsburgh Filmmakers, 3rd edition, 2000)

The Directors Guild of America (DGA)

This union is the production management team. It covers a number of different job descriptions. It is most certainly not a "creative" team in the true sense of the term. Production management is creative in other ways, and really, without a solid management team the show will never go to camera. It is a grueling side to the business, but someone has to do it.

The Directors Guild of Canada (DGC)

This is a union representing all non-technical crew such as directors, production managers, unit managers, assistant directors, trainee assistant directors (TADs), location managers, assistant location managers, trainee assistant location managers, and production assistants (the entry-level position).

The main function of any union is to maintain fair and reasonable working conditions and rates of pay for its members.

In order to obtain membership in the Directors Guild you must first obtain experience in the categories of work that the Guild represents. You must also acquire recognition from senior members of the Guild regarding your professional standing and abilities.

In order to assist, the Directors Guild has the Permit Program. This program enables individuals to gain the necessary experience and contacts needed to apply for membership as a production assistant.

Your first contact with the Guild office may seem impersonal to you. Keep in mind that you are dealing with an extremely busy office, and the staff will not have a lot of time for you. Acquire a production list from the Guild. This list outlines productions that are in production and ones that are in negotiation. You should concentrate on the shoots that are not yet in production, as they are the ones in the process of being crewed up.

Mail, email or deliver your résumé and cover letter to the location manager (LM) or the assistant location manager (ALM). If you have office experience and are interested in working in the production office, you can mail, email, or deliver your résumé to the production coordinator (PC). It is not advisable to phone the production office.

One of the requirements for membership into the Directors Guild is 90 days of work. You must report each job to the union before starting. When reporting these days, provide your name, your registration number and its expiration date, the name of the show, and the date(s) you will be working.

What to expect

At first you will be given jobs that seem menial, tedious, and lacking in responsibility, but you should realize several things before you complain about this type of work. This is a testing ground to see whether you are able to handle greater authority. Each position in production requires its own blend of endurance, communication skills, and dedication. It never gets easy.

At times you may be required to work outside in an unsheltered area for 15 hours or more, for example. Make sure you are prepared with the right clothing, raingear, etc. Make sure your clothing is not bright, or this will reflect onto surfaces that are potentially within the camera's range.

Your employer will be looking for people who are good-natured, intelligent, interested, observant, and who are able to maintain a good attitude while standing in the rain for hours, cleaning up garbage in downtown alleyways, dealing with a crowd, or guarding a lonely parking lot for hours on end.

Keep yourself informed at all times, but don't hassle your department head with every question that comes into your head. However, if you are given instructions that you don't understand, ask for more information.

Always be aware of safety and the need for good communication. Watch for potential safety hazards and report them to the department head immediately. If the production company chooses to upgrade you beyond production assistant, it is your responsibility to inform the company that you are not yet a member of the Guild and to ask for a copy of a signed permit request approved by the Directors Guild prior to commencing work.

Move to features

Once you've shot one, two, or more short films and are starting to receive the recognition you knew you deserved, you may want to move on to a more ambitious project—a feature film. Although the principles are the same, at least technically, working with the enlarged canvas of a feature requires a different approach.

Story

A short film, like a short story, is a vignette from a much larger, ongoing series of events, although complete within itself. A feature requires more exposition. Characters need to be fully developed, relationships and settings established. Telling a story in 90-plus minutes gives you the time to do this, but in that space you also have to get your idea across and keep the audience enthralled, entertained, scared, or whatever your intention is. For many filmmakers this is a natural format, one with which they feel most comfortable, while others revel in the short format. If you find short films too restricting, full length could be for you. Just make sure that you have a strong script before you start any other aspect of the production.

Shooting

If you are going to all the trouble of making a feature-length film, you want to be sure it is seen by as wide an audience as possible. You are making them sit and watch for an hour and a half, so you need to ensure that image quality is good, and this entails using the best cameras you can get. You don't have to use film—some high-profile features have been shot on digital SLRs—but the cameras do have to be of at least that standard. With the new HD DV cameras coming out, that should not be a problem. Beyond them is the new range of professional HD cameras. Manufacturers of these cameras are very eager for them to be used to gain market acceptance, so if they like your script it may be possible to negotiate special deals.

One of the big differences between shooting a feature and a short is the time it takes, and therefore the cost and commitment involved. However long your ten-minute movie took, a feature will take at least nine times as long, but realistically more—depending on the nature of the screenplay.

A lot will depend on the logistics involved in getting all the cast and crew in the same place at the same time, and that place (the location) being available on the same day as the people. This is where the time is eaten up—in preproduction—which is why it is very important to start putting into practice all the right working methods from your very first short. If you can't organize a small shoot, you don't stand a chance on something bigger. Your rehearsal time will be expanded, as there will be more scenes and more lines to learn.

The time for shooting each setup should be about the same as for the short film, unless you are going for more involved lighting or complex set pieces. You may want to shoot more coverage, especially if you are using video, which will extend your schedule. The longest job is going to be postproduction, with hours more footage to cut and a longer story to pull together. Every aspect is just going to take longer.

Budget

If you are without any funding, your job is going to be that much harder. Getting someone to give up a weekend or two is not difficult, but persuading them to commit to a feature is another matter. A lot of lo-no budget films struggle and fail because of this. If you are relying on people to work for nothing, be as flexible as you can with your shooting schedule and your projected completion date, and do as much of it as you can yourself.

Ideally, your short films should have snared you some funding or sponsorship. If you have money, don't fall into the trap of spending it all on equipment and sets, neglecting the cast and crew. They are the ones making your movie, not the camera. Remember this and they will be loyal and give you more than you expect.

Whatever you decide to do—short, feature, drama, documentary—go do it. If you don't know where to start, try stimulating your imagination with some of the projects on pages 142–155.

International arts grants

- Australian Film Commission: www.afc.gov.au/funding/
- British Council: www.britishcouncil.org/arts-film.htm
- Canada Council for the Arts: www.canadacouncil.ca/mediaarts/
- Film Arts Foundation: www.filmarts.org/grants
- Global Film Initiative: www.globalfilm.org (feature films only)
- Manitoba Arts Council: www.artscouncil.mb.ca/english/vis_grantind.html
- Moxie Films: www.moxie-films.com
- National Endowment for the Arts: www.nea.gov
- Princess Grace Awards: www.pgfusa.com/grants-program/overview
- Roy W. Dean Film and Video Grants: www.fromtheheartproductions.com
- UK Film Council: www.ukfilmcouncil.org.uk/funding/

Check your local or state arts council as they usually have film and video funding.

50 MOVIES TO SEE BEFORE YOU TRY

BEST FOR DIRECTING

1. *Giant* (1956)

Edna Ferber specialized in writing sprawling family sagas, several of them set in the West. In *Giant*, Bick Benedict (Rock Hudson) is a Texas cattle baron who marries a spirited Maryland belle, Leslie (Elizabeth Taylor). Bick's sister has left some of the property to Jett Rink (James Dean), a former employee. Rink discovers oil and becomes immensely rich, but his personal life is a disappointment and he declines into alcoholism. As Bick and Leslie grow older, they are concerned with who will run the ranch after they've gone.

At well over three hours, *Giant* certainly lives up to its title. But the performances are outstanding, not least James Dean's, who was tragically killed in a car crash shortly after completing his part. Director George Stevens does justice to the immensity of the Texas landscape, and unusually for the time the film deals interestingly with both racial and class differences.

2. *The Apartment* (1960)

Inspired by David Lean's *Brief Encounter* (1945), director Billy Wilder had to wait ten years for the necessary slackening of censorship to be able to tell the story of the "third" man, who lends his apartment to the adulterous couple. Despite its sensitive subject matter, *The Apartment* won five Academy Awards (including Best Director), and is now considered by many to be the last truly "realist" film made by its director.

Some have criticized the amorality of Jack Lemmon's character C.C. Baxter, who gets promoted because he helps some of the executives at his company in their efforts to cheat on their wives. But Lemmon brings to the role a solid touch of humanity, and Baxter appears unwillingly trapped in a situation that already exists and is beyond his control. Despite its humor, *The Apartment* is indeed a severe social critique, as well as an examination of contemporary American life and sexual mores.

3. *One Flew Over The Cuckoo's Nest* (1975)

Based on Ken Kesey's best-selling novel, the film is set in a state mental home where anti-establishment wiseguy Randle P. McMurphy (Jack Nicholson) is sent for rehabilitation. While there he falls under the watchful eye of the sadistic Nurse Ratched (Louise Fletcher), and soon stirs up a rebellion against her.

A groundbreaking film that Kesey apparently never wanted to see, *One Flew Over the Cuckoo's Nest* made Oscar-night history when it became only the second film to win five major awards. Each award was well deserved, with Czech director Milos Forman delivering a hypnotic and humanistic movie filled with eccentric characters and garnering a career-best performance from Fletcher. Nicholson, of course, is mesmerizing as the incarcerated but free-spirited McMurphy, and the scenes between him and Fletcher's contemptible Nurse Ratched are the most electric of this modern classic of American cinema.

4. *The Deer Hunter* (1978)

The second picture by director Michael Cimino, *The Deer Hunter* was immediately declared both a cinematic masterwork and a film of gross historical distortion. Somewhere between these extremes it also became a commercial hit.

Opening in a Pennsylvania steel town, three mill workers, Michael (Robert De Niro), Steven (John Savage), and Nick (Christopher Walken), are drafted for war. All three are made prisoners of war who finally escape their torment, albeit with several complications.

Over more than three hours of screen time, *The Deer Hunter* presents strong performances and a group of remarkably intense set pieces. In between are various depictions of a collapsing community, every scene of which features career-making moments from the likes of De Niro, Walken, and Meryl Streep. *The Deer Hunter* was among the first mainstream American movies to focus on

Vietnam. It provided indelible images for the pop imagination before earning a Best Picture Oscar.

5. *Ordinary People* (1980)

It is a source of indignation to some that Robert Redford's beautifully crafted directorial debut should have bested *Raging Bull* in the Academy Awards, taking the Oscars for Best Picture and Direction. But those who don't "get" this movie are missing a remarkably fine, intimate drama.

Timothy Hutton plays high-school teen Conrad Jarrett, overwhelmed by guilt and suicidal depression since his older brother drowned in an accident he survived. There is no understanding for him from his distant mother, Beth (Mary Tyler Moore), and his easygoing father, Calvin (Donald Sutherland), doesn't know how to talk to him about what matters. Only his father's love can save the boy, when connecting with him forces a painful choice.

The principals are superb, particularly Moore, and there is a radiant debut from Elizabeth McGovern as Conrad's girlfriend. Redford's films are uniquely American and always graceful. This signature production epitomizes his liberal humanism.

6. *Reds* (1981)

Warren Beatty's tribute to journalist John Reed is an intriguing look into American political radicals of the early 20th century.

Beatty worked for years on *Reds* and he is credited as producer, director, screenwriter, and performer. The film was a daring venture, mostly because Reed, its central focus, was virtually unknown to the cinema public of the late 20th century. Limited by Hollywood conventions, Beatty is able only to suggest the complex and frenetic aspects of Reed's meteoric career.

The first half of *Reds* is devoted to Reed's love affair with feminist intellectual Louise Bryant (Diane Keaton), then once Reed leaves for Russia, *Reds* does an excellent job of delineating the epic events of the developing revolution.

Beatty gives the film a documentary flair by interspersing fictional sequences with short interviews featuring eyewitnesses of the period. *Reds* is arguably Hollywood's most effective presentation of politics and ideological conflict in 20th-century America.

7. *Terms of Endearment* (1983)

Larry McMurty's novel was translated into an award-winning movie by screenwriter/director James L. Brooks. It remains a textbook example of how to make a successful mainstream American weepie.

Debra Winger stars as Emma, the stubborn daughter of possessive, often smothering mother Aurora (Shirley MacLaine). *Terms of Endearment* follows their relationship, from Emma trying to extricate herself from her mother, to a truce when Emma is dying of cancer. Brooks manages to keep sickly sentiment at bay and in doing so helps his cast deliver one of the most moving deathbed scenes in cinema history.

Subtly played by Winger, Jeff Daniels, John Lithgow, and Danny DeVito, *Terms of Endearment* features scene-stealing performances from MacLaine and Jack Nicholson that threaten to overtake the film. However, Brooks paces the movie in such a manner—cleverly mixing humor and tragedy—that their star turns only enhance this melancholy look at modern family relationships.

8. *A Passage to India* (1984)

More or less faithfully adapting E. M. Forster's story of class and cultural conflict in colonial India, David Lean's final film, *A Passage to India*, is more a movie of ideas than a movie of spectacle. In the directorial hands of Lean—ever the consummate craftsman—the film blazes by, and if he too often relies on frequent collaborator Alec Guinness for humor and James Fox to make obvious the movie's themes, Lean's respect for the script and his actors allows them to transcend the sometimes fetishistic depiction of India.

Particularly strong is the wan Judy Davis, who in her search for the "real" India—neither homogenized nor shunned by her fellow Brits—gets more than she bargained for in Victor Banerjee, whose obsequious and oblivious Dr. Aziz sparks in the mind of Davis's naïve Ms. Quested a primal aversion to "going native."

9. *Forrest Gump* (1994)
A brisk trot through events in American history from the 1950s until the 1980s, *Forrest Gump* succeeds as both epic and character study. This is thanks to clever, if occasionally sentimental, direction from Robert Zemeckis and a sensitive central performance from Tom Hanks, who won his second Best Actor Academy Award in as many years for the role.

We meet Forrest, an amiable idiot savant, sitting on a bench, waiting for a bus to take him to meet his childhood friend Jenny (Robin Wright Penn). While lingering there, he relates his life story to a succession of people who share the bench—and what a story it is. Raised by his mother (Sally Field), Forrest went on to experience many of America's most famous events of the 20th century. Over three decades he meets John F. Kennedy and Elvis; becomes a Vietnam war hero; and a shrimp tycoon, all the while he dreams he will be reunited with Jenny.

10. *The Departed* (2006)
Based upon Hong Kong action film *Infernal Affairs* (2002) and its two sequels, Martin Scorsese's *The Departed* received popular and critical acclaim, and five Academy Award nominations, including Best Director. *The Departed* features strong performances from Matt Damon and Leonardo DiCaprio as "moles" working undercover for the mob and the police respectively. The action unfolds at a steady pace, propelled by plenty of the director's trademark stylistic flourishes, from the skillful manipulation of the soundtrack, to an array of dizzying whip-pans and complex tracking shots.

What is most remarkable about *The Departed* is the intelligence with which Scorsese and screenwriter William Monahan adapted the *Infernal Affairs* films for Western audiences. The themes of deception and conflicted loyalties translated smoothly, but more difficult is the transplantation of the action from the glossy cityscape of contemporary Hong Kong to the vastly different social and geographical terrain of Boston.

BEST FOR EDITING

11. *The French Connection* (1971)
With *Bullitt* (1968) and *Dirty Harry* (1971), *The French Connection* (directed by William Friedkin) spearheaded the cop-movie revival that took place around 1970. It centers on the fanatical efforts of New York City police detective "Popeye" Doyle (Gene Hackman) to intercept a massive heroin shipment engineered by the entrepreneur Charnier (Fernando Rey). Although its view of the war on drugs as a class struggle waged by street cops against establishment fat cats now seems dated, *The French Connection* remains tremendously exciting and powerful, primarily because of its vigorous editing, epic vision of urban decay, and uncompromisingly pessimistic ending.

The editing—its rough-edged energy enhanced by jagged, truncated scene transitions—conveys both off-balance disorientation and reckless forward propulsion. The celebrated chase scene, in which Doyle's car hurtles down a busy avenue in pursuit of an elevated train, never seems overblown; it simply extends the kinetic, careering, tunnel-vision effect sustained throughout the film.

12. *The Sting* (1973)
George Roy Hill first directed Paul Newman and Robert Redford in *Butch Cassidy and the Sundance Kid* (1969). Assembled again four years later in the caper pic *The Sting*, Hill gave the actors more room to play, though this time without any tragic resonance.

Set in post-Depression Chicago, Henry Gondorff (Newman) and Johnny Hooker (Redford) are two conmen with ambition. After mobster Doyle Lonnegan (Robert Shaw) kills one of their friends, they set out for revenge. The subsequent effort, built on smoke, mirrors, and a number of situational reversals, also depends on a dense network within Chicago's criminal underworld.

Sparkling wit abounds as a supporting cast of smart men pitch personal style to other smart men. Newman and Redford look great, and into their friendship is entrenched the joy of screen masters

jousting in a comic adventure centered on loyalty and deception.

13. *Star Wars* (1977)
Writer–director George Lucas's film was not expected to be a success. A "sci-fi Western" with a virtually unknown principal cast, studio bosses were so convinced the movie would flop that they happily gave Lucas the merchandising rights to any *Star Wars* products.

After the death of the aunt and uncle who raised him, a headstrong young man, Luke Skywalker (Mark Hamill), teams up with an old Jedi Knight, Ben "Obi-Wan" Kenobi (Alec Guinness), two creaky robots, a cocky spaceship pilot named Han Solo (a star-making performance from Harrison Ford), and Solo's furry Wookie pal to rescue a princess (Carrie Fisher) from an evil guy wearing a big plastic helmet.

In giving the world *Star Wars*, Lucas succeeded in making much more than just a movie; he made a world, a new style of cinema, and an unforgettable outer space opera that has been many times imitated but never bettered.

14. *Raging Bull* (1980)
This boxing biopic was a personal project for actor Robert De Niro, who discovered the as-told-to autobiography of former middleweight champion Jake La Motta and persuaded director Martin Scorsese and writer Paul Schrader to commit to the apparently unpromising material.

After many years and setbacks, La Motta (De Niro) wins the champion's belt, but in screen time a few minutes later he is clawing off the jewels to pawn so he can bribe his way out of a morals charge.

Raging Bull is a poetic, daring exploration of the soul of an inarticulate, violent man. The miracle is that De Niro, in a textbook example of screen acting, can find as much sympathy as he does for La Motta. It's a remarkable feat, with the actor equally convincing as the wolverine-sleek punching machine of the early bouts and the fat-bellied shambles La Motta becomes when his career is over.

15. *Gandhi* (1982)
"The truth," Richard Attenborough said, "is that I never wanted to be a director at all. I just wanted to direct that film." Attenborough survived 20 years of delays, frustrations, and personal financial risk to recreate the life and times of Mohandas Kharamchand Gandhi (1869–1948), in a way that would touch audiences of East and West alike.

John Briley's script opens with the assassination of Gandhi in 1948, and then flashes back to his beginnings as a young lawyer, protesting racial discrimination in South Africa. It traces the main biographical landmarks of his battle against British imperial domination, and for an integrated Indian society.

Gandhi triumphantly disproved the general tenet that films which are long in the making usually fall short of their ambition; it found an instant response in critical acclaim and a worldwide audience. Its eight Academy Awards marked a record, surpassed only by *Ben-Hur* (1959).

16. *The Killing Fields* (1984)
Director Roland Joffe's morally earnest film depicting the disastrous aftermath of American involvement in Cambodian politics during the Vietnam War era offers a bravura performance by Sam Waterston as journalist Sydney Schanberg.

The Killing Fields divides into two parts, with Schanberg's decision to remain after the Khmer Rouge take the country occupying the first part. Schanberg's Cambodian assistant, Dith Pran (Haing S. Ngor), assists the Western journalists as they negotiate a series of harrowing encounters with the victors, but despite their attempts to pass him off as a U.S. citizen, he is left behind when they leave. In the second part, Pran endures captivity and evades death, escaping through rice paddies filled with the corpses of his countrymen—the "killing fields"—until he is reunited with Schanberg in New York.

The film does not dwell on international politics, but on the damage done to human dignity by impersonal violence.

17. *JFK* (1991)
No stranger to controversy, director Oliver Stone followed up his powerful post-Vietnam movie *Born on the Fourth of July* with his questioning conspiracy movie *JFK*.

At the picture's heart is Jim Garrison (Kevin Costner), the real-life New Orleans District Attorney who conducted an investigation into the matter from 1966 to 1969. Stone doesn't buy into all of Garrison's theories—some believe he couldn't distinguish real clues from crackpot conspiracy ideas—but uses him as the symbolic center of a film. Using documentary footage as well as flashbacks, reconstructions, quick editing, and a skillful use of words and music, Stone weaves ideas and theories together using the huge mountain of evidence and witness testimony.

Stone would not succeed in getting us to care so completely without a strong central performance from Costner, who holds your attention despite the numerous heavyweight actors who stroll in and out of small roles. A truly astonishing piece of filmmaking.

18. *Unforgiven* (1992)

Clint Eastwood's last Western is a grand one to have ridden out on: dark, gripping, and embracing complex themes, *Unforgiven* is a saga of melancholy beauty and unflinching moral, physical, and historical realism.

Eastwood's William Munny is a retired killer, reformed by the love of a good woman who has died, leaving him to raise two children on a failing farm. Munny struggles to retain his humanity when he teams up with old sidekick Ned (Morgan Freeman) to claim a bounty. Their task: to avenge a knifed prostitute in bleak Big Whiskey, where brutal sheriff Little Bill (Gene Hackman) is indifferent to the women's demands for justice.

This is as fine a piece of craftsmanship as one would expect from Eastwood, who brings to the film all his understanding of a genre he singlehandedly kept alive for 20 years when it was out of fashion.

19. *Secrets & Lies* (1996)

Secrets & Lies, Mike Leigh's gripping, multifaceted comedy-drama, may be his most accessible and optimistic film and remains the celebrated work of a writer–director who is often best known for his anger and merciless skewering of class differences in Thatcherite and post-Thatcher Britain.

Hortense, a young black optometrist (Marianne Jean-Baptiste), seeks out her white biological mother (Brenda Blethyn), a factory worker who put her up for adoption at birth. As the two become acquainted, tensions build between the mother and another illegitimate daughter (Claire Rushbrook), between the mother

and her brother (Timothy Spall), and between him and his wife (Phyllis Logan), everything leading to a ferocious climax.

The dense, Ibsen-like plotting of family revelations in *Secrets & Lies* is dramatically satisfying and the acting is so strong—with Spall a particular standout—that you're carried along as if by a tidal wave.

20. *Crash* (2004)

Crash is about the side effects of Los Angelenos interrupting each other's lives. Insert your preferred ethnic conflict, ripen with any available inciting event, and the scope is suddenly broad but clear.

There are several standout characters: Detective Waters (Don Cheadle) and his partner Ria (Jennifer Esposito) investigate a murder; power-hungry DA Rick (Brendan Fraser) and his wife Jean (Sandra Bullock) are car-jacked by crooks; and Officer Ryan (Matt Dillon) and his partner Tom (Ryan Phillippe) harass a yuppie couple. Finally TV director Cameron (Terrence Howard) and studious locksmith Daniel (Michael Pena) help convenience-store owner Farhad (Shaun Toub), which leads to unexpected consequences as more paths cross and re-cross.

Written by director Paul Haggis and Bobby Moresco, *Crash* exists between realism and fantasy. It is a study of closely held bigotry; of characters trying to navigate a post-PC age; and of how we are led to treat one another.

BEST FOR CINEMATOGRAPHY

21. *Taxi Driver* (1976)

"Some day a real rain will come and wash all this scum off the street." So mutters tormented taxi driver malcontent Travis Bickle, played with maximum intensity by Robert De Niro in the first of his lead turns for Martin Scorsese. He's become so inured to the world around him that he feels numb, invisible, and impotent.

He tries to woo beautiful Betsy (Cybill Shepherd), and when his awkward romantic advances are rebuffed, his alienation intensifies. After trying to rejoin society, Bickle's next goal is to destroy it, beginning with the planned assassination of a presidential candidate. When this plan also fails he then tries to redeem society, with the suicide-mission rescue of an underage prostitute (Jodie Foster) from her abusive pimp.

Portraits of urban malaise and anomie don't come any bleaker, or more claustrophobic than *Taxi Driver*. We view the city from Bickle's relentlessly isolated perspective, with few peripheral glimmers of hope.

22. *Close Encounters of the Third Kind* (1977)

A terrific sci-fi mystery which climaxes in first contact with extraterrestrials, *Close Encounters* incorporates themes that recur throughout director Steven Spielberg's work: rescue, redemption, and affirmation of an individual's worth.

When Roy Neary's (Richard Dreyfuss) UFO encounter is dismissed he becomes obsessed with discovering what his experience means, alienating his family in the process. The only person who understands is Melinda Dillon's Jillian Guiler, driven by her own search for her son (Cary Guffey), who was taken in a terrifying visitation at her home.

While *E.T.* (1982) may be even more revealing of his psyche, *Close Encounters* is a definitive Spielberg film in both style and substance. The five-tone greeting-cum-language musical motif by John Williams and the mashed potato mountain both directly entered popular culture, and the collective gasp of awe at the mothership coming over the mountain serves as yet another testimonial to Spielberg's gift for wonder.

23. *Fanny and Alexander* (1982)

Showing the darker side of the human spirit without flinching or melodrama, Ingmar Bergman's dreamy, allegorical films present life as it is rather than how we wish it would be.

This part-autobiography spans a stormy year in the life of a brother and sister (Pernilla Allwin and Bertil Guve) born into an aristocratic family in turn-of-the-century Sweden. Beginning at a luxurious family Christmas, it switches to their miserable life after the death of their much-loved father.

Fanny and Alexander's length and languorous, careful pace may put modern action viewers off, but Bergman's cinematographer Sven Nykvist uses lustrous lighting to make each frame a delight. The entire film has a dreamy sense of the unreal, a relief during its more tragic moments. Bergman, ever the

master, wisely structures the tale to have its most horrific and satisfying moment just when the story demands a resolution, so the viewer is left breathless.

24. *The Right Stuff* (1983)

High expectations for this celebratory, epic three-hour drama of America's early manned space program, with its ensemble of actors on the verge of stardom (Ed Harris, Dennis Quaid, and Jeff Goldblum among them), were disappointed by its modest box-office return against a hefty budget. But writer–director Philip Kaufman's offbeat take on the heroics and striking treatment of the visuals saw *The Right Stuff* rewarded with eight Academy Award nominations, four wins, and a cult of admirers for whom the film's aerial and Earth-orbiting space sequences remain sheer bliss.

Adapted from Tom Wolfe's tough, touching, and tale-telling nonfiction chronicle of the Mercury astronauts, the film contrasts the courageous but comparatively unsung exploits of sound-barrier-breaking test pilot Chuck Yeager (Sam Shepard perfectly cast as the laid-back, ruggedly individualistic fly boy) with the selection, training, and media parading of more competitive, crewcut-wearing jocks into an elite, all-American cadre with "the right stuff."

25. *Schindler's List* (1993)

Working from a script by Steven Zaillian, adapting Thomas Keneally's nonfiction novel—a fascinating account of the Nazi businessman Oskar Schindler, who saved the lives of over 1,100 Polish Jews—Steven Spielberg holds our interest over 185 minutes and shows the nuts and bolts of the Holocaust.

An enormous plus is the rich and beautiful black-and-white cinematography by Janusz Kaminski. Spielberg's capacity to milk the maximal intensity out of the terror and pathos in Keneally's book—Polish Jews could be killed at any time by the capriciousness of a labor camp director (Ralph Fiennes)—is complemented by his capacity to milk the glamor of Nazi high life and absolute power. Each emotional register is generally accompanied by a different style of cinematography, and as Liam Neeson's Schindler is our conduit to the Nazi's, Ben

Kingsley's subtle performance provides our conduit to the Polish Jews.

26. *Titanic* (1997)

With a reported budget of over $200 million, even before its release *Titanic* was the most expensive production of all time. Following the film's stupendous box-office success (more than $1 billion worldwide) and the most Academy Awards (11) since *Ben-Hur* (1959), James Cameron was christened a genius.

Both romance and disaster are explored in equal measure. Kate Winslet stars as Rose, the young socialite who falls for steerage passenger Jack (Leonardo DiCaprio) just before the world's most famous ship plunges into its watery grave. Their romance gives the movie its heart and Cameron piles on the special effects to truly convey the terror when the ship begins to sink.

A blockbuster if ever there was one, *Titanic* made a superstar of DiCaprio and boasts one of the best-selling soundtracks ever. In terms of production size and sheer epic scale, *Titanic* remains one of the most impressive films of all time.

27. *The Matrix* (1999)

A sci-fi blockbuster that fuses pop-philosophical themes with skillfully choreographed action sequences and state-of-the-art special effects, *The Matrix* was conceived of, written, and directed by brothers Andy and Larry Wachowski.

Keanu Reeves stars as a company man who doubles as a hacker named Neo. A mystery woman, Trinity (Carrie-Anne Moss), introduces him to a legendary Zen-hacker Morpheus (Laurence Fishburne) and Neo discovers that the world in which he previously "existed" is nothing but a computer-generated virtual reality program controlled by the very artificial-intelligence machines developed by mankind years before. Morpheus is certain that Neo is the Messianic "One," who, according to legend, will save the human race from eternal subjugation.

What separates *The Matrix* from other virtual reality science-fiction fare are its epic pretensions, apocalyptic overtones, and breathtaking visuals. New technologies, wire-enhanced gymnastics, and kung fu fight scenes all served to raise the bar significantly for big-budget Hollywood action sequences.

28. *Pan's Labyrinth* (2006)

Pan's Labyrinth is a summative film from Mexican director Guillermo del Toro. Having previously worked on projects that offered a high level of special effects, as well as those that created an unnervingly otherworldly atmosphere, here, in perhaps his most mature picture, the director brings the two strands together, creating a film that is both eerie and built around effects technology.

Set in 1944, *Pan's Labyrinth* tells the story of Ofelia (Ivana Baquero), a young girl who discovers a fantastical world when her mother takes her to northern Spain to join her stepfather, a bitter, twisted member of General Franco's Facist army.

Pan's Labyrinth offers much to admire. But for all its startling beauty and the strength of its performances, the allegorical elements of the story fail to fully gel the reality and fantasy elements, with the result that *Pan's Labyrinth* remains two outstanding halves rather than one spectacular whole.

29. *Avatar* (2009)

Avatar marks a decade's worth of work and hundreds of millions of dollars of investment. Though no *Gone with the Wind* in complexity of character or event, *Avatar* is of the same monumental ambition and singularity of vision. Few have attained such technical achievement in stories of such grand scope while still achieving box-office success.

The story has been told a thousand time but it's a classic. A solider tries to find inner peace during wartime by going native, finding a more grounded, loving existence among the indigenous (alien) peoples he has been taught are his enemy. By using state-of-the-art technologies, crippled Jake Sully (Sam Worthington) is able to run free in his "avatar," a genetically engineered alien body that allows him to survive in the hostile atmosphere of the moon Pandora. Similarly, writer–director James Cameron uses state-of-the-art film technologies to submerge his audience in a new world.

30. *Inception* (2010)

Christopher Nolan is a mastermind filmic architect, and *Inception* is a feat of complicated construction. Dom Cobb (Leonardo DiCaprio) and Arthur (Joseph Gordon-Levitt) are corporate spies specializing in "extraction," the art of going into someone's subconscious to extract their deepest secrets. Cobb has been exiled for espionage, forced to leave his children, and is desperate to return to them. When guaranteed safe passage back to the United States upon completion of a new job, he will stop at nothing to accomplish the task. The job is unlike any other: the implantation of an idea so deep in one's subconscious that it is believed to be one's own—"inception."

Inception is an entirely original idea, a smart action thriller, a poignant and grief-filled drama, and an examination of the deeply hidden recesses of our minds. Although *Inception* plays well on the popcorn-movie premise, its twisted mind-game undercurrents set it apart in cinematic history.

BEST FOR PRODUCTION DESIGN

31. *Metropolis* (1927)

Fritz Lang's *Metropolis* is the first science-fiction epic, with huge sets, thousands of extras, then-state-of-the-art special effects, and a heavy-handed moral.

Freder Fredersen (Gustav Frolich), son of the Master of Metropolis (Alfred Abel), learns, through saintly Maria (Brigitte Helm), of the wretched lives of the workers who keep the supercity going. The Master consults with mad engineer Rotwang (Rudolph Klein-Rogge), who has created a feminoid robot he reshapes as an evil double of Maria and unleashes on the city.

Shortly after its premiere, the film was pulled from distribution and reedited against Lang's wishes: this truncated, form remained best-known, until the 21st century, when a partial restoration made it much closer to Lang's original vision. This new-old version reveals that the futuristic setting isn't intended as prophetic but mythical, with 1920s architecture, industry, design, and politics mingled with the medieval and the Biblical to produce images of striking strangeness.

32. *Day for Night* (1973)

Day for Night is Francois Truffaut's valentine to the process of moviemaking. Truffaut paints an affectionate portrait of good-natured relations among cast and crew in place of the vicious power plays usually presented.

Gentle, bittersweet wisdom is the keynote here, as a rich ensemble of performers (from smooth Jean-Pierre Aumont to firecracker Jean-Pierre Leaud) share fleeting lessons in life, love, and loss. The film deftly sketches a wide range of characters, cleverly compared on certain points. Truffaut stresses the transience, fragility, and unreality of life on a set—even allowing an outsider to finally explode and criticize these film people for their rampant immorality. *Day for Night* gently exposes the many illusions of the filmmaking process, but also maintains our awe over the magic of movies. Characteristically for Truffaut, the brisk montage scenes express a deep affection for, and appreciation of, the mundane practicalities of his trade.

33. *Blade Runner* (1982)

Written in 1968, Philip K. Dick's novel *Do Androids Dream of Electric Sheep?* took 14 years to make it to the big screen, and it was another decade after that before Ridley Scott's jaw-dropping cinematic version was finally recognized as a masterpiece of science-fiction filmmaking. The movie was not well received on its original release and was a financial flop; only after the director's cut was released in 1992 did critics and audiences embrace it.

Acclaimed for its astonishing production design, Scott's vision of 2019 Los Angeles as bleak and neon-lit, with overcrowded streets and acid rain, has often been copied but never bettered. It is through this world that detective Rick Deckard (Harrison Ford) wanders searching out "replicants"—mutinous androids masquerading as humans—while inadvertently falling for one (Sean Young). Packed with symbolism, *Blade Runner* remains one of the most beautifully art directed and visually stunning science-fiction movies ever made.

34. *One Upon a Time in America* (1983)

Beginning during Prohibition and leading up to the late 1960s, the film follows partners-in-crime Robert De Niro and James Woods as two gangland leaders whose different approaches inevitably lead to conflict. Noodles (De Niro) is quieter and prone to depression, whereas Max (Woods) is his hotheaded opposite. The film tracks the pair at three specific dates—1921, 1933, and 1968—and each time we catch up with the characters we are reminded of their inability to change.

At nearly four hours long, *Once Upon a Time in America* is Sergio Leone's longest and most languorous film. The patient narrative drifts along with the same narcotic haze of the opium den where Noodles reflects on his wayward life. As usual, Leone pays close attention to period details and composition, emphasizing his preference for the power of images over dialogue. His story plays out in simmering glances, scurrilous squinting, and barely concealed sneers.

35. *Out of Africa* (1985)

Awesome landscapes nearly overpower this Best Picture winner shot on location in Kenya. "Nearly," however, is the operative word, because Meryl Streep and Robert Redford fulfill an uncommon love story to counterbalance this absurdly beautiful spectacle.

Every frame is a marvel, every set piece a gem. A memoir's translation to the big screen, *Out of Africa* sidesteps charges of racism with fidelity to its source. Demonstrating how First World storytelling technique can subdue all else in pursuit of profits and art, Sydney Pollack's epic exists as a sharply produced romance-cum-travelogue.

When Karen Blixen (Streep) is forced into a marriage of convenience with Baron Bror Finecke (Klaus Maria Brandauer), her dowry affords him a farm in Kenya. Afflicted with wanderlust he disregards her, so she finds sustenance in the adventurer Denys Hatton (Redford) until World War I and other personal complications interrupt the affair.

36. *The Piano* (1993)

Sweetie (1989) and *An Angel at My Table* (1990) taught us to expect startling and beautiful things from director Jane Campion, and this assured and provocative third feature offers yet another lush parable about the perils and paradoxes of female self-expression. Set in the 19th century, this story by Campion focuses on a Scottish widow (Holly Hunter) who hasn't spoken since childhood, and whose main form of

self-expression is her piano playing. She arrives with her daughter (Anna Paquin) in the New Zealand wilds to enter into an arranged marriage, which gets off to an unhappy start when her husband-to-be (Sam Neill) refuses to transport her piano. A local white man living with the Maori natives (Harvey Keitel) buys the piano from him and, fascinated by and attracted to the mute woman, agrees to "sell" it back to her a key at a time in exchange for lessons—lessons that have ultimately traumatic consequences.

37. *Braveheart* (1995)

Producer, director, and star Mel Gibson's gigantic historical epic combines brutal action, derring-do, and romantic tragedy so wholeheartedly that all are pleased by at least one half of its three hours.

Financed heavily by Gibson himself, *Braveheart* is a panegyric for Scottish warrior William Wallace, whose loss of his love (Catherine McCormack) triggers a handkerchief-wringing sequence of events in spectacular locations with a cast of thousands. Wallace's grassroots revolt against Edward I (dastardly Patrick McGoohan) at the turn of the 14th century climaxed with the Scots' victory at Stirling but ended in tears, betrayal, and butchery.

Punctuated by battle sequences that run from thrilling to repulsively gory, the story is a good old-fashioned swashbuckler with vengeance and historical figures. Gibson took Best Picture and Best Director Oscars (among *Braveheart*'s five wins) for a film made with gusto that retains a sense of humor and exhibits a flair for the mythic.

38. *The English Patient* (1996)

Anthony Minghella's epic adaptation of Michael Ondaatje's novel owned Oscar night, winning nine Academy Awards in the most sweeping victory since the 1987 film *The Last Emperor.*

A pilot (Ralph Fiennes) is found in the wreckage of his biplane near the end of World War II. Apparently amnesiac, and unidentified, he is in the care of nurse Hana (Juliette Binoche). They are joined by Willem Dafoe's vengeful torture victim and two bomb disposal experts for an intimate exploration of memory, loss, and healing. The mystery patient recalls his past gradually, and Almasy's tragic

love affair with the married Katharine Clifton (Kristin Scott Thomas) unfolds.

The story is convoluted but classically, passionately romantic. And the production is meticulously artful, likened to the style of David Lean, from dreamlike aerial sequences to sensuous love scenes. *The English Patient*'s scale and majesty on screen demanded recognition for its artistic and technical achievements.

39. *Crouching Tiger, Hidden Dragon* (2000)

Ang Lee has said that his intention with *Crouching Tiger, Hidden Dragon* was to make the best martial arts movie possible, and the success of the end result indicates he achieved just that.

Chow Yun Fat plays a warrior in search of a stolen sword. Aided by Michelle Yeow, he discovers that the theft of the sword is connected to issues of honor and revenge. For all the gravity-defying stunts and inventive violence, Lee keeps the focus firmly on the film's three central characters, whose philosophies on fighting and bloodshed have been shaped by their radically different experiences.

Lee modulates each scene with sensitivity. His fight sequences play like psychological confrontations as much as sword fights, the clash of innocence and experience, peace and anger. Even so, Lee leaves as much room for levity as he does for visual poetry, achieving a rare balance of thrills, beauty, humor, and smarts.

40. *Moulin Rouge!* (2001)

Writer–director Baz Luhrmann effectively reinvented the movie musical with this brash, gaudy, and unique tale.

Moulin Rouge! is a 21st-century version of an 1890s Paris romance. Christian (Ewan McGregor), a young Englishman, comes to Paris to be a writer. He makes contact with a group of artists led by Toulouse Lautrec (John Leguizamo) who want to stage a show, and who enlist Christian to write it. He approaches Moulin Rouge owner Harold Zidler (Jim Broadbent) for funds and falls in love with the beautiful star of the Moulin Rouge, Satine (Nicole Kidman). McGregor is wide-eyed, charismatic, and sensitive as Christian, and Kidman is a joy to watch as Satine— sexy, strong, and ravishing.

Besides being a celebration of show business, life, and color, *Moulin Rouge!*

is also a celebration of music, which Luhrmann uses to ingenious effect. The featured songs are all recognizable but used in a very unusual manner.

BEST FOR ACTING

41. *The Man Who Knew Too Much* (1956)

In Alfred Hitchcock's only remake of one of his own films, James Stewart plays an American doctor on vacation in Morocco with his family who accidentally learns of a political assassination to take place in the near future. A friendly English couple are in fact spies in on the plot, and they kidnap Stewart's son to ensure his silence.

As in most Hitchcock films, the international intrigue is less important than the odyssey of the hero. Stewart indeed "knows too much," not valuing his wife's (Doris Day) capabilities. As the plot unfolds, however, her assistance proves essential, despite his fears of her emotional collapse. The film climaxes in London's Royal Albert Hall, one of Hitchcock's best-ever set pieces. *The Man Who Knew Too Much* features excellent performances by Stewart and Day, and by Bernard Miles and Brenda De Banzie as the British agents.

42. *North by Northwest* (1959)

Mistaken for a spy and suspected for the murder of a U.N. diplomat, Cary Grant's Roger O. Thornhill flees across the country pursued by villains and shadowed by government agents. Somewhere in between is the stunningly beautiful Eve Kendall (Eva Marie Saint), whose allegiances wobble warily between the good guys and bad guys.

Working from one of the all-time great scripts by Ernest Lehman, and featuring several of cinema's greatest action sequences—the crop duster attack, the chase across the face(s) of Mount Rushmore—Hitchcock ended his golden period on the highest of notes with *North by Northwest.*

Saint is one of Hitchcock's more vulnerable female leads, and Grant is made to surmount various threats not just for his life but implicitly for his and Saint's future life together. Hitchcock— ever the romantic sadist—has a hoot putting up the roadblocks.

43. *Who's Afraid of Virginia Woolf?* (1966)

Based on a screenplay that keeps much of the dialogue from Edward Albee's Broadway smash, Mike Nichols's film is one of the finest adaptations of a stage play ever produced.

The casting was a coup, with the world's most tempestuous couple, Richard Burton and Elizabeth Taylor, cast as George and Martha, whose unremitting verbal and mental fencing constitutes the main action. George and Martha invite a younger couple (George Segal and Sandy Dennis) for an evening of games: First "Humiliate the Host," and then, more destructively, "Get the Guests." The young marrieds come off second best, with the less-than-honorable aspects of their marriage laid bare.

Of the many attempts to use the Burtons effectively in a film, *Who's Afraid of Virginia Woolf?* is by far the most successful, as Nichols elicited the best performance of Taylor's career and Burton is effective as a weak man possessed of enormous emotional strength.

44. *Midnight Cowboy* (1969)

Texan dishwasher Joe Buck (Jon Voight in a star-making performance) heads for New York City believing wealthy women will be eager to pay a strapping stud for sex. His tragicomic progress is punctuated by disturbing flashbacks and his "career" is a string of dispiriting encounters.

Destitute and lonesome, Joe bonds with the crippled, consumptive Enrico "Ratso" Rizzo (Dustin Hoffman, a compelling study of "street weasel"), who invites him to share his squat. Although the film is often called cynical and bleak, director John Schlesinger's view that it is a story of hope is justified by Joe's abandonment of his gigolo fantasy for the sake of a real, human relationship.

Arguably the bravest choice ever made by Academy Award voters, *Midnight Cowboy* is the only X-rated movie to have won the Oscar for Best Picture. The distinction prompted a rethink, and the film's US rating was changed to an R.

45. *Body Heat* (1981)

The controversial directorial debut of writer Lawrence Kasdan, *Body Heat* generated powerful and divergent reactions upon its initial release.

Ned Racine (William Hurt) is a lazy, womanizing lawyer who works in a small town in Florida. In the midst of a terrible heatwave, he meets Matty Walker (Kathleen Turner), a rich, married woman from a nearby suburb and a steamy affair quickly develops. Soon enough, Matty has convinced Ned to murder her husband so they can be together. After Matty fakes her own death, Ned is sent to jail and learns that she had taken on another woman's identity and set him up. But it's too late to do anything.

Over time, positive response to Kasdan's film has won out, with subsequent neonoirs paying homage to *Body Heat*.

46. *Raising Arizona* (1987)

The Coen brothers' second feature abandoned the noir mood of *Blood Simple* (1984) for this larger-than-life, intricately plotted comedy. Nicolas Cage is the convenience-store robber who falls for and weds prison officer Holly Hunter; their blissful marriage is blighted when they find she's infertile and, to keep her happy, he kidnaps one of the quintuplets born to a local tycoon. As if it weren't bad enough that the father hires the biker from hell (Randall "Tex" Cob) to bring back his baby and wreak vengeance on the abductors, Cage's fortunes take a turn for the worse when he is visited by escaped former cellmates John Goodman and William Forsythe.

The farcical improbabilities of *Raising Arizona* are as nothing to the absurdly overpoetic voiceover the Coens brilliantly concoct for their hapless hero. The aura of heady hysteria is sustained with considerable expertise, not least in the perfectly pitched performances.

47. *Rain Man* (1988)

Numerous writers and directors had tinkered with the script of *Rain Man* before Barry Levinson came on board. Many believed the story of a used-car salesman trying to befriend his autistic brother so he can get his hands on the latter's multimillion dollar inheritance just too difficult to bring to the screen. Levinson luckily didn't balk at the idea of making a film with little dramatic story, instead focusing on the human development that is at the picture's heart.

Traveling across country with the autistic Raymond (Dustin Hoffman), Charlie Babbitt (Tom Cruise) gradually gets to understand the brother he hardly knows and in the process develops a sense of decency he didn't have before. Hoffman captures his character's autism without going overboard, but most impressive is Cruise, who holds his own alongside a more experienced actor and expertly depicts a shallow man who finally finds some depth in his life.

48. *Fargo* (1996)

Joel and Ethan Coen are the foremost filmmakers to emerge from America in the 1980s and devilishly clever *Fargo* is among their very best.

Desperately in-debt car salesman Jerry Lundergaard (William H. Macy in the performance that lifted him from everuseful to eagerly sought) hires two ex-cons to abduct his wife. His wife's ransom is to be paid by her rich father (Harve Presnell) with the woman going free none the wiser but things go horribly and grotesquely awry in the hands of psychopath Grimsrud (Peter Stormare), and agitated bungler Showalter (Steve Buscemi). Enter Frances McDormand, absolutely fantastic as the very pregnant, comically ordinary but sharp police chief, Marge Gunderson, easily the most engaging character conceived by the Coens (along with, later, Jeff Bridges' "The Dude" Lebowski).

The Coens' witty expertise results in a quirky, bizarre tragi-comedy that manages to be wildly funny and violently distressing by neatly accomplished turns.

49. *American Beauty* (1999)

If *Blue Velvet* peeked behind the curtains of modern-day suburbia, *American Beauty* yanked them completely away and gave us an unsettling view inside.

American Beauty is a dark comedy about what life is really like for those people supposedly living the American Dream. This is Lester's story, and with Kevin Spacey in the role it is an extremely fascinating one—on the surface a tale of one man's midlife crisis as he tries to rediscover the freedom he has lost in the face of marital and parental responsibility. He becomes transfixed by the Lolita-esque Angela (Mena Suvari) and is soon having erotic visions of her that lead him to completely change his life.

Written by Alan Ball, this is a funny, sad, wistful, and even hopeful movie that never goes quite where you think it will. Beautiful and brooding, *American Beauty* is a truly remarkable debut from director Sam Mendes.

50. *The Queen* (2006)

The heart of Stephen Frears's *The Queen* is the complexity of public performance, about which the film holds varying degrees of antipathy and admiration. The central figure is Queen Elizabeth II (Helen Mirren) upon Lady Diana's death in 1997, when royalty, and its stiff formality, went at loggerheads with the Internet age. *The Queen* presents Elizabeth walking a tightrope between necessary tradition and what innovation she might affect.

Written by Peter Morgan, *The Queen* is equally about the ascent of Tony Blair (Michael Sheen), who is as pleasant and attractive as Elizabeth is intimidating and distant.

A crafty fable about old versus new, Frears lets performance lead our reflections, sympathizing with both Elizabeth and Tony since both are undeniably influenced by the waxing and waning interests of their sovereign people. James Cromwell, Alex Jennings, and Helen McCrory, are also excellent in subtly critiquing modern class distinctions.

GLOSSARY

ADR (automatic dialogue replacement) Re-recording dialogue in a studio to match what is onscreen. Used to improve sound quality.

Alpha mask/channel Provides transparency around an object on a digital image.

Ambient sound Background noise recorded to add atmosphere to a soundtrack. Also known as "atmos" and "wildtrack."

Animatics Storyboard filmed with sound to give sense of a movie's pacing. Can also be simple 3-D animation to demonstrate complicated action sequences.

Animation Films made from a sequence of individual images that are either drawn, modeled, or created on a computer.

Audition Test piece by an actor to get a role in a film or play.

Auteur A somewhat pretentious name given to certain filmmakers/directors.

CCD (charge-coupled device) Simply put, this is what converts light into image in a DV camera—but it's much more complicated than that. The best cameras have three CCDs. The latest cameras come with 16:9 chips for filming native widescreen.

Cel (cellulose acetate) A sheet of transparent material used in traditional animation.

Chroma key Replacing a large area of flat color (usually blue or green) with another image. Also known as blue screen or green screen.

Cinematography Cinema photography—the art of using lights and cameras for motion pictures.

CGI (computer-generated imagery) Any images created by a computer, usually 3D, for special effects or animation.

Color grading Balancing color to improve continuity between different shooting times or lighting. Also used for adding color effects to film or video. Also called color correction or color timing.

Continuity Ensuring that everything onscreen looks the same from take to take.

Copyright An artist's legal right to control the use and reproduction of his or her work. In some countries it is seen as the right to copy.

Crane Grip equipment with a long jib that allows the camera to be moved to a greater height.

Credits List of who did what on a movie.

DAT (digital audio tape) Digital recording system that uses small cassettes.

DAZ Studio 3D software for creating character animation. Poser is a similar program.

Dialogue The spoken words in a movie.

DigiBeta Short for Digital Betacam, a proprietry high-resolution video format from Sony.

Digital zoom Enlarges an image to make it appear as though a long lens was used. Causes degradation of the picture.

Distribution Getting your movie shown in as many cinemas or broadcasts as possible.

Documentary A factual film on any topic that is not a work of fiction.

Dolly A camera support with wheels, or running on a track, to give smooth movement.

Dubbing Adding extra sounds on top of other sounds. Replacing one language dialogue with another language. Copying from one tape to another.

DV (digital video) Any system that records moving images as digital information (ones and zeroes). Does not lose quality when copied. Popular formats are miniDV, HDV, DVCAM, DVCPro, Digital Betacam.

Editing Putting all the various shots and elements of the movie together into a coherent whole.

Feature film A movie that is usually anywhere between 75 and 200-plus minutes in length.

Film A motion picture.

Filter Either a piece of glass or gelatine that goes over the lens and changes the color and/or the amount of light reaching the film or tape.

Software filters serve a similar function but after shooting. They can also apply special effects.

Focus Adjusting the elements in a lens so that an image is sharp, or not, depending on requirements.

Foley Sound effects recorded in a studio. Usually sounds made by people in the movie, such as footsteps.

fps (frames per second) The number of images captured every second on film or video. PAL video is 25fps, and NTSC is 30(29.97)fps.

Gaffer tape Sticky black cloth tape, similar to duct tape—indispensable on a film set. Camera tape is similar, but thinner and white, so it can be written on.

HDV (high-definition video) The latest video format that gives extremely high-resolution images in a 16:9 (widescreen) format.

ILM (Industrial Light & Magic) Huge special effects company run by George Lucas.

Jib See crane.

Kelvin A measuring system used for color temperature or the color of light in the visible light spectrum.

Keyframe A frame used to show the extreme part of a movement in animation.

LCD screen Liquid crystal diodes that light up to produce a color image. They are very thin, making them ideal for use as screens on digital cameras.

Lip-sync Synchronizing sound recording of dialogue with the mouth movements of the actors.

Location An existing set that has not been created in a studio. Can be interior or exterior. Favored by lo-no budget filmmakers.

Medium (plural: media) Material onto which your movie will be shot or stored; film, videotape, or DVD.

Microphone A device for converting sound to electrical impulses that can be recorded onto a suitable medium.

MiniDV A digital tape format used in consumer and professional digital video cameras.

Monitor Television or computer screen. A field monitor is a small, high-resolution, color-corrected screen for checking lighting and exposure on location.

Monopod An easily transported, single-legged camera support. Not entirely suitable for movies.

NLE (non-linear editing) Editing system that lets you insert footage anywhere in the edit without having to remove what was there before. Applies to digital and film editing.

NTSC (National Television Standards Council) The television and video format used in North America and Japan that runs 525 lines at 29.97 or 30fps. Sometimes called "No Two Similar Colors" because of its dubious reproduction quality.

Optical zoom The range of a lens as defined by the minimum and maximum focal lengths. *See* zoom.

Outtakes Takes that are discarded, usually because the actor(s) made a mistake, but also for technical reasons such as the mic being in shot.

PAL (Phase Alternation Line) Television and video system used in Europe and other countries that don't use NTSC. Runs 625 lines and 25fps.

Pan Following action that moves across the scene, with the camera fixed on a tripod.

Photoflood Artificial light designed for use with film and video.

Polaroids Instant photos made from film produced by the Polaroid Corporation. Killed off by digital cameras, although still used by professional film-based stills photographers for test shots.

Poser A 3D software for creating character animation. DAZ Studio is a similar program.

POV shots Point of view—showing on camera/screen what the actor is seeing.

Props Items used by actors in a film.

Reflector A shiny surface used to reflect light onto an actor or location as a boost to the existing light, usually to remove excessive shadow areas.

Rough cut The first edit of the film, also called assembly, as it puts all the elements roughly in the right order.

Rushes Raw footage screened so the director and DP can check the footage they shot. Can also be on videotape.

Script/screenplay The blueprint for a movie, with scene descriptions and dialogue.

Shot list List of shots to be completed for the film, usually broken down into a daily schedule.

Slapstick Physical comedy with a lack of subtlety.

Soundtrack Audio part of a movie containing dialogue, sound effects, and music. Often refers to just the music.

Sprocket Evenly spaced holes in the side of film to allow a gearing mechanism to pass the film evenly and consistently through the camera and projector.

Static shot Scene filmed with the camera in a fixed position on a tripod or other type of support.

Stock *See* medium.

Storyboard Visual representation of the script, using drawings to show key moments of action in a scene.

Syncing Synchronizing, usually pictures and sound.

Telephoto lens Lens with a long focal length that brings everything nearer (like a telescope).

Tilt Following action vertically with the camera mounted on a tripod.

Time code Numbering system for measuring frames to help with editing. Shown as HH:MM:SS:FF (hours:minutes:seconds:frames).

Titles Creative way to show the name of the film. Sometimes includes credits if major talent is involved.

Track/tracking A smooth camera movement with the camera mounted on a dolly. Often used on rough surfaces.

Trailer Short preview of a film showing the best parts to entice an audience. A van where actors go to rest between takes.

Tripod Three-legged camera support with a pan and tilt head for smooth and stable shots. Known as "legs."

Tungsten A traditional incandescent light that has its filament made from tungsten, which has a low color temperature that will appear orange with daylight film or white balance.

Video Relating to the visual element of television. Short for videotape. The electronic capturing of images onto videotape.

Voiceover Recorded dialogue that is added to a film after it has been shot.

White balance The control on video cameras that is adjusted to match the light's color temperature.

Wide-angle lens A lens with a large field of view. Particularly useful for interiors and other confined spaces.

Widescreen A screen ratio where the width is significantly greater than the height. The ratio of 16:9 has been adopted for high definition televisions. Cinema formats are even wider.

Zoom A camera lens of various focal lengths. On movie and video cameras this is usually from wide angle to telephoto. Originally designed so only one lens was needed on the camera, allowing the camera operator to get the exact framing. On movie cameras it was found that changing focal length while shooting gave a sense of movement without having to move the camera.

RESOURCES

STORYTELLING

Adventures in the Screen Trade, William Goldman (Warner Books (reissue ed.), 1989): Top Hollywood screenwriter's story of working in the system.

The Art of the Matrix, Wachowski Brothers (Newmarket Press (reissue ed.), 2000): Probably the best storyboards ever drawn for a movie.

Hero with a Thousand Faces, Joseph Campbell (Bollingen (reprint ed.), 1972): The book on myths and archetypes. Apparently the inspiration behind *Star Wars*.

On Writing, Stephen King (Pocket, 2002): A master storyteller explaining how he does it. If only it were that easy.

Screenplay, Syd Field (Dell, (revised ed.), 1984): The standard book on writing screenplays.

Story, Robert McKee (Regan Books, 1997): A standard text on story structure.

What Lie Did I Tell? William Goldman (Vintage, 2001): More adventures.

Worlds of Wonder, David Gerrold (Writer's Digest Books, 2001): Great ideas for sci-fi and fantasy stories.

The Writer's Journey, Christopher Vogler (Michael Wiese Productions (2nd ed.), 1998): Campbell's work adapted for use with movies.

PRACTICAL

Behind the Seen, Charles Koppelman (New Riders Press, 2004): A look at Walter Murch's adoption of digital NLE.

The Blink of an Eye, Walter Murch (Silman-James Press (2nd ed.), 2001): Master editor imparts wisdom.

The Digital Filmmaking Handbook, Ben Long and Sonja Schenk (Course Technology PTR (4th ed., 2011): A general overview of video/film production and editing.

Digital Video for Dummies, Keith Underdahl (For Dummies (4th ed.), 2006): A good starting point with simple, clear explanations on almost everything about digital video.

Directing Actors, Judith Weston (Michael Wiese Productions, 1999): How to work with the talent.

Every Frame a Rembrandt, Andrew Laszlo (Focal Press, 2000): A guide to cinematography by a working DP.

Film Directing Shot by Shot, Steve Katz (Michael Wiese Productions, 1991): Another standard filmmaker's text book.

From Reel to Deal, Dov S-S Simens (Warner Books, 2003): A guide to successful independent filmmaking.

From Word to Image, Marcie Begleiter (Michael Wiese Productions, 2001): Making effective storyboards.

The Guerilla Film Maker's Blueprint, Chris Jones (Continuum International Publishing Group, 2003): Everything you practically need to know about making a film.

Raindance Producers' Lab Lo-to-no Budget Filmmaking, Elliot Grove (Focal Press, 2004): Aimed at producers but invaluable just the same.

Scene by Scene, Mark Cousins (Laurence King, 2002): Illustrated talks with renowned directors on their most famous scenes.

The Technique of Film Editing, Karl Reisz and Gavin Miller (Focal Press (2nd ed.), 1995): Practical information on cutting a film.

What They Don't Teach You at Film School, Camille Landau and Tiare White (Hyperion, 2000): Lots of practical tips from the real world.

INSPIRING

Gilliam on Gilliam, Ian Christie (Editor) (Faber and Faber, 2000): One of the more imaginative directors and filmmakers.

Make Your Own Damn Movie, Lloyd Kaufmann (L.A. Weekly Books, 2003): He's been around independent filmmaking for a long time. Lots of practical advice too.

Making Movies, Sidney Lumet (Vintage (reprint ed.), 1996): One of the great masters of cinema.

My First Movie, Stephen Lowenstein (editor) (Pantheon, 2001): Established directors talk about their first major movies.

Rebel without a Crew, Robert Rodriguez (Plume Books, 1996): If this doesn't inspire you, nothing will.

Silent Bob Speaks, Kevin Smith (Miramax Books, 2005): He's funny and can make good films.

Spike, Mike, Slackers and Dykes, John Pierson (Faber and Faber Ltd, 1997): The story behind the success of some of the great independent films and their directors.

American Cinematographer, Magazine and Handbooks: The handbook on video is a must and reading the monthly magazine will keep you up to date on the latest processes and tools of the big shows.

DVDS TO SEE

Adventures in Shorts: How a low-budget film ended up with an Oscar nomination (www.little-terrorist.com).

Anything by Robert Rodriguez. They all feature different 10-Minute Film School lessons.

Cinema 16: Shorts by internationally renowned directors (www.cinema16.org).

Lost in La Mancha: The making and collapse of Terry Gilliam's Don Quixote film.

Palm Directors Label: The works of commercials and music video directors, including a book.

Requiem for a Dream: Includes an excellent making of documentary.

WEBSITES

As well as the Web sites you'll find referenced in the text and in "Check these out" panels throughout the book, here are some great Internet resources that are worth checking out.

TECHNOLOGY

www.adobe.com Photoshop, Premiere, After Effects.

www.apple.com Macintosh computers. Final Cut, Soundtrack, iMovie, Shake.

www.avid.com Avid editing systems.

www.canon.com DV cameras.

www.discreet.com Combustion effects and compositing.

www.dvfilm.com "Progressive scan" after you've shot the movie.

www.finaldraft.com Screenwriting software.

www.frameforge.com 3D storyboard software.

www.glidecam.com Camera stabilizers.

www.jvc.com DV and HDV cameras.

www.kodak.com The film source.

www.miller.com.au Fluid head tripods.

www.panasonic.com DV and HD cameras.

www.powerproductions.com Storyboard Quick software.

www.screenplay.com Screenwriting software.

www.sony.com DV, DVCAM, and HDV cameras.

www.steadicam.com Camera stabilizers.

RESOURCES

www.amazefilms.com Short film site.

www.crime-scene-investigator.net Great for making authentic crime stories.

www.filmeducation.org Theory and practice of filmmaking for schools.

www.filmmaking.net Links and resources.

www.filmmaker.com/DUMPS.html Everything you need to avoid when making a film.

www.raindance.co.uk Courses for the independent filmmaker.

www.shootingpeople.org Networking site for filmmakers.

www.simplyscripts.com Screenplays to download and study.

FILM FESTIVAL LISTINGS

www.cultureunplugged.com An online community which houses eight online film festivals.

www.festivalofilm.com Online community for viewing licensed short and feature length films onilne.

www.filmfights.com Filmmakers submit a film to suit a given title and genre and the public vote

www.haydenfilms.com Premier online film festival.

www.openfilm.com Film festivals are searchable by category, date, and region so you can find the festival that's best for you.

www.renderyard.com Short film and animation network where filmmakers can upload their films and interact with other filmmakers across the globe.

www.tribecafilm.com/tribecaonline/ Making the Tibeca Film Festival available and accessible online, with award categories such as Best Online Feature and Best Online Short.

www.withoutabox.com List of film festivals and how to enter.

INDEX

CREDITS

© 2012 SHOOTING PEOPLE, shootingpeople.org, p.44

© Courtesy of University of the Arts, p.93b

© Elaine Perks, courtesy of University of the Arts, p.85t

© Mario Alessandro Razzeto, courtesy of University of the Arts, p.103

© Reed, Phillip, courtesy of University of the Arts, p.2, 49bc

A BAND APART / MIRAMAX / THE KOBAL COLLECTION, p.59

AD HOMINEM ENTERPRISES / THE KOBAL COLLECTION, p.73c

Alamy, p.11, 15t/c/b, 94, 95, 101, 114bl/br

Andrushko, Galyna, Shutterstock, p.43br

ARRI, www.arri.com, p.71

ARTE / BAVARIA / WDR / THE KOBAL COLLECTION / SPAUKE, BERND, p.22

Bentow, Joel, www.joelbentow.com, p.120

Bettles, Stevie, www.steviefx.com, p.96

Brimm, David, Shutterstock, p.89bl

Broer, Steve, Shutterstock, p.48bc, 71t

Corbis, p.64

Costen, Chad & CITIZEN 11 ENTERTAINMENT, www.citizen11.com, p.24–25, 26, 35

Courtesy of Vancouver Film School, p.3, 4, 35, 48bl, 51tl, 51tr, 51b, 52, 55, 63, 67, 72t, 76bl/r, 85b, 87t, 93tr, 122, 123, 124, 148–149b, 152, 159

Dangerous Parking 2008 (Flaming Pie Films), directed by Peter Howitt, p.28–29b

De Burca, Sean, Shutterstock, p.31

Diament, Dario, Shutterstock, p.48br

digitalreflections, Shutterstock, p.88tr

Everett Collection, Shutterstock, p.88bl, 89cr

Farina, Marcello, Shutterstock, p.46bcl

Featureflash, Shutterstock, p.46bl, 46bc, 46bcr, 46br

Garlick, Rachel, p.28–29t

Hibbert, Richard, http://vimeo.com/user778540, p.134–135b

Hunt, Nigel, MD of London Visual Effects Studio, Glowfrog, www.glowfrog.com, p.117

Hunt, Roxy, LES graphis, LES Film Festival, lesfilmfestival.com, p.130–131, 132–133, 136t

iStock Photos, p.86tl, 86br

Junial Enterprises, Shutterstock, p.89tcr

Kristensen, Lasse, Shutterstock, p.88cl

Location Managers Guild of America (LMGA), Lori Balton, President, LMGA and Tony Salome, First Vice President, LMGA, p.43tr

LOS HOOLIGANS/COLUMBIA / THE KOBAL COLLECTION, p.32bl

Man, Kenneth, Shutterstock, p.66

MARVEL/PARAMOUNT / THE KOBAL COLLECTION, p.73b

Mayskyphoto, Shutterstock, p.97

Mirra, Caitlin, Shutterstock, p.77t,c,b

NEW LINE CINEMA / THE KOBAL COLLECTION, p.73t

Northfoto, Shutterstock, p.54, 91t

nsm, Shuttersock, p.43bl

Onida, Chiara, www.chiaraonida.com, 124b

PhotoSky 4t com, Shutterstock, p.88tl

Pierce, Kevin, www.kevstar.com, p.53

riekephotos, Shutterstock, p.49br

S.Borisov, Shutterstock, p.43cr

Sabo, Dennis, Shutterstock, p.50tr, 50b

Seer, Joe, Shutterstock, p.157

Shawshamk, p.16, 17

Sodhi, Gunpreet (Preeti), p.37, 38, 41, 60, 79

Spence, John, Shutterstock, p.65tl

StockLite, Shutterstock, p.89tl

Stone, Laura, Shutterstock, p.43tl

Trigger Street Labs, labs.triggerstreet.com, p.138t

TTphoto, Shutterstock, p.43cl

Vimeo, www.vimeo.com, p.139t

WALT DISNEY / THE KOBAL COLLECTION / VAUGHAN, STEPHEN, p.32br

Wilson, Rob, Shutterstock, p.43ct

YouTube, www.youtube.com, p.139b

All other illustrations and photographs are the copyright of Quarto Publishing plc. While every effort has been made to credit contributors, Quarto would like to apologize should there have been any omissions or errors—and would be pleased to make the appropriate correction for future editions of the book.

Thanks to Joe Wilby for contributing to "Editing your movie" (pages 104–112) and Philip Rodrigues Singer for contributing to "Postproduction sound" (pages 122–125).

"50 Movies to see before you try" is taken from *1001 Movies You Must See Before You Die* (Barron's Educational Series, Inc.).